T0214622

# Computational Thinking

Paolo Ferragina • Fabrizio Luccio

# Computational Thinking

## First Algorithms, Then Code

Paolo Ferragina
Dipartimento di Informatica
University of Pisa
Pisa, Italy

Fabrizio Luccio
Dipartimento di Informatica
University of Pisa
Pisa, Italy

ISBN 978-3-030-07424-1     ISBN 978-3-319-97940-3   (eBook)
https://doi.org/10.1007/978-3-319-97940-3

This Springer imprint is published by the registered company Springer Nature Switzerland AG
The registered company address is: Gewerbestrasse 11, 6330 Cham, Switzerland

# Preface

The main purpose of this text is to introduce readers to algorithms and their coding for solving problems in different fields, some of which are of major importance in today's world. The presentation is accessible to anyone with elementary mathematical knowledge and is made as simple as possible, without giving up the scientific rigor that is indispensable for transforming general ideas into executable algorithms. In the course of the discussion, however, arithmetic notions that are particularly relevant for the construction of algorithms are referred to as needed.

To make it as usable as possible, the text is divided into substantially independent chapters that can be read separately, leaving the reader the freedom to choose the topics he or she prefers. In a few cases more challenging side arguments have been reported which can be omitted without affecting the understanding of the main text.

In addition, readers interested in implementing the algorithms described in the text on a computer may, even without any knowledge of "programming", examine their operation and perhaps try to build their own programs through a very accessible website created for this purpose.[1] It contains the coding of these algorithms in Python and provides everything a reader would need to execute them and, perhaps, construct new examples.

Pisa,
February 2018

*Paolo Ferragina*
*Fabrizio Luccio*

---

[1] https://github.com/ComputationalThinking-Springer/FirstAlgorithmsThenCode

# Contents

# Chapter 1
# A Brief Historical Outline

Computation, in the sense of computing numbers, has existed since ancient times. In a papyrus written around 1650 B.C., the scribe Ahmes described to Egyptians how to multiply by doubles, halves, and additions according to a method known long before his writing. We begin with a modern version of this method, as an unconventional introduction to our work. In Ahmes's papyrus the product factors are two positive integers, say $a, b$. The calculation is based on the following considerations:

1. if $a = 1$, $a \cdot b = b$;
2. if $a$ is even, $a \cdot b = (a/2) \cdot (2b)$; and
3. if $a$ is odd and greater than 1, $a \cdot b = ((a-1)/2) \cdot (2b) + b$.

The product $p = a \cdot b$ is obtained by iterating steps 2 and 3, whichever applies. At each iteration the value of the first factor of the multiplication decreases ($a$ becomes $a/2$ or $(a-1)/2$), and the iterations go on until the value of this factor becomes 1. At this point step 1 applies and the process ends. For example, to calculate $p = 6 \cdot 7$ proceed as follows:

- 6 is even (step 2), so $p = (6/2) \cdot (7 \cdot 2) = 3 \cdot 14$   (now $a = 3$ and $b = 14$);
- 3 is odd and greater than 1 (step 3), so $p = ((3-1)/2) \cdot (2 \cdot 14) + 14 = 2 \cdot 14 + 14$;
- 2 is even (step 2), so $p = (2/2) \cdot (14 \cdot 2) + 14 = 1 \cdot 28 + 14$;
- the first factor has become 1 (step 1), so $p = 28 + 14 = 42$.

The method described by Ahmes is what is now called an "algorithm," a term unknown to most people until a decade ago and very fashionable nowadays, even though those who use it may not know what it exactly means. Its "realization" is an example of "coding." It was done in the past by means of an abacus, which made it easy to double, halve, and add, and is executed today by the electronic circuits of a computer.

Algorithms and coding are the absolute protagonists of this book. The former establish the logical rules to be used for solving problems, and the sequence in which these rules must be applied. The latter commands a particular computing device to execute the steps of that sequence. In our case, the reference device will be a computer and the coding will consist of a "program," but the device may be

© Springer Nature Switzerland AG 2018
P. Ferragina, F. Luccio, *Computational Thinking*,
https://doi.org/10.1007/978-3-319-97940-3_1

different and the border between algorithms and coding may not be sharply defined. Computational thinking is based on the understanding of these concepts.

The history of science, especially the history of mathematics, is full of computing processes conceived before the concept of an algorithm had been precisely defined. In all these studies, whether they had a practical purpose or were abstract speculation, arithmetic and geometry were almost the only protagonists. Nowadays, the situation has changed substantially. Even those who use a *smart phone* to make phone calls, listen to music, take pictures, or access the Internet, put into action a completely invisible but very complicated "computation" that allows them to operate on sounds, pictures, or sequences of characters. This computation on data of any kind is essential in the present world, even though numbers still play an important role. In fact, no other field of knowledge developed with the extraordinary speed that has characterized the *science of computation*. The origins are found in the studies of mathematics and mathematical logic developed between the end of the nineteenth and the beginning of the twentieth century, and the key turning points occurred in 1936, with the formal definition of algorithms and computable functions, and in 1971, with the discovery of problems that are intractable in practice. These were two moments in which fundamental definitions were laid down and the limitations of computation were specified. Let us summarize some phases of this initial development, which constitute the cultural basis of our field.

At the end of the nineteenth century, the German mathematician Georg Cantor formulated his theory of infinite sets, initially rejected by many, and then assumed as one of the basics of mathematics. In particular, Cantor proved that there cannot be a one-to-one correspondence between integers and real numbers: intuitively, there are infinitely "fewer" integers than real numbers. Within this theory it can easily be shown that the sequences of finite (but a priori unlimited) length constructed with an arbitrary but finite alphabet are *numerable*, that is, they can be put in one-to-one correspondence with the integers. An obvious example is given by the sequences constructed with the digits 0 to 9 that describe the integers themselves, each of which has a finite length, without, however, the possibility of fixing a limit to the length of the sequence representing an integer. Similarly, all the infinite "words" that can be constructed with arbitrary sequences of the letters of our alphabet are numerable, leaving aside whether or not they are meaningful. Whereas, the sequences of infinite length are not numerable, that is, there are (many) more of them than there are integers. In particular, real numbers typically require an infinite number of digits to be represented, so they are not numerable, as Cantor showed.

All of this has an immediate consequence on the use of algorithms for calculating mathematical functions. In fact, even before formally defining them, we may note that algorithms must be described with finite sequences of characters in a natural or artificial language. These sequences can be of any length and, according to what we said above, the algorithms must be numerable. By contrast, functions such as $y = f(x)$, i.e. laws that establish a correspondence between infinite values of $x$ and the corresponding values of $y$, are not numerable because the two infinite sequences for $x$ and $y$ must be fully specified if there is no rule to establish the value of $y$ for any value of $x$. Since, as previously mentioned, the sequences of infinite length are not numerable, the functions are not numerable either. It follows that there are functions for which no computing algorithm can exist because all possible algorithms are infinitely "fewer" than all possible functions. That is, there must be non-computable functions and these are the absolute majority of all possible functions.

This conclusion had a fundamental impact on the emerging theory of algorithms. In fact, you can calculate a function by specifying which rules to use among the known ones. For example, to calculate $y = x^2$ you can use Ahmes's algorithm to multiply $x$ by itself, but it is obviously not possible to find a non-computable function without giving a general definition of an algorithm. In 1936, the American logician Alonso Church and the English mathematician Alan Turing independently defined two computing models, respectively known as $\lambda$-*calculus* and the *Turing machine*, which constitute two formal definitions of an algorithm. It quickly became apparent that the two models were equivalent in the sense that they were able to calculate exactly the same functions, and there is strong evidence that in fact they can calculate all the functions that could be calculated with pen and paper. In the same studies, the first examples of non-computable functions were presented.

The two models have served as a basic reference for the development of computers and their programs. In fact, the definition of an *algorithm* is fundamental to the field of theoretical computer science but too subtle and complex for the purposes of this book. It will suffice to indicate a simpler but substantially correct definition, that is: an algorithm is a finite sequence of elementary steps leading to the resolution of a problem. In addition, an algorithm satisfies the following properties: (1) it can be used on different inputs generating corresponding outputs, (2) each step allows a single unambiguous interpretation and is executable in a finite amount of time, and (3) whatever the input, its execution eventually stops.

The *Science of Computation* is a specific field of study developed from Church's and Turing's models. It is addressed to solving problems in the broad sense and not just calculating mathematical functions, but this distinction does not really exist. Just as the calculation of a function $y = f(x)$ transforms $x$ values into $y$ values, so a problem resolution processes data to generate results. This amounts to calculating a function in Church's and Turing's models because data and results are treated as character sequences from an arbitrary alphabet, and arithmetic data processing does not differ in principle from that of other genres. After this was made clear, particular attention was paid to the resources needed to make a calculation, in particular the time and the space required by an algorithm, leading to studies on *computational complexity*. At first glance, it may seem contradictory that dizzying advances in hardware have required increased attention to the quality of software, because a more powerful computer should cushion lower efficiency in its use. However, the need to deal with bigger data has stimulated the development of efficient algorithms, partly because advances in hardware only marginally influence calculation time if the quality of the algorithms employed is low, as we will explain below. In 1971, the Canadian computer scientist Stephen Cook and the Russian mathematician Leonid Levin independently identified a family of problems that, while solvable by computable functions, are in fact *intractable* because the number of operations required for their resolution with the best available algorithms grows exponentially with the size of the data processed. The existence of more efficient algorithms to solve them, or the demonstration that such algorithms cannot exist, is considered to be one of the major open scientific problems today.

On these theoretical bases the science of computation has developed, accompanied by the constant advancement of electronic engineering. The two fields of study have progressed in parallel to create the extraordinary tools available to us today. This is the world to which we now turn. Of course, this book does not aim to train experts in computation, because this requires a long period of study and even longer practice, but to present general principles on which the computational activity hidden behind a computer screen or a mobile phone display is based. Readers unaware of this subject will encounter new lines of reasoning and unexpected situations. They will find problems that seem difficult but are actually very easy to solve, and problems that seem easy but are in fact rather difficult to solve. They will also have the satisfaction, great for those who have not already tried it, of gaining access to short "pieces of software" or designing their own, and making them run on a computer.

# Chapter 2
# A Problem with Which to Begin

*PROBLEM. Among three coins of identical appearance one could be false and of different weight from the other two. Using a twin-pan balance to compare the coins' weights, find the false coin if there is one, and in this case determine whether it weighs more or less than the other two with no more than two weighings.*

The solution is very simple. We invite you to find it on your own before going on in our discussion, which will become progressively more complicated and, we hope, more interesting.

If you have tried it, let us now start. To solve the problem we are looking for an *algorithm*, in the most general sense of the term, relying for the moment on an improvisation. Number the coins from one to three. The operations to use are the placement of the coins on the balance pans, the interpretation of the result of each weighing, and the decision as to whether the problem has been solved. To do this, we choose a graphic representation, that we will now explain.

The comparison of the weights of two coins, for example 1 and 2, is indicated with the notation 1 : 2 enclosed in a circle. The three possible results, i.e. coin 1 weighs more than coin 2 ($1 > 2$), coin 1 weighs the same as coin 2 ($1 = 2$), and coin 1 weighs less than coin 2 ($1 < 2$) are indicated by the symbols $>, =, <$ on the three arrows coming out of the comparison circle, thus opening three computation paths (Figure 2.1). Each of these results allows you to gather some "information" (singular in math) about the possible solutions that can be reached following that path. As we will see, all of the collected information is essential to solving the overall problem.

The problem has seven possible solutions, namely: coin 1, 2, or 3 is false and weighs more or less than the other two; or the coins are all authentic and have the same weight. Let's denote these solutions as 1L (coin 1 is false and lighter), 1H (coin 1 is false and heavier), 2L, 2H, 3L, 3H (all with similar meaning), or A to indicate that all coins are authentic. With this notation, the information collected in the three computation branches after comparing 1 : 2 is as follows:

- For $1 > 2$ we have 1H or 2L. So a false coin exists and in fact either 1 is false and weighs more than the others, or 2 is false and weighs less than the others. Coin 3 is authentic because at most one coin may be false.

© Springer Nature Switzerland AG 2018
P. Ferragina, F. Luccio, *Computational Thinking*,
https://doi.org/10.1007/978-3-319-97940-3_2

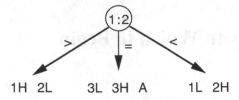

**Fig. 2.1** Comparison between coins 1 and 2 and information on possible solutions collected in the three branches of the computation.

- For $1 = 2$ we have 3L, 3H, or A. Coins 1 and 2 are authentic and nothing is known about coin 3.
- For $1 < 2$ we have 1L or 2H, symmetrical to the first case. A false coin exists and in fact either coin 1 is false and weighs less than the others or coin 2 is false and weighs more than the others, while coin 3 is authentic.

The seven solutions are divided between the three branches of the computation and each of them appears only once in one of the branches (Figure 2.1). Let's see now how we can continue our algorithm. Each arrow that leaves a comparison circle points either to a possible next comparison or to a square where the final result, if reached, is written. Let's consider $1 > 2$. Based on the information that we have acquired and knowing that coin 3 is authentic, we have to determine whether the solution is 1H or 2L. For that we make the new comparison $1 : 3$ (Figure 2.2).

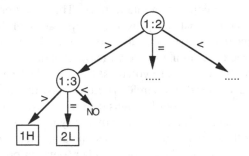

**Fig. 2.2** Continuation of the algorithm for three coins in the case $1 > 2$. The event $1 < 3$ cannot occur and the label "NO" is assigned as the descendant of the arrow $<$.

The result $1 > 3$ indicates that the final solution must be 1H as coin 3 is authentic. The result $1 = 3$ indicates that coin 1 is authentic and leaves only the alternative 2L open. Finally, the result $1 < 3$ cannot occur because coin 3 is authentic and if coin 1 is false it must weight more than the others while $1 < 3$ would indicate that it weighs less: we register this third alternative by writing NO in the destination of the arrow to indicate that this event is impossible.

The algorithm can thus be completed as shown in Figure 2.3. We invite you to verify this on your own, especially for the central branch $1 = 2$. In particular, since

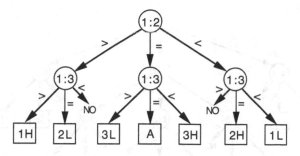

**Fig. 2.3** An overall algorithm to solve the three coins problem.

we know that in this branch coins 1 and 2 are authentic, the event $1 = 3$ shows that coin 3 has the same weight as the others, and thus it is also authentic (solution A). Note also that the third branch, $1 < 2$, is perfectly symmetrical to the first one.

We think that no further comments are needed except for noting an implicit and very important condition, namely that the instruction that the problem be solved with no more than two weighings must apply to each of the seven possible solutions. This actually occurs in Figure 2.3, in which each one of these solutions is at the end of a path that includes exactly two comparisons.

We have identified a correct algorithm for solving our problem without claiming it to be the only one. For example, in the initial comparison instead of coins 1 and 2 we could have engaged any other pair. Alternatively, starting with $1 : 2$, we could have chosen $2 : 3$ as the next comparison. Or, we could sometimes use a different comparison in the second step of the algorithm (in Figure 2.3 we used the $1 : 3$ comparison in all three branches).

Let's see how we can generalize the problem.

*PROBLEM. There are five coins. Identify the false coin, if any, with no more than three weighings.*

With the same reasoning as above, you should be able to solve the problem by yourself, though it is not easy. Figure 2.4 shows a possible algorithm, not necessarily the same as yours, which requires a few comments. When comparing two coins (4 and 5 in the example) and they are of equal weight, it can be concluded that they are both authentic and the problem is transferred to the other three coins. This is what happens in the central path in Figure 2.4, where the remaining coins 1, 2, and 3 are compared via the algorithm in Figure 2.3, after a comparison is done to establish that $4 = 5$. The two branches for $4 > 5$ and $4 < 5$ are identical to those in Figure 2.3 except for replacing the coins. Note that this algorithm performs at most three comparisons for any solution and in some cases it requires only two.

Many different algorithms can be devised for five coins, but a reflection is in order at this point. Without saying it explicitly, it is conceded that the weight of the false coin differs only slightly from those of the other coins, so that the same number of coins must always be placed on the two pans of the balance. Otherwise, the pan

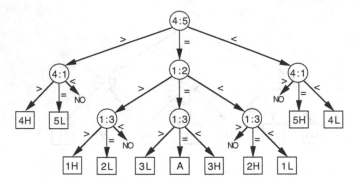

**Fig. 2.4** An algorithm for solving the problem of five coins using the algorithm of Figure 2.3 to compare coins 1, 2 and 3, after having determined that coins 4 and 5 are authentic (result $4 = 5$ of the first comparison).

containing more coins would certainly drop, without providing any new information (in effect, a weighing would be wasted). In the previous algorithms we have always compared individual coins, but with five coins we could place two coins on each pan, e.g. starting with the comparison $1, 2 : 3, 4$. This would still respect the limit of three weighings, but it turns out to be a bit more complicated. We invite you to try this on your own.

*If there were still* five *coins, could the problem be solved with no more than* two *weighings?*

Try thinking about it, but you will not find a solution because there is none. And here the reasoning becomes much more subtle.

The computational structure shown in Figure 2.3 and Figure 2.4 is called a *decision tree*. It shows an algorithm and all the computational paths that result from its execution in relation to the given input data. In the case of the three coins, for example, if coin 2 is false and heavier than the others, the algorithm in Figure 2.3 makes the comparison $1 : 2$ obtaining $1 < 2$, then $1 : 3$ obtaining $1 = 3$, thus returning the correct response 2H. Weighing has three possible results because the pans may be unbalanced in one direction or the other, or stay at the same level, so each comparison opens three different paths in the computation, or fewer than three if some result cannot occur. This means that one weighing opens up to three paths, two weighings open at most $9 = 3^2$ paths, three weighings open at most $27 = 3^3$ paths, until after the generic $i$-th weighing the opened paths are at most $3^i$.

Observe now that the five-coin problem has in total 11 solutions (1L, 1H, 2L, 2H, …, 5L, 5H, or A) and that each solution must appear at the end of a path in the computation. Any algorithm that performs only two weighings would correspond to a decision tree that opens up to nine paths: it follows that to solve the problem, no matter how the input data are presented (i.e., how the coins are put on the balance pans) two weighings are not enough. Three weighings, instead, open up to 27 paths and may therefore be sufficient for five coins, although this does not imply that such a solution actually exists. To decide whether this is the case the solution has to be identified, just as we did in the previous pages.

This reasoning leads to the recognition of two essential concepts in the science of computation, called the *upper bound* on the time complexity of an algorithm, and the *lower bound* on the time complexity of a problem. The *upper bound* measures the ability of an algorithm to provide a solution in a given number of steps, for example the three weighings in Figure 2.4. This is an upper bound in the sense that, once determined through the construction of an algorithm, it establishes a number of steps sufficient to solve a problem and, therefore, that it makes no sense to exceed using less efficient algorithms. The *lower bound* indicates a feature of the problem that makes it possible to determine a number of steps below which the problem cannot be solved: in our example, a minimum of three weighings are needed for five coins. Note that *the lower bound is intrinsic to the problem* (therefore it applies to any resolution algorithm), while *the upper bound is relative to the chosen algorithm*. When, as in the present case, the upper bound established by an algorithm coincides with the lower bound of the problem, the algorithm is said to be *optimal*. The algorithm of Figure 2.4 is therefore optimal because it requires three comparisons as the lower bound indicates.

Let us now ask a new question, the answer to which should be clear at this point:

*If there were* four *coins, could the problem be solved with no more than* two *weighings?*

The problem should be seen as an exercise, for which we offer a partial solution.

1. For computing the lower bound, remember that two weighings can open up to nine paths and there are in fact nine solutions to the problem. Therefore, a lower bound is two weighings and the problem could then admit such a solution. However, an algorithm that solves the problem with two weighings requires that all comparisons generate exactly three alternatives so that the entire decision tree contains exactly three *nodes* (circles corresponding to weighings) at the first level, and nine *nodes* (squares corresponding to solutions) at the second level: in the theory of algorithms such a tree is said to be *perfectly balanced*.
2. However, alas, for this particular problem a perfectly balanced tree cannot exist. In fact, in the first weighing you can compare two coins (for example 1 : 2) or four coins (for example 1,2 : 3,4). In the first case if 1 = 2 (therefore, these two coins are authentic) one of the five solutions 3L, 3H, 4L, 4H, or A is still to be determined and this cannot be achieved with one further weighing that opens only three paths leading to three solutions. In the second case, if the 1,2 : 3,4 comparison leads to the result 1,2 = 3,4, the solution A is immediately determined (all the coins are authentic) but the remaining eight solutions, though divided into two branches, cannot all be identified with only one further comparison because at least one of the branches would have to lead to more than three solutions.

We conclude that for the problem of four coins the limit of two weighings is insufficient, so at least three weighings are needed. And, indeed, an algorithm for this is easy to build.

It is now time to reveal that this stems from a famous problem born in a mathematical field known as Information Theory, in which there were 12 coins and even in this case at most three weighings were permitted. For this problem there are 25 solutions and this makes it possible to set a lower bound of three weighings that can open up to 27 paths of computation. In fact, an algorithm that requires only three weighings does exist but it is rather difficult to build. We have to start with the comparison between two groups of four coins and then, if the weights are different, swap some coins between the pans and check whether the pan that went down before is still the lower one or now goes up. In the first case the coins that have changed pan are certainly authentic, while in the second case they are responsible for the new imbalance and the false coin must be sought among them. This is an important example because it shows how all the information acquired with each subsequent weighing should be stored and used in subsequent steps.

You may change the number of coins as desired to find that the problem has an innocuous appearance but is in fact very complicated. The second algorithm presented (Figure 2.4) uses the first one (Figure 2.3) within it, but this generalization cannot readily be extended to any number of coins. It is generally not easy to determine an efficient, albeit not optimal, algorithm that is valid for any number $n$ of coins, as would be very desirable in algorithm design. On the other hand, an interesting lower bound can easily be established for the general problem, which does not happen for many other problems. In mathematical terms it requires introducing a function known as *logarithm*, which we will discuss later. As far as we have seen, however, we can say that $p$ weighings open up to $3^p$ computation paths and that the solutions are $2n + 1$ if the coins are $n$. Then we must have $3^p \geq 2n + 1$ to ensure that different solutions are at the ends of different paths, and we can determine a lower bound as the smallest value of $p$ that satisfies the relationship above. For example, for $n = 12$ coins we have $2n + 1 = 25$ solutions and then $p = 3$ weighings are needed because $3^3 = 27 > 25$, while the values $p < 3$ are too small to satisfy the relationship and thus less than 3 weighings are insufficient to solve the problem on 12 coins.

# Chapter 3
# Algorithms and Coding

The word "algorithm" (from the medieval Latin "algorismus") appeared for the first time in an important document dated 1202, in fact on the very first page of the mathematical treatise "Liber Abaci" written by Leonardo Fibonacci. Today, the word is firmly established in almost all languages together with the English word "coding." The two words together indicate how to organize and describe a series of actions to achieve a desired result: the algorithm constitutes the stage of designing and evaluating the strategy on which to build single actions, while coding reflects the operational phase that leads to the execution of those actions on a particular computing device, such as a PC, tablet, smartphone, or smartwatch.

Algorithms and coding generally target the sequence of commands to be given to a machine, especially a computer, although it would be fair to extend their use to any activity: from the order in which to put on clothes in the morning, to the sequence of operations for handling a document in an office. However, while traditional day-to-day operations do not require special attention, dealing with a machine is much more delicate.

For at least two centuries, most machines have been modified to make them increasingly "friendly" (a word used today in a technical sense) with the aim of requiring less knowledge of their internal functioning on the part of the user. For machines of all kinds, successive coding levels have been developed, which approximate better and better their users' understanding. Today, you start a car by turning a key or pressing a button without having to know what is actually happening under the hood and this greatly simplifies the "coding" of driving. A century ago, drivers started their cars' engines by manually turning an external crank that rotated the crankshaft: the coding action was expressed in an "engine language" that was comprehensible to any user with some technical knowledge, who could immediately realize that turning the crank spun the driveshaft. Today, pressing the ignition button connects the battery to an electric motor that in turn carries out a mechanical action on the shaft, a chain of operations that can be understood almost exclusively by an auto mechanic. This same approach to computer coding was crucial to the spread of computers, which are the machines referred to in this book.

© Springer Nature Switzerland AG 2018
P. Ferragina, F. Luccio, *Computational Thinking*,
https://doi.org/10.1007/978-3-319-97940-3_3

To fix some preliminary ideas, let us imagine that we need to search for a word in a dictionary. If we do the search by hand, the dictionary we use is a printed book and we take it for granted that the words in it appear in alphabetical order. We will randomly open the dictionary at a reasonable place with respect to the beginning of the word we are looking for (e.g., looking for mother we will open the dictionary close to the center, looking for aunt we will open it close to the beginning); we will compare a random word on the selected page with the word of interest to determine whether one precedes or follows the other in the alphabetical order; we will move on to previous or subsequent words by skipping a group of pages if we are still too far away; finally, we will examine in succession a few words alphabetically close to the one sought for, until we find it or decide that it is not there. This is the scheme of a "search algorithm" that will serve as a basis for a formalization that can be used by a machine. We will see this formalization at the end of the chapter because it is good to proceed gradually.

To address the problem with a computer we need to specify every operation to be done with absolute precision, at least with the machines we have access to today. Computers, more than any other machine, have seen the development of successive coding levels: from those that explicitly refer to the internal structure, written in *machine language* and reserved for specialized technicians, to those in *high-level languages* accessible to all users, who may also ignore how the commands they provide translate into internal operations, but must know their effects on the computational process as a whole. This book refers to the use of high-level languages, observing that such use, known as *programming*, is not simple: it is far more difficult than driving a car, but is rich in satisfaction when you begin to master it.

## 3.1 The Pseudocode

After such a long preamble, we begin to "program" by introducing the commands as needed. We learn much better this way, without discussing *a priori* the many formal properties of the language used. Although it may seem strange, these properties are more attractive after one has gained a little bit of intuitive experience on very simple examples; this is useful when we have to study the subtleties of the language in order to deal with more complicated problems.

Among the many coding levels we have chosen one that does not employ any specific language that can be executed on a computer, but in some sense represents them all. It is called *pseudocode*. A program formulated in pseudocode is not accepted directly by any machine but is so close to the commonly accepted high-level languages that can easily be translated into any of them. In this text, programs in pseudocode will then be translated into the *Python* language that is in vogue today. While Python, like all of its peers, can be quickly replaced by other languages at any time, the formulation in pseudocode offered in this text will remain valid, to be transformed into a new language. So let's begin.

*PROBLEM. Searching for a word in a sequence.*

In essence, this is similar to the dictionary problem we have already introduced, but our present ignorance in programming prevents us from using the algorithm described above for manual use: an algorithm that has a simple logical structure but is too complicated for a first attempt at coding. So let us look at how to deal with the problem in the simplest possible way.

First we assume that the sequence of words is not ordered (the problem of how to sort a sequence of arbitrary elements will be the topic of a later chapter). In the first instance we imagine that the sequence has already been stored in the computer, and here we encounter the first difference between the internal structure of the machine and the view of it we have from the outside. Let's say that the sequence is made up of eight two-letter codes of Italian cities: FI, MI, PA, NA, BO, TO, VE, and CA (Figure 3.1). The computer has a memory consisting of cells numbered in succession (these numbers are called *addresses*). Analyzing the memory's contents we find the number of elements in the sequence and their data, recorded one after the other starting from an address known to a user working in machine language, but not known to a programmer using a high-level language. The latter will know that the sequence is contained in a suitable *data structure*, called a *vector*, to which an arbitrary name, such as CITY, must be assigned. The data stored in the vector, which in this case has eight cells because this is the length of the sequence, are referred to in the program as CITY[0] = FI, then CITY[1] = MI, and so on up to CITY[7] = CA. That is, for the programmer, the address is relative to the position in the vector, not to the position in the memory.

| Address in memory | ⋯ | 48 | 49 | 50 | 51 | 52 | 53 | 54 | 55 | 56 | 57 | 58 |
|---|---|---|---|---|---|---|---|---|---|---|---|---|
| CITY | ⋯ | ⋯ | 8 | FI | MI | PA | NA | BO | TO | VE | CA | ⋯ |
| Position in the vector | | | | 0 | 1 | 2 | 3 | 4 | 5 | 6 | 7 | |

**Fig. 3.1** Storing a sequence in the form of a vector (middle row) in the cells of addresses from 50 to 57 of a computer's memory. Cell 49 contains the number of vector elements. Access to the sequence is obtained by specifying the name assigned to the vector and a position within it: commonly, these positions start from zero.

We are now at the heart of *problem solving*, which consists of the following steps:

1. establish the broad structure of an *algorithm* to solve the general problem; in the present case, finding a datum in a sequence regardless of the number of its elements;
2. choose the *data structures* best suited to describe to the machine the required form of the input and output. In addition to the initial data and the final results, some intermediate structures may be used to represent facts emerging during the computation and necessary for its continuation;

3. formalize a program in *pseudocode* that describes the algorithm in a clear and appropriate way for its implementation on a computer; and
4. translate the program into a high-level and *executable* language, for example Python.

In this chapter and the following ones we limit our programs to a pseudocode formulation, referring to the website mentioned at the beginning of this text for the equivalent versions of these programs written in Python.

Contrary to common belief, the most important step is the first one, namely establishing the structure of the algorithm. It does not make sense to start writing a program before setting out the strategy to follow and evaluating its efficiency, although this can be affected by the computer features and programming languages used. To write a general search algorithm applicable to our city codes example, we denote the sequence with a generic name such as SET, and the element to be searched for with the name DATA. Once the program is formalized, this will be used, for example, to search for the city-code NA in the sequence CITY by replacing these two words for DATA and SET, as we will see below.

Since the sequence is not ordered, the placement of any element inside it is independent from that of all the other elements. Therefore, examining an element and finding that it is different from the one specified in DATA does not provide any information as to whether DATA is in SET, and, if so, where. As a result, the search algorithm has to scan one by one all the elements of SET stopping only when it finds DATA, or deduces that the element is not present after examining the entire content of SET with a negative result. This allows us to reaffirm a fundamental concept:

*An algorithm must solve the problem for which it has been designed, with the level of efficiency that we predetermined, for each form in which the input data can occur and therefore even in the worst case.*

For the present problem we can admit that the worst case is the one that requires the maximum number of comparisons and this occurs when the element being searched for is the last one to be examined, or is just not there. In relation to the concepts introduced in Chapter 2, we use $n$ to indicate the number of elements in the sequence and count the number of data comparisons as a criterion to judge the quality of the algorithm. It is easy to find that $n$ comparisons is an *upper bound* for a set of $n$ elements since it is established by an algorithm that examines each element of the sequence exactly once. On the other hand, $n$ is also a *lower bound* because if an algorithm executed fewer than $n$ comparisons without finding the datum sought for it could not conclude that it was not one of the other ones.

In conclusion, we can say that all the elements of the sequence must be examined in the worst case, and any algorithm examining them all exactly once is *optimal*. This concludes the first step of the computational approach to a problem, which is establishing the basic ideas on which an algorithm has to be built.

The second step – that is, the choice of data structures to be used – is in this case immediate because we already know about vectors whose elements can be numbers, alphabetical sequences, etc., in essence "words" in a general sense. So the sequence

```
program SEARCH1 (SET, DATA)
// Finding an element DATA in a set SET
// n indicates the number of elements of SET
    i ← 0;
   while i ≤ n − 1
      if SET[i] = DATA
         print DATA "is present";
            stop;
         else i ← i + 1;
      print DATA "is not present";
```

**Fig. 3.2** Program to detect the presence of an element in a set.

will be contained in a vector SET, the element to be searched for will be the value of a variable DATA specified by the user at the time the program is used, and the result of the search will be returned through a printout or shown on a screen.

The basic structure of the pseudocode program SEARCH1 is shown in Figure 3.2. Let's now explain the meaning of the program and of its "keywords" (in boldface) in no particular order, noting that what is said here will remain valid in the rest of the book.

- The **program** SEARCH1 is defined with two input parameters: an arbitrary sequence of elements allocated to a vector named SET and an element to be searched for stored as a variable named DATA. The number $n$ of the elements of SET is stored together with their values and is automatically read by the computer when the program is initiated.
- The double slash // indicates that the following text is an explanatory comment and does not affect the execution of the program.
- $i \leftarrow 0$ means that a variable $i$ is used and initialized to the value 0. The statement $i \leftarrow i + 1$ indicates that the current value of $i$ (to the right of the arrow) is added to 1 and the new value is assigned to $i$.
- **while** is a fundamental command in the pseudocode. The portion of the program to which this command applies, or the *body of* **while**, is indicated by indenting the subsequent lines of code. When another line with the same indentation as **while** is encountered, the body of **while** is terminated. In the example, the command has effect until the line beginning with **else**, included in the body. Indentations are used in the same way for any other programming construct.
- **while** requires a part of the program (the *body*) to repeat according to a boolean condition specified at its beginning: in our case, $i \leq n - 1$. The values of the variables in that condition must be changed in the **while** body to allow its termination: when the condition is no longer verified the program proceeds with the line of code following the **while** body. In our program each repetition (or loop)

compares DATA with the element of the sequence contained in SET[$i$] (see the meaning of the construct **if-else** in the next point): if the two are different, the value of $i$ is incremented by 1 and the next loop is executed, provided that the condition $i \leq n - 1$ is still verified.

- The construct **if-else** is also controlled by a boolean condition indicated at its beginning: in our case, SET [$i$] = DATA. If that condition is verified, the commands that follow the **if** line with an indentation are executed (this is the *body of* **if**: in our case, the commands **print** and **stop**); otherwise, the commands in the *body of* **else** are executed. In our example, the body of **if** prints a message indicating to the user that DATA was found, while the body of **else** increments the variable $i$ and starts another execution of the **while** loop.

- The command **print** writes on a screen the sentence that follows the command. The words in quotes are printed identically while for the other ones, typically variable names or parameters (DATA in our case), the *value* that they have at that time is printed. If in SEARCH1 the **while** loops are completed without finding DATA (and thus we have $i = n$), the **print** command at the bottom of the program is executed.

- The command **stop** determines the end of the computation by blocking any other operation present in the pseudocode. In our case, if DATA is present in SET, the command **stop** interrupts the search for it (thereby interrupting the execution of SEARCH1) regardless of the boolean condition driving the **while** loop. Alternatively, the computation ends after the last command in the program has been executed.

- Once written, the program can be used on arbitrary input data, by specifying as input parameters the sequence and the element to be searched for. So, to search for NA in the vector CITY of Figure 3.1 we will execute the program *call*

    SEARCH1(CITY, NA)

that prints "NA is present" after four repetitions of the **while** loop. Whereas the execution of the call

    SEARCH1(CITY, RC)

prints: "RC is not present" after eight repetitions of the **while** loop.


## 3.2 A More Useful Program

The usefulness of the SEARCH1 program is very limited. Typically an element is searched for in a sequence not only to establish its presence, but as a task preliminary to other ones that include extracting some information about the element itself, for example, searching for a word in a dictionary to find its meaning or its translation into another language. In relation to the CITY sequence, you may want to specify a city code to see whether it appears in the sequence and, if so, to find out the corresponding area code. Fortunately, as we will now see, SEARCH1 can be immediately extended for this purpose.

First of all we need to enlarge the data structure to contain area codes. In addition to the vector CITY there will be another vector AREA, also of eight elements, contained for example in the memory cells from 65 to 72 (see Figure 3.3) where the city code in position $i$ of CITY is associated with the area code in position $i$ of AREA. For example we have CITY[3] = NA and its area code is AREA[3] = 081.

| Address in memory | 63 | 64 | 65 | 66 | 67 | 68 | 69 | 70 | 71 | 72 | 73 |
|---|---|---|---|---|---|---|---|---|---|---|---|
| AREA | | $\cdots$ 8 | 055 | 02 | 091 | 081 | 051 | 011 | 041 | 070 | $\cdots$ |
| Position in the vector | | | 0 | 1 | 2 | 3 | 4 | 5 | 6 | 7 | |

**Fig. 3.3** The vector AREA stored in the memory cells from 65 to 72, preceded by its size in cell 64. As usual the vector is accessed using a high-level language by specifying the vector's name and the location of the elements.

The new program SEARCH2 for searching the information associated with the elements of a sequence is shown in Figure 3.4. As in SEARCH1 the element names are contained in a vector SET while the information associated with them is contained in a vector INFO, both of $n$ elements. DATA indicates the element whose associated information is searched for: and the result of the search will be returned through only a printout. The program is an immediate extension of SEARCH1 where the lines marked with an asterisk have been modified.

```
* program SEARCH2 (SET, INFO, DATA)
* // search for the information associated with an element of a set of cardinality n
    i ← 0;
    while i ≤ n − 1
        if SET[i] = DATA
*            print " the information of " DATA "is" INFO[i];
            stop;
        else i ← i + 1;
    print DATA "is not present";
```

**Fig. 3.4** The program to extract the information, stored in a vector INFO, associated with the elements of a vector SET.

To get the area code of NA we make the call

SEARCH2 (CITY, AREA, NA)

that generates the printout "the information of NA is 081".

## 3.3 Interacting with the Machine

The two examples seen so far give an initial idea as to the structure of a program and some standard constructs, but leave us at an uncomfortable distance from its practical use in a computer even if it solves a very simple search problem. In fact, we have not yet clarified how the program can be materially used.

Let's look at SEARCH2. First, the program and the sequences must be physically stored (*uploaded*) into the computer's memory. If we assume that we have written names and area codes in an address book the parallel with manual processing is immediate. The search algorithm is present in our head where we implicitly loaded it, thinking of how to solve the problem. However, the task is different with a computer, due to the inflexible precision required to perform the loading operations, which may be quite monotonous.

As for the program, we can trust that someone has uploaded it for us, though, after trying to write it or at least understand it, we would probably have preferred to have done so on our own. However, it is an old story because, as we will see, modern high-level languages are charged with automatically loading the programs into memory. In addition to the program, the data on which to operate—i.e. the vectors CITY and AREA in our example—should be stored in the computer's memory. This can be achieved as a *file transfer* if the two vectors are already present on another device connected to ours, or by entering the values for the first time according to a series of commands shown in Figure 3.5.

```
// loading the vector CITY
   get CITY [8] = { FI, MI, PA, NA, BO, TO, VE, CA };
// loading the vector AREA
   get AREA [8] = {055, 02, 091, 081, 051, 011, 041, 070};
```

**Fig. 3.5** Commands for uploading the vectors CITY and AREA.

Note that the pseudocode of Figure 3.5 has introduced other features in the coding:

- The command **get** captures input data introduced by the user, for example through a keyboard. Such data may be of various kinds (in our case it will consist of names or numbers) and are subject to the specific formatting rules of the particular programming language used.
- The command **get** uses the notation CITY[8] to indicate that CITY is a vector of eight elements, and the sequence that follows contains the names that must be stored inside it. The computer does not proceed to the next line of the program until it has received eight elements. The uploading of the vector AREA follows, obviously, the same rules.

Once the program and the data have been uploaded into the computer's memory, we must tell the computer that we want to make a search through SEARCH2 by specifying the element to search for and by receiving the area code in reply. This is achieved with the program LOAD_SEARCH in Figure 3.6, which includes the commands for loading the vectors and interacting with the computer, and the call of program SEARCH2 that we assume to be present in memory.

```
program LOAD_SEARCH
    get CITY [8] = {FI, MI, PA, NA, BO, TO, VE, CA};
    get AREA [8] = {055, 02, 091, 081, 051, 011, 041, 070};
    SEARCH ← GO;                          // SEARCH is a control parameter
    while SEARCH = GO                     // the search goes on
        print "State the data to search for";
        get CODE;                         // CODE is a parameter specifying a city code
        SEARCH2 (CITY, AREA, CODE);
        print "Do you want to continue searching?";
        get SEARCH;
```

**Fig. 3.6** A program to get information associated with the names in a sequence. The program calls SEARCH2, which retrieves and prints the required information.

A call of LOAD_SEARCH performs the following steps that relate to a sample interaction with the user:

- the program prints the message "State the data to search for",
- the user enters the city code NA,
- the program prints the message "The information of NA is 081",
- the program prints the message "Do you want to continue searching? ",
- the user enters GO,
- the program prints the message "State the data to search for",
- the user enters the city code VR,
- the program prints the message "VR is not present",
- the program prints the message "Do you want to continue searching?",
- the user enters HALT (or any word other than GO),
- the program stops.

## 3.4 Binary Search

At the beginning of this chapter, we referred to the usual method of searching for a word in a dictionary in which words are printed in *alphabetical order*. This is a very different and faster method than the ones seen previously, which scanned the dictionary from its beginning in a sequential manner. Let's now see how to formalize the former schematic description in an algorithm and its program.

The general problem is to look for an element in a set for which a *total ordering* is defined: that is, for every pair of elements $a, b$ it happens that $a$ *equals* $b$, or $a$ *precedes* $b$, or $b$ *precedes* $a$ (in symbols $a = b, a < b$, or $b < a$). Of course, this relationship applies between numbers, or between words according to the alphabetical order. However, it also applies to any set of character sequences if you define a total ordering on their characters and then apply the alphabetical order to the sequences.

The new search algorithm, known as *binary search*, works on a vector SET whose $n$ elements are arranged in "increasing" order according to an ordering relationship defined for them. In other words, those elements, which we assume for simplicity to all be different from each other, are stored in the vector with $SET[i] < SET[j]$ for each pair $i, j$ with $0 \leq i < j \leq n - 1$. For example, our list of cities will be stored in alphabetical order in the new vector CITORD shown in Figure 3.7. Consequently, the sequence of the corresponding area codes will be reordered in the vector AREAORD, which does not follow the numerical ordering within it, but is related to the ordering of the city codes. In computer language CITORD is called the *index* and is used to access the information contained in AREAORD.

| CITORD | 8 | BO | CA | FI | MI | NA | PA | TO | VE |
|--------|---|----|----|----|----|----|----|----|----|
| AREAORD | 8 | 051 | 070 | 055 | 02 | 081 | 091 | 011 | 041 |
| Position | | 0 | 1 | 2 | 3 | 4 | 5 | 6 | 7 |

**Fig. 3.7** Vector CITORD with city codes arranged in alphabetical order, and the corresponding vector AREAORD of area codes. Of course, the two vectors are contained in two different groups of memory cells. The number 8 at the beginning of the two vectors indicates their length.

Binary search on a computer differs from "manual" coding as to the ease or difficulty of performing some manual or machine operations. It is natural for us to open a dictionary at a point that we believe to be close to the word sought for due to its initial letter, then move by groups of pages, or rows, chosen with common sense depending on the words encountered. With a computer, this would require it to access some statistics about the frequency of initials, which depend on the language used. While this may significantly complicate the process, it can take advantage of a computer feature that is unavailable to humans: to access the central element of the vector containing the dictionary with a simple arithmetic operation.

The central word, denoted by $C$, of the dictionary will then be the first one to be compared with the search word, denoted by $K$. If the two words match, the search ends successfully; otherwise, if $K < C$, the search is repeated with the same rule in the half of the dictionary preceding $C$; if instead $C < K$ the search is repeated in the half of the dictionary following $C$. This way the portion of the dictionary to be examined is halved at each step. If the word $K$ is contained in the dictionary, it is certainly encountered in the center of one of these portions, otherwise the search

---

**program** BINARY_SEARCH (SET, DATA)

// binary search of an element DATA in a vector SET of $n$ elements

$\quad i \leftarrow 0; \; j \leftarrow n-1;$

$\quad$ **while** $i \leq j$

$\qquad m \leftarrow \lfloor (i+j)/2 \rfloor; \quad$ // $\lfloor x \rfloor$ specifies the largest integer $\leq x$

$\qquad\qquad\qquad\qquad$ // $m$ is the middle position between $i$ and $j$

$\qquad$ **if** DATA = SET $[m]$;

$\qquad\qquad$ **print** DATA "is present" ;

$\qquad\qquad$ **stop**;

$\qquad$ **if** (DATA < SET $[m]$) $\; j \leftarrow m-1$;

$\qquad$ **if** (SET $[m]$ < DATA) $\; i \leftarrow m+1$;

$\quad$ **print** DATA "is not present";

---

**Fig. 3.8** The BINARY_SEARCH program which searches the element DATA in the vector SET.

ends unsuccessfully when the last portion examined is reduced to a single word different from $K$.

The pseudocode of the BINARY_SEARCH program is shown in Figure 3.8 as an alternative to SEARCH1 in Figure 3.2. The search word $K$ is transmitted through the variable DATA, the dictionary is stored in ascending order in the vector SET, and its central element is SET$[m]$ at every step. We notice that:

- Each iteration of the **while** loop considers the portion of the vector SET within the indices $i, j$. In the initial iteration, we have $i = 0$ and $j = n - 1$, so the portion coincides with the entire vector.
- $m = \lfloor (i+j)/2 \rfloor$ is the central position of the vector portion between positions $i$ and $j$. If the number of elements in the portion is odd, the center is uniquely identified and the approximation inherent in the $\lfloor \; \rfloor$ notation does not produce any effect. If the number of elements in the portion is even, the position preceding the non-integer value $(i+j)/2$ is taken as the central position. For example, the center between the five positions from 3 to 7 is $\lfloor (3+7)/2 \rfloor = \lfloor 5 \rfloor = 5$; the center between the four positions from 3 to 6 is $\lfloor (3+6)/2 \rfloor = \lfloor 4.5 \rfloor = 4$.
- If DATA = SET$[m]$ the computation ends, otherwise it will repeat on a new portion of the vector in the next iteration of the **while** loop. If, instead, DATA < SET$[m]$ the new portion is the "left half" of the current one: so the value of $i$ remains unchanged while $j$ takes the value that precedes the central point, that is $j = m - 1$. Finally, if SET$[m]$ < DATA, a new search is symmetrically repeated in the "right half" of the current portion, with $j$ unchanged and $i$ taking up the value $m + 1$.
- If the current portion contains only one element, i.e. $i = j = m$, and DATA $\neq$ SET$[m]$, either $j$ or $i$ is updated as indicated in the previous point. In any case we

have $i > j$ so the **while** loop ends. The following line of the program indicates that DATA is not present in SET, and the program execution terminates.

For example, in order to search for FI in the set CITORD (see Figure 3.7) we call

      BINARY_SEARCH(CITORD, FI)

that computes $m = \lfloor(0+7)/2\rfloor = 3$ and compares FI with CITORD [3] = MI getting FI $<$ MI; it then updates the value of $j$ as $j = 2$ ($i$ remains equal to 0), and repeats the **while** loop; now the new value $m = \lfloor(0+2)/2\rfloor = 1$ is computed and FI is compared with CITORD [1] = CA obtaining FI $>$ CA. A new update sets $i = 2$ ($j$ remains equal to 2) and the **while** loop is repeated giving $m = \lfloor(2+2)/2\rfloor = 2$ and FI = CITORD [2] that produces the final printing: "FI is present".

The call BINARY_SEARCH(CITORD, GR) generates the same steps until it finds GR $>$ CITORD[2], then the values $i = 2 + 1 = 3$ and $j = 2$ are computed corresponding to the condition $i > j$, which blocks the **while** loop and produces the printing: "GR is not present".

Similarly to how we extended the program SEARCH1 (in Figure 3.2) to the program SEARCH2 (in Figure 3.4), the pseudocode of BINARY_SEARCH can be transformed into a new program BINARY_SEARCH2 that works on the two sets SET and INFO by substituting the line of code

**print** DATA "is present";

with the new line:

**print** "the information of" DATA "is" INFO[$m$];

The program LOAD_SEARCH (of Figure 3.6) can also be adapted to upload in the computer's memory the vectors CITORD and AREAORD (in Figure 3.7), and to call BINARY_SEARCH instead of SEARCH2.

Once again we underline that binary search is equivalent to the hand-made search, but the jump between dictionary words is now established by a precise arithmetic rule (the calculation of the value $m$) instead of moving heuristically. It can be shown that the number of steps performed by the two methods is comparable. But how many steps are there? That is, what is the number of comparisons between the element DATA being searched for and the elements in the vector SET? Calculation of this number is difficult for the manual algorithm but is simple for BINARY_SEARCH. The worst case occurs when the search arrives at a portion that consists of a single element, and this is equal or not to the searched element, namely DATA. The number of comparisons leading to this condition is equal to the number of times an integer $n$ (the number of elements of SET) can be divided by 2 until it becomes equal to 1. This can be an alternative definition of the logarithm function calculated to the base 2, which will be discussed in detail in a later chapter. For the time being, we notice that the value of this function is much smaller than $n$ and that it grows very slowly as $n$ increases. For example, searching in the phone book of a small town with 1,000 entries requires 10 comparisons because ten halves reduce the search set to one element; the phone book of a small city with 30,000 entries requires 15 comparisons; that of a metropolis with 1,000,000 entries requires 20 comparisons.

Therefore, the binary search is much faster than the sequential search, and this difference in efficiency increases quickly with the increase of the input size $n$. Furthermore, from the previous examples it can be seen that the slow growth of the logarithm function with $n$ implies that the number of comparisons required by BINARY_SEARCH is not much influenced by the size of SET.

# Chapter 4
# The Tournament

The final phase of the football World Cup is played as a knockout stage: those who lose are eliminated, so at each round the number of teams is halved. The number of teams, say $n$, is initially a power of 2, for example $n = 2^4 = 16$. In this case, the sixteen teams play in the octofinals from which eight winning teams emerge that meet in the quarterfinals; the four winning teams play in the semifinals, and finally two teams play in the final from which the world champion team emerges. Note that these numbers 16, 8, 4, 2, and 1 are all powers of 2 with decreasing exponents: the last one is $2^0 = 1$.

Is all this correct? Whoever understands a bit about football, or any other sport that includes a knockout tournament, knows that many facts can affect the result of a match so that nobody can assert with absolute certainty that the stronger of the two contenders will win. Therefore, without taking anything away from the glory of the champion team, there is always doubt that it may not be the overall best. And, as we will see, this doubt is far more serious regarding the second place reserved to the team that comes to play, and loses, the final.

Let us examine the problem by proceeding gradually, setting up a strict mathematical formulation to leave nothing to chance. We indicate the teams with different positive integers, and assume that team $a$ wins against team $b$ if $a > b$.

*PROBLEM. Given an arbitrary set of n different positive integers, find the greatest of them, called the* maximum.

Of course this problem is very similar to the one of the tournament, but now the comparison between two elements has a fixed result that will always be the same if the comparison is repeated. Another very important feature for our purposes is the "transitive property of skill" that sometimes may not hold in sports, namely that if $a > b$ and $b > c$ then certainly $a > c$. This means that, if the first two comparisons have been made, the result of the third one is implicitly known.

We must now design an algorithm for solving the problem, that is we must decide in which order the elements are to be compared and how to accumulate the information obtained from the results of the comparisons, up to determining the maximum. First note that the set is arbitrarily chosen, so if an element has not yet been consid-

© Springer Nature Switzerland AG 2018
P. Ferragina, F. Luccio, *Computational Thinking*,
https://doi.org/10.1007/978-3-319-97940-3_4

ered, we do not know its relationship with the other ones. Once this element enters a comparison, however, we can use the transitive property, if it applies, as in the case of element $c$ in the previous example. We also establish that the maximum element must be determined with the fewest total number of comparisons, as is reasonable in a sports tournament. Of course, we will set up this number as a function of the number $n$ of participants.

Before proceeding, an algorithm designer should consider what is a *lower bound* to that number of comparisons, as we have seen in Chapter 2 for the problem of coins. In fact, if the problem cannot be solved with fewer than a certain number of comparisons, it makes no sense to look for an algorithm that does so. Since this reasoning is not easy we put it aside for a moment and try to build a first, albeit naïve, algorithm. We also postpone the pseudocode formalization of the standard tournament algorithm, that is, the one that ends up with the final, because even this task is not easy.

Consider a set of $n$ integers that we can examine consecutively. The first element is provisionally declared the maximum of the set. Compare this element with the second one and provisionally state that the greater of the two is the maximum. Compare this element with the next one and again declare that the greater one is the maximum. Continue comparing each new element with the current and temporary maximum. The final solution is determined when all the elements have been compared.

| **24** | 15 | 7 | 9 | 20 | **49** | 33 | 35 | 22 | 40 | **52** | 12 | **62** | 30 | 8 | 43 |
|------|----|---|---|----|------|----|----|----|----|------|----|------|----|---|----|
| 0 | 1 | 2 | 3 | 4 | 5 | 6 | 7 | 8 | 9 | 10 | 11 | 12 | 13 | 14 | 15 |

**Fig. 4.1** A vector SET of $n = 16$ elements. In the left-to-right scanning, the numbers in boldface indicate the temporary maximum MAX. The final value at the end of the scanning is MAX = 62. As always, the positions in the vector range from 0 to $n - 1$.

Let us see, for example, how this algorithm behaves on a set of $n = 16$ elements that, as we know, will be contained in a vector SET as illustrated in Figure 4.1 above. The temporary maximum, updated through the comparisons, will be indicated with MAX. Start by setting MAX = 24. This value stays unchanged until the element 49 is encountered and the new value MAX = 49 is established after the comparison between 24 and 49. We will then have MAX = 52 and then MAX = 62, which remains the maximum value until the end.

The pseudocode formulation of the algorithm, called MAXIMUM, is shown in Figure 4.2. We have introduced a new command:

- The command **for** requires the iteration of the lines contained in its body, as usually indicated by the indentation of the following lines, for all the values fulfilling a condition attached to the word **for**. The condition has the form $x = a$ **to** $b$ (in our example $i = 1$ **to** $n - 1$), where $x$ is a control variable and $a, b$ are two integers

```
program MAXIMUM (SET, MAX)
// search for the maximum in a set of n integers
    MAX ← SET[0] ;
    for i = 1 to n − 1
        if SET[i] > MAX
            MAX ← SET[i] ;
    print "the maximum element is" MAX ;
```

**Fig. 4.2** The program MAXIMUM to find the maximum in a set of integers.

with $a \leq b$. Starting with $x = a$, the lines in the **for**-loop are executed for all the values of $x$ between $a$ and $b$, incrementing $x$ by 1 in each iteration of the loop.

- We also note that the construct **if** is used here without the **else** part: this is interpreted by executing the commands contained in its body, or skipping them all, if the control condition is, or is not, verified. In our example, if SET[$i$] $\leq$ MAX (the **if** condition is not verified) the next iteration of the **for**-loop is run by incrementing $i$ by one.

The algorithm coded in MAXIMUM is apparently very rudimentary. Certainly it would not be used in a tournament: in the example of Figure 4.1, if team 62 were the first of the list, it would have to play $n - 1$ matches with all the others to be declared the winner. But let us examine it closer.

First of all, the algorithm is correct because we have accepted that the transitive property of skill holds. In our example 24 beats 15, 7, 9, and 20 one after the other, before meeting 49, and since 49 beats 24, it is implicitly greater than 15, 7, 9, and 20 without the need to be compared with them directly. It is clear that the maximum would be found by comparing all the possible pairs of elements, but here we do a lot fewer comparisons. How many in total?

This is a fundamental question because we have committed to evaluate (and then compare) the algorithms for finding the maximum by counting the number of comparisons between elements that they make. And it is immediately apparent that MAXIMUM executes $n - 1$ comparisons because, after each comparison, the losing element is no longer considered: after discarding $n - 1$ elements, only the winner remains. So $n - 1$ is an *upper bound* to the number of comparisons.

It is worth noting that checking all pairs of elements would execute $n(n-1)/2$ comparisons. In fact, each of the $n$ elements would be compared with the other $n - 1$ ones, for a total of $n(n - 1)$ comparisons, each of these is however counted twice because it is there both as $x$ vs $y$ and as $y$ vs $x$. For the 16 elements of Figure 4.1 we would have $(16 \cdot 15)/2 = 120$ comparisons instead of the 15 comparisons executed by the algorithm MAXIMUM. For a set of 100 elements the comparisons would be 4,950 instead of 99. In fact, an algorithm performing all the possible comparisons between $n$ elements would lead to a value of about $n^2/2$ comparisons, which, as $n$

grows, becomes much higher than the value of about $n$ comparisons of MAXIMUM. We can now start considering MAXIMUM with a little more confidence.

Can we do better? More importantly, what is a *lower bound* to the number of comparisons for solving the maximum problem? Now things become much more interesting.

## 4.1 A Lower Bound to the Problem of Maximum

Recall the problem of the coins with which we began this book. A lower bound to a problem where comparisons play an important role can be found by means of a *decision tree*, where a branch corresponds to the result of a comparison and the problem solutions are arranged at the end of the computational paths as leaves of the tree. In the case of searching for the maximum, the solutions are $n$ because the maximum can be the first, or the second .... or the $n$-th element. Since in our problem each comparison has two possible results (one element is larger or smaller than another but the two cannot be equal), one comparison opens two paths, two consecutive comparisons open four paths, and so on until $k$ comparisons open up to $2^k$ paths (note that some paths may terminate before the $k$-th level) at the end of which the $n$ solutions are found. For this problem, the bound obtained with a decision tree is very low, for example, to reach our 16 solutions, four comparisons would be enough since $2^4 = 16$, while the algorithm MAXIMUM requires 15 comparisons.

Mathematically we have to impose $2^k \geq n$ and the function to express $k$ is called the *logarithm to the base 2*. That is $k \geq \log_2 n$. Without going deep into the mathematical details, we recall that $\log_2 n$ progressively becomes much less than $n$ as $n$ increases. That is, the lower bound $\log_2 n$ to the number of comparisons is much smaller than the $n - 1$ upper bound established by the proposed algorithm MAXIMUM. For example, for $n = 1,024$ we have $\log_2 n = 10$.

At this point, there are three possibilities: either there is a better algorithm than the one expressed by MAXIMUM, requiring less than $n - 1$ comparisons thus approaching the lower bound stated above, or a different reasoning indicates that there is a higher lower bound, or both of these facts are possible. Generally, we do not know what the most plausible hypothesis is but in this case the second one will prevail. Note, however, that determining a higher lower bound does not at all mean that the previous bound is "wrong" but that, considering a different aspect of the problem, a more significant (larger) bound may emerge than the (smaller) one determined using the decision tree. And indeed this is the case with the tournament.

First of all we notice that, in order to determine the maximum, all elements of the set must enter into at least one comparison. In fact, if an element $x$ is never compared with other ones, we would never know whether $x$ is the maximum. This leads us to establish the new lower bound $n/2$ because we need at least $n/2$ comparisons to get all the elements into a comparison. Warning: we are not saying that $n/2$ comparisons *suffice*, which has to do with building an algorithm that employs exactly that number of comparisons, but that the problem cannot be solved with fewer than $n/2$

comparisons regardless of the chosen algorithm. So we have the new lower bound $n/2$ that is larger than $\log_2 n$ and thus this latter bound is not significant (though, again, it was not wrong). The lower bound $n/2$ is closer to the number of comparisons required by MAXIMUM.

Now a further reasoning that will perhaps be surprising. Determining the maximum in a set of $n$ elements also implies that the other $n-1$ elements are found not to be the maximum. Therefore, no algorithm can stop before this property has been verified. However, to ensure that an element is not the maximum it will have to be the loser in at least one comparison. (If $x$ has never lost, who can say that it is not the maximum?) And since exactly one loser comes out of each comparison, it takes at least $n-1$ comparisons to determine $n-1$ different losers. Therefore, the new lower bound $n-1$ prevails over the other ones (which are smaller, i.e. $n/2$ and $\log_2 n$), and this allows us to conclude that the algorithm MAXIMUM is optimal with regard to the number of comparisons. Who would have thought this?

## 4.2 The Knockout Stage

Although the algorithm MAXIMUM is computationally optimal, the proposed approach is neither elegant nor useful in a tournament in which the knockout stage is adopted, as we will now precisely describe in algorithmic terms. Of course, even the standard representation of the knockout stage and its interpretation that we all know describes an algorithm, but it is not that simple to turn it into a computer program. For this reason it is first necessary to define exactly what is meant by a tree in mathematics because the knockout stage is actually a tree.

A *tree* is an abstract mathematical entity composed of *nodes* (or *vertices*), and of *arcs* (or *edges*) joining nodes in pairs, such that any two nodes are linked through a *path* of consecutive arcs but no path touches a node twice (that is, there are no *cycles*). A tree node constitutes the *root*. The root is the *parent* of the nodes directly connected to it, which are its *children* and are in turn roots of smaller trees (or *subtrees*) in which the tree can be naturally partitioned. Proceeding in the division, nodes that have no children are called *leaves* of the tree. The number of arcs in the path that links two nodes is the *distance* between them. Nodes located at the same distance $d$ from the root are at *level d* in the tree (then the root is at level zero).

As shown in Figure 4.3 the knockout stage is a tree in which the leaves (24, 15, 7, etc.) are associated with all the participants; each tree level above that of the leaves includes the participants who have so far won the previous comparisons (games), so that the champion is placed at the root. Mathematical trees are in fact turned upside down compared to their plant homonyms as their roots are on top. Notice that the knockout stage is a *binary tree* since all nodes, except the leaves, have exactly two children. It is also a *balanced tree* because all the leaves are at the same level (removing, say, nodes 24 and 15 the tree would remain binary but would not be balanced). Of course, the decision tree we saw in Chapter 2 was also a tree, but *ternary* rather than binary since each node had three children.

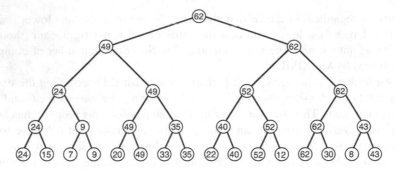

**Fig. 4.3** Knockout stage of a tournament between the sixteen elements of Figure 4.1 placed in the leaves of a tree. Compared elements are arranged in pairs next to each other, and the winner appears in the level above as the parent of the two contenders. For example 24 wins the comparison with 15 and becomes the parent of the leaves 24 and 15, etc. 62 is the tournament winner being the maximum of the contenders, and indeed it appears at the tree root.

After so many definitions we finally examine the algorithm formalizing the knockout stage. Maybe our interest is slightly decreased by knowing that it cannot beat MAXIMUM as far as the number of comparisons is concerned. Or, that it might execute more comparisons than MAXIMUM. So let us count them inside the tree. Every node in all levels above the leaves contains a winner, so the number of comparisons is equal to the number of these nodes; 15 in our example, that is $n - 1$ again for $n = 16$. However, this result is true for every number of participants because in each comparison one participant is discarded, so after $n - 1$ comparisons only the champion remains. Consequently, the knockout stage algorithm is optimal, too, and makes crucial use of the transitive property of skill: if 49 has beaten 24, and then 62 beats 49, 62 would certainly have beaten 24 if the match had been played (in sports it is not always so, therefore the knockout strategy is a bit unjust; in fact we will see that in some cases it is absolutely unjust).

It is also worth noting that to have a balanced knockout stage the leaves of the tree, therefore the number of participants, must be a power of 2. There are $2^4 = 16$ in our example, with the leaves at level $k = 4$. However, going up one level the number of nodes halves, it is $2^3$ and so on. Generally speaking, if at a tree level the nodes are $2^k$, then at the level above the nodes become $2^k/2 = 2^{k-1}$, until this number becomes $2^0 = 1$ at the root. Here we can point out an interesting property of the powers of 2: the sum of the first $k - 1$ powers is $2^0 + 2^1 + 2^2 + \ldots + 2^{k-1} = 2^k - 1$ (in our example we had $1 + 2 + 4 + 8 = 16 - 1 = 15$). This relationship shows the extraordinary power of the *exponential growth* of which we will speak again: any power of two, say $2^k$, is greater than the sum of all the powers that precede it. If the human population doubled every 20 years (which, unfortunately, is close to the truth), the world of the living would be more numerous than the world of the dead, that is the world of all the preceding generations together.

Let us now see how to represent in pseudocode the knockout stage mechanism which is formalized in the program TOURNAMENT shown in Figure 4.4. The input

```
program TOURNAMENT(SET)
// search the maximum in a knockout stage with n = 2^k participants
1.    for i = 0 to n − 1                              // copy the input vector SET in P
2.        P[i] ← SET[i];
3.        h ← k;                                      // h is the current level
4.    while h ≥ 1                    // performs the comparisons at level h, from k to 1
5.        i ← 0; j ← 0;
6.        while i ≤ 2^h − 2                           // loads the winners in W
7.            if P[i] > P[i + 1]                      // P[i] is the winner
8.                W[j] ← P[i]
9.            else W[j] ← P[i + 1];                   // P[i + 1] is the winner
10.               i ← i + 2; j ← j + 1;
11.       for i = 0 to 2^{h−1} − 1                    // transfers the winners to P
12.           P[i] ← W[i];
13.       h ← h − 1;                                  // moves to the higher level
14.   print "the maximum is" P[0];
```

**Fig. 4.4** The program TOURNAMENT to find the maximum in a set of integers by simulating the matches of a tournament knockout stage.

vector SET containing all of the participants is the same as in MAXIMUM. This new program is more difficult than the previous one and requires some attention.

The nodes in the tree levels, starting from the leaves, are represented in vectors whose length gradually halves, which requires defining an arbitrary number of large vectors for increasing $n$. However, the vectors are reduced to two: the one containing the participants at a certain level (i.e. the participants not yet eliminated in the preceding levels), and the one holding the winners of the matches among them (i.e. the participants in the next level). These vectors will be progressively used in shorter portions: $P$ for the participants still in the tournament and $W$ for the winners of the matches between them, respectively containing $2^k$ and $2^{k-1}$ elements to store all the participants at level $k$ and all the winners at level $k − 1$.

First note that it is of no importance what elements are originally contained in the vectors $P$ and $W$ (i.e. in the memory cells chosen for them) because they will be re-loaded through the program automatically deleting any previous content. The lines of the program are numbered for future reference. The input elements of SET are transferred to vector $P$ with the **for**-loop at lines 1 and 2. Once the loop is over, the variable $i$ can be reused in subsequent cycles.

The "external" **while**-loop (lines 4–13) is repeated $k$ times (four times in our example) starting with $h = k$ and decreasing the value of $h$ at each cycle (line 13). This loop determines the matches, in the successive stages of the tournament, between pairs of consecutive elements contained in the first $2^h$ cells of vector $P$, recording the winners in vector $W$ through the "internal" **while**-loop at lines 6–10. Then, still in the external **while**-loop, these winners are copied to the first $2^h/2 = 2^{h-1}$ cells of $P$ (lines 11 and 12), ready to be used in the next iteration of the loop. Recall that at every iteration of the external **while**-loop, the variable $h$ decreases by 1 so the portion used in the two vectors halves. After $k$ of these iterations, the used portion of $P$ is reduced to the first cell that contains the maximum, then printed at line 14.

## 4.3 The Problem of the Runner-up

When a tournament ends the final winner is declared champion and the other finalist gets the runner-up prize: but is this all right? In other words, is the second finalist really superior to all the other contenders apart from the champion, even though the transitive property of skill holds? As we will now see, the answer is decidedly negative because more or less in one case out of two the wrong contender is rewarded. Tournament injustice!

The problem was raised in 1883 by Lewis Carroll, the author of "Alice in Wonderland," who proposed an elegant solution. In the knockout stage of Figure 4.3 element 49 plays the final, while element 52 holds the second largest value. In fact, the real second finalist reaches the final only if it starts in the "half" stage opposed to the maximum (52 should have been among the first eight elements because 62 is among the other eight). The probability of this happening is $\frac{n/2}{n-1} \approx \frac{1}{2}$ because there are $n/2$ positions in the stage favoring the legitimate second finalist out of a total of $n-1$ possible positions excluding the one of the maximum.

How can this injustice be corrected? Once the champion is determined, we could run a second tournament among the other $n-1$ elements, whose winner would certainly be the legitimate runner-up. Such an algorithm would require $n-1$ comparisons to find the maximum plus $n-2$ comparisons to find the second largest integer, for a total of $2n-3$ comparisons. Surprisingly enough, the algorithm proposed by Lewis Carroll requires much less.

We must first determine who, at the end of the tournament, could be the real runner-up. You are invited to think about it for a moment … and now we unveil it. The real second finalist must be sought among all the participants who lost in a direct comparison with the champion; in the example, they are 30, 43, 52 and 49. In fact, each of the other elements was eliminated by another one that is not the maximum, so it cannot be the second finalist because there are at least two elements greater than it. The number of candidates is therefore equal to the number of levels in the tournament tree because the champion plays exactly one match per level; that is there are $k$ candidates for $n = 2^k$. We have already seen that the function involved is the logarithm to the base 2, so the candidates for being the second finalist are $k = \log_2 n$. A second tournament is then run with these elements only, which requires $(\log_2 n) - 1$ new matches. So the total number of matches will be $n - 1 + (\log_2 n) - 1 = n + \log_2 n - 2$, far below the previous bound of $2n - 3$ (for $n = 16$ we have $16 + 4 - 2 = 18 \ll 32 - 3 = 29$).

We omit the coding of this algorithm, which is a bit complicated. This is a typical case where the wordy description of the algorithm and a preventive analysis, based on this description, as to how many operations it will execute is much more important and easy to understand than the coding. We add that there is a very subtle proof that $n + \log_2 n - 2$ comparisons are indeed necessary to determine the first and the second elements of a set, that is, that this value is also a lower bound for the problem. So we can conclude that Lewis Carroll's algorithm is optimal. Too bad that the author was not able to establish it: the proof came almost a century later!

# Chapter 5
# A Financial Problem

How many times has this happened to you? You read in a newspaper the closing prices of the New York Stock Exchange (NYSE), notice the trend of a specific company's share price $\mathscr{S}$, and angrily exclaim: "Had I known it before, I would be rich now!"

The problem is not as simple as it seems because, in order to become rich this way, we should buy a number of shares of $\mathscr{S}$ and then resell them after a reasonable time interval to maximize our gain. This actually means choosing the buy-in instant $b$ (purchase) and the buy-out instant $s$ (sale) to ensure that the price difference between the sale and the purchase is maximum. This value clearly depends on the trend of $\mathscr{S}$'s quotes, which are unknown *a priori*, and makes the problem of *automatic trading* of stock exchanges (also known as a *forex robot*) one of the most interesting areas of algorithmic research of recent years. This problem has seen the design and implementation of sophisticated hardware and software platforms that quickly and efficiently determine daily the instants $b$ and $s$ above.

In this chapter we deal with a simpler situation by assuming that one night the genie of the lamp, which we found in an attic, revealed to us the performance of $\mathscr{S}$ for the next few years, writing it on a sheet of paper that would disintegrate at dawn. The goal is therefore to determine the *best* instant $b$ (buy) and $s$ (sell) by taking advantage of the knowledge of that secret and with the constraint of finishing the computation before sunrise. The adjective *"best"* refers to the maximum possible gain that we would achieve by buying a fixed number of shares of $\mathscr{S}$ in the instant $b$ and selling them in the instant $s$, with $b$ and $s$ denoting, clearly, instants that follow the night appearance of the genie.

What is computationally challenging in this problem is to determine the *best* instants $b$ and $s$ *fast enough* to enable us to examine as many daily prices of $\mathscr{S}$'s shares as possible before the sun rises and the genie's writing disappears. This should ensure that we will be able to identify a particularly favorable investment.

In this chapter we will formalize our "dreams of wealth" as a computational problem and design three algorithms that show increasing sophistication and elegance. They will also solve the problem more and more efficiently, up to the third algorithm, which will achieve optimality in the number of executed steps and in its

© Springer Nature Switzerland AG 2018
P. Ferragina, F. Luccio, *Computational Thinking*,
https://doi.org/10.1007/978-3-319-97940-3_5

occupancy of space. Moreover, this last algorithm will result in a surprisingly simple program consisting of only a few lines of code. Overall, these three algorithms will offer us the chance to introduce and discuss two fundamental questions:

- The first question concerns a salient requirement of algorithm design, namely, that the elegance of the solution (which we have already mentioned in Chapter 4) is not only tied to the quest for "beautiful math," an aspiration perhaps of the *problem solving* purists; rather, it has a strong practical relevance because the more elegant and simple the solution is, the more easily programmable it is, which reduces errors in the coding process. This is therefore an unexpected link between a *qualitative* property of the algorithm (i.e. elegance) and a *quantitative* property of the corresponding code (i.e. the cost associated with its implementation and maintenance).
- The second question, which emerges from the discussion of the previous problem, concerns the *inverse* link that exists between the efficiency of an algorithm and the amount of data that it can process within a predetermined time interval, in our case indicated with $t$. Until now, we have expressed the time efficiency of an algorithm as a function of the input size $n$ capturing the number of steps executed by the algorithm to solve a problem. Hence, it is a positive and non-decreasing function of $n$. For example, in Chapter 3 we introduced binary search and counted its number of steps as a logarithmic function of type $T(n) = \log_2 n$. In the present chapter, we will focus on the *inverse function* that expresses the amount of data that can be processed by the algorithm within an available time interval. In the previous example, we set $T(n) = t$, solve with respect to $n$, and thus get $n = 2^t$. Therefore, binary search can process an amount of data that grows exponentially in $t$. This statement is not surprising to those familiar with the analysis of functions, but we think that the considerations that will arise in Section 5.4, where we will indissolubly tie technological advances with the importance of developing efficient algorithms, are *stunning*.

Let us proceed gradually and start by introducing some notation and definitions that will help us first to formalize our financial problem and then to deal with its computational solution.

It is common to characterize the performance of a share with a plot in which the $x$-axis is indexed by days and the $y$-axis is indexed by the price of a stock share, as shown in Figure 5.1. Day 0 corresponds to the day in which the genie of the lamp appeared in our attic, and the integer 10 specifies the value in Euro of the price of the stock $\mathscr{S}$ at the end of that day. For ease of illustration, the figure reports only 11 days of stock quotes for $\mathscr{S}$, but we have to remember that the sequence written by the genie is *arbitrarily long*.

To design an algorithm that solves our financial problem we assume that the input is stored in a vector $D[0 : n]$, where $D[0]$ contains the initial price for the stock $\mathscr{S}$, and $D[1 : n]$ stores the *differences* between the quotations on contiguous days. Referring to Figure 5.1 we have that $D[0] = 10$ and $D[1 : 11] = [+4, -6, +3, +1, +3, -2, +3, -4, +1, -9, +6]$. The vector $D$ stores the value 4 in its second entry $D[1]$ because this is the difference between the price of $\mathscr{S}$ on day 1 (= 14) and its price on

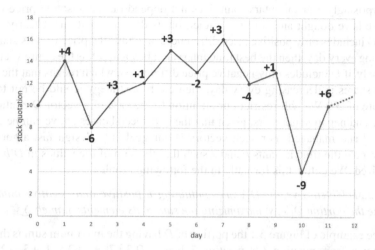

**Fig. 5.1** Example of share price performance that, for ease of exposition, is assumed to be a sequence of integer numbers. Close to every point, the difference in the price of a stock between two consecutive days is indicated.

day 0 (= 10); similarly, $D[2] = -6$ because this is the difference between the price on day 2 (= 8) and the one on the previous day (= 14), and so on for all $n$ subsequent days stored in $D$. Vector $D$ has size $n$ which is, nevertheless, assumed to be arbitrarily large because it stores the sequence of share prices written by the genie. As the reader already knows, the analysis of the time efficiency of algorithms is done in *asymptotic* terms, meaning that we will analyze and compare algorithms based on the number of steps that they will execute for a growing input size $n$, thus fitting perfectly the computational context that we have framed for this financial problem.

Before entering into the formal definition of our problem, let us state three important observations that will simplify the pseudocode of our algorithms:

- The number of shares to buy and sell is not relevant for the computation of the instants $b$ and $s$, so in the rest of this chapter we will concentrate on the purchase of a single share of $\mathscr{S}$.
- The quotation of one share of $\mathscr{S}$ at the beginning of a day $t$ is the price of that share at the end of the previous day $t - 1$. For example, the price of $\mathscr{S}$'s shares at the beginning of day 3 equals 8 euro, according to the plotting in Figure 5.1.
- The monetary gain due to a financial trade that buys one share of $\mathscr{S}$ at the *beginning* of day $b$ and sells it at the *end* of day $s$ can be computed by summing the values in the portion $D[b : s]$. For example, with reference to Figure 5.1, if we buy one share at the beginning of day 3 (at the quote of 8 euro, see the previous item) and sell it at the end of day 7 (at the quote of 16 euro), then we would gain $16 - 8 = 8$ euro and this value can be computed by summing the entries in $D[3 : 7] = [+3, +1, +3, -2, +3]$.

Not surprisingly, our monetary gain does not depend on the absolute price of the share we have bought and sold but, rather, on its daily fluctuations. Clearly, if the vector $D$ includes only positive price differences, and thus the price of $\mathscr{S}$'s shares is increasing every day, then the best time interval to buy and sell is the entire vector $D$; conversely, if $D$ includes only negative price differences, which means that the price of $\mathscr{S}$'s shares is decreasing every day, then the best strategy would be not to buy any share of $\mathscr{S}$! We will restrict our attention to the case of a vector $D$ containing positive and negative numbers, given that the two special cases above can be easily identified and managed. For such vectors $D$ our goal is to design fast algorithms that compute the time instants $b$ and $s$ such that the sum of the values in $D[b:s]$ is maximized. We define this formally in the following problem.

PROBLEM. *Given a vector $D[1:n]$ containing $n$ positive and negative numbers, compute the portion $D[b:s]$ maximizing the sum of its elements, namely $\sum_{i=b}^{s} D[i]$.*

In the example of Figure 5.1 the portion of $D$ having the maximum sum is the one that extends from position 3 to position 7; hence, $D[3:7] = [+3, +1, +3, -2, +3]$, where the monetary gain is 8 euro if $\mathscr{S}$'s share is bought at the beginning of day 3 and sold at the end of day 7. The reader can verify that every other portion of $D$ induces a smaller monetary gain. Indeed, the reader can also visually verify over the plot of Figure 5.1 that this maximum gain is achieved in the time interval during which the quotations of $\mathscr{S}$ experience the maximal increasing fluctuation.

How do you find that interval? In what follows, we introduce three algorithms of increasing sophistication and elegance, evaluate their time efficiency (also called *time complexity*), and comment on their algorithmic properties.

## 5.1  A "Cubic" Algorithm

The design of the first algorithm we present in this chapter derives directly from the problem's formulation. Its pseudocode is very simple and is reported in Figure 5.2. It is characterized by three nested **for**-loops: the first two loops examine all possible intervals $[i, j]$ contained in $[1, n]$, while the third loop (lines 5–6) computes the sum of the values in $D[i:j]$ using the auxiliary variable $Tmp$ that is initially set to zero (line 4). If the total sum of $D[i:j]$ is greater than the best result computed so far, and saved in $MaxSum$ (line 7), then this variable is updated and the interval $[i, j]$ is saved in $[b, s]$. Notice that we have initially set $MaxSum$ to the *value* $-\infty$, meaning that it is a value smaller than any possible sum. This guarantees that the first execution of line 7 updates it; we could have achieved the same result by setting $MaxSum$ to one minus the minimum value in $D$.

The correctness of the algorithm should be obvious, because it is a sort of "brute-force solution" that computes the sum of all possible subintervals of $[1, n]$. The evaluation of its time efficiency deserves instead some extra comments in order to familiarize the reader with the terminology and its computing practices. The two **for**-loops analyze all intervals $[i, j]$ in $[1, n]$, so their number can be (roughly) upper

```
program CUBIC (D)

// Vector D[1 : n] consists of n positive and negative numbers

1.    MaxSum ← −∞; b ← 1; s ← 0;

2.    for i = 1 to n

3.        for j = i to n

4.            Tmp ← 0;                          // Tmp is an auxiliary variable

5.            for k = i to j

6.                Tmp ← Tmp + D[k];

7.            if Tmp > MaxSum

8.                MaxSum ← Tmp; b ← i; s ← j;

9.    print "The maximum gain is" MaxSum;

10.   print "It occurs in the time interval" [b, s];
```

**Fig. 5.2** The program computes the portion $D[b : s]$ achieving the maximum sum of its elements by evaluating all possible intervals $[i, j]$ in $[1, n]$, and storing the best solution in the variables *MaxSum, b* and *s*.

bounded by the quadratic function $n^2$ because the iterators $i$ and $j$ can assume no more than $n$ values each. We could have actually been more precise in this calculation, but this is not important at this point because we only wish to derive an upper bound. For every such interval, we have to compute the sum of the values in $D[i, j]$ (**for**-loop at lines 5–6) and this takes $j − i < n$ additions. Therefore, algorithm CUBIC executes at most $n^3$ steps, hence its name. It is not difficult to derive a *lower bound* to the number of steps executed by CUBIC: it is enough to observe that there are more than $n/2$ intervals in $D[1 : n]$ with a length between $\frac{n}{4}$ and $\frac{n}{2}$ and, for each of them, the algorithm executes at least $n/4$ additions at line 6. This means the total number of additions (steps) is at least $\frac{n}{2} \times \frac{n}{4} \times \frac{n}{4} = \frac{n^3}{32}$. The reader should not be confused by our use of the expression "lower bound," which refers here to the complexity of the algorithm CUBIC and not to the inherent complexity of the financial problem. By this we mean that CUBIC executes more than $\frac{n^3}{32}$ steps, whatever the input data is; instead, as we will see immediately from the next section, the problem admits faster solutions.

## 5.2 A "Quadratic" Algorithm

The key inefficiency of the previous algorithm is located at lines 4–6 where it computes the sum of the sub-vector $D[i : j]$ by executing $(j − i)$ additions. However, if we consider two consecutive iterations of the **for**-loop – say $j$ and $j + 1$ at line 5 – we notice that the sums computed for $D[i : j]$ and $D[i : j + 1]$ differ only by the

```
program QUADRATIC (D)
// Vector D[1 : n] consists of n positive and negative numbers
1.      MaxSum ← −∞; b ← 1; s ← 0;
2.      for i = 1 to n
3.          Tmp ← 0;
4.          for j = i to n
5.              Tmp ← Tmp + D[j];
6.              if Tmp > MaxSum
7.                  MaxSum ← Tmp; b ← i; s ← j;
8.      print "The maximum gain is" MaxSum;
9.      print "It occurs in the time interval" [b,s];
```

**Fig. 5.3** This program computes the portion $D[b : s]$ achieving the maximum sum in $D[1 : n]$ via the analysis of all intervals in $[1,n]$ and an *incremental computation* that needs one addition per interval. At each step, the algorithm stores the best solution in the variables $MaxSum, b$ and $s$.

value $D[j + 1]$ (the rightmost item in them). Consequently, it is very inefficient to restart from scratch (line 4) the calculation of the sum of $D[i : j + 1]$, given that we have $D[i : j]$ in the value currently stored in $Tmp$. So, it suffices to add to $Tmp$ the value $D[j + 1]$ and thus obtain the sum for $D[i : j + 1]$. In Figure 5.3 we report the pseudocode of the algorithm QUADRATIC which, with respect to the algorithm CUBIC, introduces two changes: the reset to zero of the variable $Tmp$ every time the algorithm changes the iterator $i$ in the first **for**-loop (line 3), and the addition of the value $D[j + 1]$ (line 5) to the variable $Tmp$, which inductively stores the sum of the elements in $D[i : j]$.

As in the case of CUBIC, the proof of correctness for QUADRATIC is easy to derive; on the other hand, the evaluation of its time complexity, which we detail here, is more involved. The algorithm consists of two nested **for**-loops that analyze all possible intervals $[i, j]$ included in $[1,n]$: there are $n$ intervals of length 1, $n - 1$ intervals of length 2, $n - 2$ intervals of length 3, and so on until we consider the unique interval of length $n$. The total number of intervals is thus $1 + 2 + \ldots + (n - 1) + n$, which is a well known summation whose explicit value equals $n(n + 1)/2$. This value was determined by Gauss at the age of 8 while performing a class assignment via the following elegant observation: we write the summation twice, the second time as $n + (n - 1) + \ldots + 2 + 1$, align vertically the terms of the two summations, and sum the aligned term pairs. In other words, $[1 + n] + [2 + (n - 1)] + [3 + (n - 2)] + \ldots + [(n - 2) + 3] + [(n - 1) + 2] + [n + 1]$. Each square bracket sums to $n + 1$, and the number of square brackets is equal to the number $n$ of terms in the original summation. So the total sum is $n(n + 1)$. This value is twice the sum we are interested in, because we have summed up twice the first $n$ integers (first in increasing order and then in decreasing order), thus it is enough to divide $n(n + 1)$ by two and get the result. Since the number of intervals is quadratic in $n$, and for each of them the algorithm QUADRATIC executes a constant number of operations at lines 5–7, its time complexity can be described with a function that grows as $n^2$.

We can thus conclude that the two simple changes introduced in the pseudocode of QUADRATIC, with respect to the pseudocode of CUBIC, induce a significant improvement in its practical performance. For instance, if our computer is able to execute one billion ($= 10^9$) operations per second then CUBIC would take 1 second to process one thousand quotations ($= (10^3)^3 \times 10^{-9} = 1$), while QUADRATIC would take just one millisecond ($= (10^3)^2 \times 10^{-9} = 10^{-3}$). The difference in performance between these two algorithms becomes more and more evident as the vector $D$ grows in size; for example, if $D$ consists of one million quotations, the algorithm CUBIC would take $(10^6)^3 \times 10^{-9} = 10^9$ seconds (namely more than 30 years), while QUADRATIC would take $(10^6)^2 \times 10^{-9} = 10^3$ seconds (about 15 minutes).

The reader might at this point observe that $n = 10^6$ elements is a fairly unreasonable value since $n$ denotes the number of daily quotes revealed by the genie of the lamp, and this time window would allow us to find a fruitful investment for our descendants, frustrating our most material and imminent dreams of wealth! On the other hand, however, it should be noted that nothing prevents the genie from adopting a much finer granularity in detecting the quotations of $\mathscr{S}$'s shares: these could be sampled per minute, per second, or even more frequently. A large $n$ also occurs if the name of the company $\mathscr{S}$ whose stock we were to buy and sell were not known in advance, and so our financial trading were open to any company in the NYSE. These scenarios are far more realistic because there are currently *online trading platforms* implementing algorithms that buy and sell millions of shares extremely fast and for many stock markets.

The next section will present an algorithm that is much faster than QUADRATIC. It will offer many interesting properties and will be *optimal* in its asymptotic time complexity, because its number of steps will match the problem's lower bound, which will be proved to be *linear* in the input size $n$.

## 5.3 A "Linear" Algorithm

In order to improve the efficiency of QUADRATIC we must change the algorithmic approach and *discard* portions of vector $D$ that do not contain the best interval $[b, s]$ *without examining* them. For simplicity of exposition, and without compromising the correctness of our algorithmic design, we will assume that no portion of $D$ has a sum equal to zero. The new algorithm is called LINEAR because its time complexity grows linearly with the vector size $n$, as we will prove next. LINEAR is based on two key properties satisfied by the optimal portion $D[b : s]$ that we state and prove by referring to Figure 5.4.

**Property 1:**   *Every portion that ends just before the optimal one, i.e. has the form $D[i : b - 1]$ where $1 \leq i < b$, has a negative sum of its elements.*

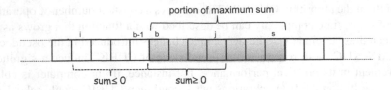

**Fig. 5.4** An illustrative example of properties 1 and 2 stated in the text.

Looking at our running example where $D[1:11] = [+4, -6, +3, +1, +3, -2, +3,$
$-4, +1, -9, +6]$ and the optimal sub-vector given by $D[3:7] = [+3, +1, +3, -2,$
$+3]$, we have that any portion identified by property 1 has the form $D[i:2]$, with
$i \le 2$. These portions have a negative sum of their elements; in fact $D[1:2] =$
$[+4, -6]$ and $D[2:2] = [-6]$.

We prove the correctness of Property 1 by contradiction assuming that there is,
in fact, a portion $D[i:b-1]$ of positive sum (by hypothesis, no portion of $D$ has
a sum of zero). Then, the sub-vector $D[i:s]$ obtained by juxtaposing $D[i:b-1]$
with the portion of maximum sum $D[b:s]$ would have a sum larger than this
latter one, and thus larger than the maximum possible sum in $D$!

**Property 2:**   *Every portion that starts where the optimal portion starts and is included in it, i.e. has the form $D[b:j]$ where $b \le j \le s$, has a positive sum of its
elements.*

In our running example above $b = 3$ and $s = 7$, so the sub-vectors identified by
Property 2 have the form $D[3:j]$, where $3 \le j \le 7$, so there are five: $D[3:3], D[3:$
$4], \ldots, D[3:7]$. The reader can verify that the sum of the elements in each of these
portions is positive.

We prove the correctness of Property 2 by contradiction assuming that there is,
in fact, such a portion $D[b:j]$ having a negative sum (by hypothesis, no portion
of $D$ has a sum of zero). Then, the sub-vector $D[j+1:s]$ obtained by removing
that portion from the one of the maximum sum, i.e. $D[b:s]$, would have a sum
larger than this latter one, and thus larger than the maximum possible sum in $D$!

We are now ready to design the algorithm LINEAR which computes the sub-vector
of maximum sum in $D[1:n]$ via a simple rightward scan executing a constant number of operations on each element (namely, comparisons and additions). Thus, the
time complexity will be linear in $n$, as promised. Figure 5.5 reports its pseudocode,
which deserves some comments in order to convince you of its correctness.

The algorithm consists of a single **for**-loop that stores in the auxiliary variable
$Tmp$ the sum of the sub-vector of $D$ currently under analysis, computed incrementally from left to right and without passing twice through the same position. This
feature ensures the linearity of the time complexity but poses the need to prove that
the optimal portion $D[b:s]$ is actually among the ones examined by the algorithm.
This guarantees that, at some step, line 4 computes in $Tmp$ the maximum sum,
which is then saved in *MaxSum* at line 6, and finally printed at lines 9–10.

```
program LINEAR (D)
// Vector D consists of n positive and negative numbers
1.    MaxSum ← −∞; Tmp ← 0;
2.    b ← 1; btmp ← 1; s ← 0;
3.    for i = 1 to n
4.        Tmp ← Tmp + D[i];
5.        if Tmp > MaxSum
6.            MaxSum ← Tmp; b ← btmp; s ← i;
7.        if Tmp < 0
8.            Tmp ← 0; btmp ← i + 1;
9.    print "The maximum gain is" MaxSum;
10.   print "It occurs in the interval" [b, s];
```

**Fig. 5.5** Program that computes the portion $D[b : s]$ of a maximum sum by examining $n$ intervals in $[1, n]$ and storing the best solution in $MaxSum, b$ and $s$.

Before digging into the formal proof of this statement, let us follow the running of LINEAR on the example in this chapter, hence on the vector $D[1 : 11] = [+4, −6, +3, +1, +3, −2, +3, −4, +1, −9, +6]$. The reader can verify that the values stored in $Tmp$ are $0, 4, −2(0), 3, 4, 7, 5, 8, 4, 5, −4(0)$, and 6, where parentheses contain the result of executing line 7, which, having verified $Tmp < 0$, will set its value to zero. The steps in which $Tmp < 0$ are also the ones in which the algorithm stores in $btmp$ the left extreme of the interval under analysis. When $Tmp$ is set to zero, $i = 2$, so that LINEAR sets $btmp = 3$ (line 8). In the following steps $i = 3, \ldots, 7$, the algorithm computes sums that are greater than zero (Property 2) and so it does not modify the variable $btmp$ but changes the temporary sum stored in the auxiliary variable $tmp = 3, 4, 7, 5, 8$. When $i = 7$, $tmp = 8$ and $MaxSum = 7$, so the **if**-statement at line 5 saves correctly the new best interval by setting $MaxSum = 8$, $b = btmp = 3$ and $s = i = 7$ (line 6).

Formally, the proof that this is correct can be derived as follows. At every iteration $i$ of the **for**-loop, the algorithm LINEAR computes in $Tmp$ the sum of the portion under consideration (line 4) and checks whether this value is greater than $MaxSum$ (line 5) or smaller than zero (line 7). In the first case, the new maximum-sum portion is saved (line 6); in the latter case, the variable $Tmp$ is reset to zero (line 8). Property 1 ensures that LINEAR executes this resetting at the position $b − 1$, just before the beginning of the portion of maximum sum. In our example, $Tmp$ is negative at iteration $i = b − 1 = 3 − 1 = 2$ (because this position precedes the one where the portion of maximum sum starts, i.e. $b$). Consequently, lines 7–8 reset $Tmp$ and execute the assignment $btmp = i + 1 = 3$. After that the subsequent iterations of the **for**-loop will examine the positions $i = 3, \ldots, 7$ and, for each of them, they will compute in $Tmp$ the sum of the scanned elements. This sum (and hence $Tmp$) will be positive in these steps because of Property 2. As soon as $i = 7$, $Tmp$ will contain the value of the maximum sum that will be stored into $MaxSum$ together with the extremes $b = btmp = 3$ and $s = i = 7$ (lines 5–6). The algorithm will continue its computation until the vector $D$ is fully examined. In any case, the maximum sum has been identified and saved so that the last lines 9–10 will print in output the correct information about $D[b : s]$.

The proposed algorithm shows many interesting properties. We already commented on some of them earlier and two more follow. Its time complexity is linear in the number of quotes, and thus it is clearly optimal because every element in $D$ has to be examined by any algorithm in order to be included or excluded from the optimal solution. Moreover, the computation is *incremental* in the sense that the elements of vector $D$ are examined once and from left to right; hence, the genie of the lamp could indicate the price of $\mathscr{S}$'s shares one-by-one until sunrise and the algorithm would still have the best solution to date in $MaxSum$. This is a precious feature that the previous algorithms, CUBIC and QUADRATIC, cannot offer because they need to operate on the entire vector $D$.

## 5.4 Algorithm Efficiency Versus Hardware Efficiency

We concentrate in this section on the frequent question of whether it is *better* to design a more efficient algorithm *or* to buy a faster computer in order to solve a given problem at hand. We will base our discussion on our example of the financial problem, discussing this issue in the context of the three algorithmic solutions presented in this chapter, namely CUBIC, QUADRATIC, and LINEAR.

For simplicity of exposition we assume that the number of steps executed by these algorithms can be described *exactly* by the functions $T_C(n) = n^3$, $T_Q(n) = n^2$ and $T_L(n) = n$, where the subscripts $C, Q$, and $L$ denote the first letters of the corresponding algorithms' names. These functions allow us to compute immediately the time taken by each algorithm to solve a problem for a given input of size $n$. It is "sufficient" to know the time cost of *each single algorithmic step* and multiply it by those functions. We have put that word in quotes because that information is not so simple to derive since it depends on many subtle and sophisticated software and hardware features, and, therefore, we have to forego an explanation of it here. Nevertheless, in order to develop our discussion as simply as possible without diminishing its soundness, we assume that *every* step costs 1 and disregard whether the time unit is seconds, milliseconds, or nanoseconds.

We are interested in evaluating how many elements can be processed by each algorithm within a bounded time window $T$ which corresponds, in our illustrative example, to the time between the appearance of the genie of the lamp in our attic and sunrise, when the paper reporting $\mathscr{S}$'s quotes disintegrates. To deal with this calculation we equal, in turn, each one of the three functions above to $T$ and then solve them with respect to the variable $n$. The solutions are: $n_C = \sqrt[3]{T}$, $n_Q = \sqrt[2]{T}$, and $n_L = T$, where we have appended to $n$ the subscripts denoting the names of the algorithms to which the calculations refer. These values are interesting because they show that the number of elements processed by each algorithm grows with a *different polynomial speed* in the time window $T$. This growth is even more explicit if we run the same algorithms on a computer that is $k$ times faster than the previous one. This now corresponds with solving the equation $T_*(n) = kT$, which is equivalent to running the algorithms on the original (slower) computer for a $k$-times longer time window. We get $n'_C = \sqrt[3]{kT} = \sqrt[3]{k} \times \sqrt[3]{T} = \sqrt[3]{k} \times n_C$ for CUBIC, $n'_Q = \sqrt[2]{kT} = \sqrt[2]{k} \times \sqrt[2]{T} = \sqrt[2]{k} \times n_Q$ for QUADRATIC, and $n'_L = kT = k \times n_L$ for LINEAR. Therefore, each algorithm is able to process an increased number of elements with the faster computer whose *multiplicative factor* is given by $\sqrt[3]{k}$ for CUBIC, $\sqrt[2]{k}$ for QUADRATIC, and $k$ for LINEAR.

Therefore the *advantage* obtained by buying a faster computer *increases with the time efficiency* of the executed algorithm, and this advantage is considerable. To see this, let us compare two cases: executing a slower algorithm on a faster computer and executing a faster algorithm on a slower computer. We instantiate this question on CUBIC and QUADRATIC and thus consider the equation $n'_C = n_Q$. We rewrite it as $\sqrt[3]{kT} = \sqrt[2]{T}$, solve by $k$, and thus get $k = \sqrt[6]{T}$. This means that CUBIC needs a $\sqrt[6]{T}$-times faster computer in order to process the same number of elements processed by QUADRATIC running on the original (slower) computer. More significantly, CUBIC needs a $T^2$ faster computer to process the same number of elements processed by LINEAR running on the original (slower) computer.

To make this reasoning even more stunning we add the observation that, according to Moore's Law, the performance of computers doubles every 18 months (this has been the case for many years now). Therefore, it is not convenient to wait for these hardware improvements; rather, it is much more effective to search for an asymptotically faster algorithm, provided that it does exist and that we are able to design it!

## 5.5 Some Interesting Variants of the Problem

What would happen if we had a budget $B$ to invest rather than buying a pre-set number of $\mathscr{S}$ shares, as we assumed at the beginning of this chapter? Algorithm LINEAR would not work in this case because the number of shares bought at some time instant depends on $\mathscr{S}$'s quote at that time and this can impact the overall gain achieved when selling these shares sometime in the future. For example, let us assume we have a budget $B = 16$ euro and a sequence of quotes $[16, 18, 4, 5]$. If we apply LINEAR on the input vector $D[1:3] = [+2, -14, +1]$, we find the "best" interval as $b = 1$, $s = 1$, and $MaxSum = 2$. But in the present scenario we have a budget to spend, equal to $B = 16$ euro, so if we buy $\mathscr{S}$ on day 0 (at the price of 16 euro) we get $B/16 = 1$ share. Since we sell this share on day $s = 1$ (at the price of 18 euro) we gain 2 euro. However, we notice that if we bought shares on day $b = 2$ (at the price of 4 euro) and sold them on day $s = 3$ (at the price of 5 euro), we would gain 4 euro because we could buy $B/4 = 16/4 = 4$ shares with a gain per share equal to 1.

The example clearly shows that LINEAR has to be modified in order to take into account the budget $B$ and the individual quotes of $\mathscr{S}$'s shares at every instant of time. This can be managed as follows. We recall that the auxiliary variable $Tmp$, for every instant $i$, computes the sum of the portion of $D$ under analysis, and if this sum is negative then we are in a local minimum of the quotes' sequence (see Fig. 5.1). More precisely, those resetting instants for $Tmp$ do not include all the minima of the sequence but *only* the ones that form a *decreasing sequence of minima*. Therefore, they correspond to instants in which the quote is particularly low and thus it could be advantageous to invest our budget $B$. However, such investment is really only advantageous if the share will fetch a higher price in the future that induces a significant gain when the *group of purchased shares* is sold. Consequently, the new goal is to determine $D[b,s]$ such that it is maximum the product between the number of shares bought at the beginning of day $b$ (hence at the prize on day $b-1$, according to our notation) and the gain per share at the end of day $s$. Finding these two values requires a change at line 5 in the pseudocode of LINEAR so that it compares $MaxSum$ with the gain $Tmp \times (B/S[btmp-1])$, where $btmp$ is the day subsequent to the one in which $Tmp$ has been reset to zero and $S[btmp-1]$ is the price of the share at the beginning of day $S[btmp]$ (or, equivalently, at the end of day $btmp-1$). $Tmp$ is updated as indicated in the original LINEAR pseudocode but $MaxSum$ is updated in line 6 to store the gain and not just $Tmp$. In our example above, $Tmp$ is reset to zero at the beginning and then at instant $i=2$. At the beginning (i.e. $i=btmp=1$), the program computes the gain function as $Tmp \times (16/S[0]) = Tmp \times (16/16) = Tmp$, which gets the value 2 at instant $i=1$, and stores it in $MaxSum$ (with $b=s=1$). At the next instant, $i=2$, $Tmp$ is negative and reset to zero, so $btmp$ is set to 3 by line 8. Here the gain function is computed as $(16/S[2]) = Tmp \times (16/4) = Tmp \times 4$, which gets the value $1 \times 4 = 4$ at instant $i=3$ because $Tmp = D[3] = 1$. We leave to the reader the task of proving that this new algorithm correctly solves the problem with budget $B$ and we dedicate the remaining lines of this chapter to investigating two variants of the problem inspired by genetics.

The first variant assumes that the sequence to analyze is a DNA sequence consisting of the bases A, T, G, and C. Portions are called *segments* and the problem consists of identifying the segments which are *rich* in occurrences of G and C. Biologists believe that these segments are biologically interesting since they often contain genes. Surprisingly enough we can turn the problem of detecting those segments into our maximum sum problem: it suffices to assign a penalty $-p$ to bases A and T, and a bonus $1-p$ to bases G and C, where $p$ is a value between 0 and 1. The sum of the values occurring in a given segment of length $L$ and containing $x$ occurrences of G or C is then equal to $x - p \times L$. Nicely enough, all three previous algorithms solve this biological problem by finding the segment richest in G and C.

The second variant considers the same scenario but the goal now is to maximize the *density* of bases C and G in a segment, computed as the ratio between the number of occurrences of C and G in that segment and its length. We notice immediately that every segment consisting of a single C or G has maximum density (i.e. 1). So the problem gets biologically interesting if we introduce a lower bound to the length of the segments to search. Unfortunately, however, this variant of the problem cannot be solved with our three algorithms above and, more surprisingly, the known solutions are rather involved.

These variants of the original problem show that there are some *dangerous computational traps*, namely, problems that appear similar to the ones for which efficient solutions are known but in which their tiny differences make known solutions inapplicable. A strong algorithm designer possesses the knowledge of a large number of algorithmic techniques and a deep "computational sensibility" that suffices to catch the small but salient differences among the problems she has to solve so that she can establish whether her algorithmic toolbox can be used effectively or she has to design new efficient (and, hopefully, optimal) solutions.

# Chapter 6
# Secret Messages

The art of exchanging secret messages has probably fascinated humankind from the earliest times, but the information we have today is related to writing only because nothing has been recorded about cave-dwellers' secret messages. It is precisely to written messages that this chapter refers: in the end they are sequences of characters and their transformation into a disguised form, and their subsequent interpretation, require appropriate algorithms. Let's then enter into the field of *cryptography*, etymologically "hidden writing", where we will find new interesting forms of coding.

It is not our intention to go into a historical exposition, for which many sources are available, but some examples related to the past are suitable to begin with because of their simplicity. Then we will address some aspects of contemporary encryption. This is a very complicated matter that cannot be seriously dealt with in a book such as this one. However, some concepts that have emerged in current times can be easily exposed, giving rise to interesting examples.

The most illustrious cryptographer of the past was Julius Caesar who is often cited as the father of encryption (but there were many other cryptographers before him). Like all the ancient methods, his was of disarming naïveté. One might argue that reading and writing was quite difficult at that time, so it was enough to secretly change the rules, even in a very simple way, to confuse those unauthorized to know the contents of a message. Caesar, as the historian Suetonius explains, wrote important messages by replacing each letter of the alphabet with another one, according to a rule known only to the recipient. This transformation, which today may make us smile, consisted in replacing each letter with the one three positions ahead in the Latin alphabet, with the last three letters cyclically transformed into the first three.

Using the English alphabet, we can imagine that the transformation is carried out using two concentric circles on the perimeter of each of which a copy of the alphabet is written, then translating the internal alphabet counter-clockwise by three positions, as shown in Figure 6.1. The letters of the message to be sent are read on the outer circle and are transformed one by one into the letters of the *cryptogram* (i.e. of the encrypted message) by reading the corresponding letter in the inner circle. To decrypt the cryptogram and reconstruct the original message the reverse transfor-

© Springer Nature Switzerland AG 2018
P. Ferragina, F. Luccio, *Computational Thinking*,
https://doi.org/10.1007/978-3-319-97940-3_6

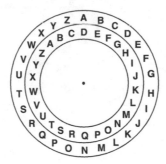

**Fig. 6.1** Two concentric disks implementing Caesar's cipher. The message BONUMVESPERUM (good evening, in Latin) is converted to ERQXPYHVSHUXP.

mation is performed, that is, the letters of the cryptogram are detected in the inner circle and are transformed into the corresponding letters of the outer circle. We have thus described two algorithms, one for encrypting and one for deciphering. However, instead of programming them in pseudocode or in Python, which is of course possible, we have indicated a much simpler manual coding—perhaps precisely the one used by the Romans.

Unlike all the ciphers that followed it, Caesar's did not require a *secret key*, that is, an additional piece of information known only to the two partners that could be changed as needed. Secrecy, therefore, depended on the knowledge of the method: if this had become public knowledge, secrecy would have been irretrievably compromised. However, a simple variation allows us to use the two circles of Caesar's cipher more intelligently. Let a key agreed by the two partners be the degree of rotation of the inner circle: if instead of by three positions that circle were rotated by four, the letter A would correspond to E, B to F, and so on, and the cryptogram for BONUMVESPERUM would become ERQXPYHVSHUXP. The two partners would have 25 different keys to choose from, that is the numbers from 1 to 25, to indicate possible rotations as the alphabet contains 26 letters. Note that key 26 would leave the message unchanged, and 27, 28, ... would have the same effect as 1, 2, .... In addition, the key could be changed from time to time in agreement between the two partners to confuse any eavesdroppers. In the following, this method will be enhanced with some transformations of the circles.

To continue with the discussion of ciphers, we will have to recall, whenever necessary, some simple arithmetic properties that are the basis of building algorithms more complicated than those seen so far, and which are essential to understanding the very essence of encryption. Don't worry, we will tackle these issues with levity.

## 6.1 Modularity

Caesar's cipher triggers a discussion on *modularity* which is an arithmetic concept that we often apply without even realizing it. Consider an analog watch and the way we determine the time according to the position of the hour hand. If the hand moves from 3 to 5, we conclude that two hours have passed. However, without an innate feeling of the passing of time we could equally say that the interval was 14 hours, or 26 hours, and so on. That is, it was any possible interval of 2 plus a multiple of 12 hours, since every 12 hours the hand returns to the same position.

In fact, we have given up on accepting that there are infinite integers by establishing that in our universe there are only numbers from 0 to 11 (12, noon or midnight, is more correctly replaced by 0 as in digital clocks). Thus an integer $n$ between 0 and 11 represents infinite integers $N$ expressed by the simple formula $N = n + 12h$, with $h = 0, 1, 2, \ldots$. Additionally, since we can move the hour hand manually counterclockwise by however many complete turns we want, the correspondence with the infinite integers remains $N = n + 12h$ but now $h$ varies between $-\infty$ and $+\infty$, that is $h = \ldots -2, -1, 0, 1, 2, \ldots$. We are counting the hours *module* 12.

Assuming that the module is a positive integer $m$ and referring to the integers $n$ between 0 and $m - 1$, the operation that transforms an arbitrary $N$ into its modular value $n$ is indicated by $N \bmod m$ and this value coincides with the remainder of the division between $N$ and $m$. For example: 25 mod 12 = 1, because $25 = 1 + 2 \times 12$. The operation is also defined for negative numbers, in fact: $-25 \bmod 12 = 11$, because $-25 = 11 - 3 \times 12$.

The phenomenon seen for the hours repeats with the ciphering disks described earlier. A relative rotation of 0 positions (key $k = 0$) leaves the two facing alphabets identical to each other. A rotation of 3 positions (key $k = 3$) reproduces Caesar's cipher (Figure 6.1). And so on, until a rotation of 26 positions (key $k = 26$), or of one of its multiples, places the alphabets back at the initial position. For a letter in position $i$ of the alphabet, and a key $k$, the encrypted letter is in position $j = (i + k) \bmod 26$. In essence we are "counting" module 26 thereby canceling the effect of the complete rotations of one disc over the other. This reflects the fact that the last letters of the alphabet are cyclically encrypted with the first ones. In Caesar's cipher, starting with letter A in position 0 of the alphabet, Y is in position 24 and is replaced by B in position $(24 + 3) \bmod 26 = 1$.

We can now present the algorithms for encryption and decryption of messages in pseudocode, even though the "mechanical" coding is simpler in this case. We store the characters in alphabetic order in a vector ALPHABET of 26 cells already loaded in the memory (ALPHABET[0] = A, ALPHABET[1] = B, etc.). We stipulate, for simplicity, that only the characters of the alphabet appear in the message and the words are not divided by spaces or punctuation marks, as is common in many ciphers, in order to avoid giving a possible eavesdropper any information as to the division of the words in the text.

The transformation of a character of the message into an encrypted one is achieved with the program TRANSFORM in Figure 6.2. This program is called

```
program TRANSFORM (k, C, T)

    // transforms the input character C into the encrypted output character T
    // by translation of k positions in the alphabet
        i ← 0;
        while ALPHABET[i] ≠ C
            i ← i + 1;
        j ← (i + k) mod 26;
        T ← ALPHABET[j];
```

```
program CIPHER

    // transforms a message into the corresponding cryptogram
        print "communicate the key";
        get k;
        print "communicate the message";
        get MSG;                          // MSG is a vector of 140 characters
                                          // containing the message
        for h = 0 to 139
            TRANSFORM (k, MSG[h], T);
            CRT [h] ← T;                  // CRT is a vector of 140 characters
                                          // containing the cryptogram
        print CRT;                        // print the cryptogram
```

**Fig. 6.2** The program TRANSFORM transforms a character of the message into an encrypted character by translation of k positions in the alphabet, where k is the cipher key. The program CIPHER encrypts a block of the entire message by calling TRANSFORM inside it.

from within the program CIPHER, shown in the same figure, which encrypts the entire message. The message is divided into blocks of 140 characters and input by the user through a vector MSG of 140 cells; the corresponding cryptogram is built by the program in a vector CRT. For a long message the operation is repeated with the next blocks. A shorter message is extended up to 140 characters by adding to it a useless phrase, which the recipient will easily recognize as such but will not provide an intruder with any information about the length of the message. For the program TRANSFORM we note:

- k and C are *input* variables to the program; T is an *output variable* used by the program CIPHER.
- For simplicity the search for the position $i$ where the character C is placed is done by a **while**-loop that scans the vector ALPHABET. In fact it could have been done

much more efficiently using the binary search mechanism discussed in Chapter 3 because the characters are stored in ALPHABET in alphabetic order.

- Character encryption is executed using a modular operation for computing the position $j$ of the encrypted character. Modular operations can be executed directly in high-level languages.

The interpretation of the two programs should be clear. The deciphering program (i.e. reconstructing the message from the cryptogram) is left to the reader as an exercise. Note that, instead of adding $i$ and $k$ module 26, you will have to make a subtraction with the same module that, as already mentioned, still produces a result in the interval between 0 and 25.

## 6.2 Exponential Growth

Here is a mathematical concept that has invaded common language while losing its most interesting features. In fact, it is usually limited to indicating a phenomenon that grows very quickly, while in reality that growth is a great deal faster than anyone who described it that way, more or less unknowingly, could probably imagine. This property gives it a very close relationship with the design of algorithms.

In the mathematical description of the evolution of a phenomenon under consideration, an *exponential growth* occurs with reference to a numeric variable that appears as the *exponent* of a *base* greater than 1. The most famous formula that describes it is $2^n$, an expression that denotes a doubling value at every step for a sequence of consecutive integers $n$. We have $2^0 = 1$ (by definition), $2^1 = 2, 2^2 = 4, 2^3 = 8 \ldots$.

In Chapter 4 we have already seen a property of this expression, that is, that each of its values is greater than the sum of all previous ones. Other examples, however, show much more impressive effects. Let us take one of many. Paper sheets used in publishing generally have a thickness between 0.07 mm and 0.18 mm. For convenience of calculation we consider a sheet of medium thickness to be 0.125 mm, such that eight overlapping sheets reach the thickness of 1 mm. If we fold our sheet in half the thickness doubles, and continuing with the folds, it doubles at every step, so that after three folds the thickness has become precisely $0.125 \times 2^3 = 1$ mm. The experiment described hereafter is virtual because we want to continue folding the sheet in two and this quickly becomes impossible for practical reasons. However, if we could fold the sheet 10 more times, the overall thickness would become $1 \times 2^{10} = 1,024$ mm. That is, our sheet folded 13 times would have reached a thickness of more than 1 meter. Now the game is clear: considering that $2^{10} > 1,000$, with another 10 folds the sheet would be more than 1 km thick. With 20 additional folds the thickness would be multiplied by $2^{20} > 1,000,000$, that is, with a total of 43 folds, the thickness would become more than a million kilometers, more than twice the distance between Earth and the moon!

Of course, with every folding of the sheet its surface is halved, and then after 43 folds it would be reduced to $1/2^{43}$ of the original. That is, its linear dimensions would be reduced to about one thousandth of those of an atom. In short, the experiment cannot be done. However, this surface reduction is the counterpart of the thickness increase, and represents the inverse phenomenon of exponential growth.

If the base in the formula were greater than 2 the values would grow even faster. The values of $3^n$ are in succession 0, 3, 9, 27, 81 ..., much higher than the ones of $2^n$. We are always in the realm of exponential growth with a constant base, but something more impressive is showing up.

Let's consider a new function known as *factorial*, indicated by the exclamation point and defined as:

$$n! = n \times (n-1) \times (n-2) \times (n-3) \times \ldots \times 2 \times 1.$$

The sequence of values grows in a way that is enormously greater than $c^n$, where $c > 1$ is an arbitrary constant. The initial factorial values are: $0! = 1$ (by definition), $1! = 1$, $2! = 2$, $3! = 6$, $4! = 24$, $5! = 120, \ldots 10! = 3,628,800$. Compared to this last value, the values $2^{10} = 1,024$ and $3^{10} = 59,049$ are small potatoes. A rather complicated formula indicates that the growth of $n!$ is a function of the form $n^n$, that is, in addition to the exponent, the base also grows progressively, resulting in an overall growth of a different nature from the one with a constant base.

To understand what all this has to do with cryptography, we will start from the factorial function. The most immediate phenomenon related to it is the number of ways in which the items of a set can be ordered. For one element, let's say A, there is only one ordering. If there are two elements, A and B, the orderings are BA and AB obtained by placing the new element B before and after A. For three elements A, B, and C, there are six orderings: CBA, BCA, BAC, CAB, ACB, and ABC, built from the two orderings of A and B by inserting in each of them the new element C in the first, second, or third position. Therefore, from 2 orderings for A and B, exactly $3 \times 2 = 6$ orderings for A, B and C can be built. Note that 2 (orderings) = 2!, and 6 (orderings) = 3!. Generally, from the orderings of $n - 1$ elements we can construct those of $n$ elements by inserting the new element into each of the previous orderings, in all the $n$ possible positions, so that the new number of sequences is equal to the previous one multiplied by $n$. Then, the orderings of $n$ elements are $n \times (n-1)!$ and thus, according to the factorial definition, they are $n!$. In math these orderings are called *permutations* of the set.

Now consider the encryption made with the two disks containing the alphabet, or with the equivalent program CIPHER. Since there are 25 usable keys (omitting the key 0), the cipher could be easily attacked by trying to decrypt the message with all the keys and examining the sequences obtained, looking for a meaningful one. Using the disks, this would consist of trying 25 shifts of the internal one. A deciphering program would add a cycle **for** $k = 1$ **to** 25 outside the other operations, to try out all the possible keys. It is easy to do both by hand and with a computer.

As a defense from these attacks one should then use a much larger number of keys to be virtually immune from any attempt to try them all, that is, a number that is exponential in relation to a parameter that characterizes the problem. For this reason, the factorial function is offered as an immediate alternative because 26

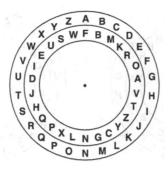

**Fig. 6.3** Character transformation using an internal disk that contains an arbitrary permutation of the alphabet. The message BONUMVESPERUM is encoded as BLNDGIRHXRQDG.

characters can be arranged in 26! permutations of the alphabet and each of them can be used as a key.

Referring to Figure 6.1, a new internal disk can be built that contains in due order the characters of a permutation chosen as a key instead of using the alphabetical order. Additionally, it is advisable that the new permutation is randomly chosen to prevent an adversary from guessing it based on knowledge of the preferences of the user who established the key. A new internal disk attached to the center of a standard external disk is shown in Figure 6.3. No rotation is required: the correspondence between characters in encryption and deciphering is performed by matching the characters facing each other. We went from the translation (i.e., shifting) of the alphabet by a fixed amount, used in the early methods, to the permutation of its characters where a cryptographic attack by trying all the keys is impossible because the value of 26! is close to $10^{27}$.

Here, however, the use of disks becomes impractical because the internal disk itself constitutes the key: changing the key requires changing the disk. It works better with a program where the key is given in a vector PERMUTATION of 26 cells containing a permutation of the alphabet, such as

F, B, M, K, R, O, A, V, T, Z, Y, C, G, N, L, X, P, Q, H, J, D, I, E, U, S, W

as given in Figure 6.3. The reader can easily write this program, to be used instead of the program TRANSFORM in Figure 6.2, by introducing the command line **get PERMUTATION** for communicating the key.

Of course, storing a 26-character key is inconvenient but you might think that, in return, all danger of eavesdropping is avoided. Unfortunately, it is not so! The lesson that encryptors have learned over the centuries is that a particular type of attack can be avoided, but there is no telling whether the opponents can find a different one, as is the present case.

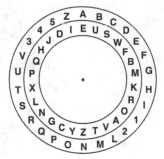

**Fig. 6.4** A disk based on Leon Battista Alberti's principle, at the beginning of the operation and after a key change.

## 6.3 Leon Battista Alberti's Disk

The weakness of all ciphers that replace a character with another, but always with the same (and are therefore called *monoalphabetic*), lies in the fact that the messages usually sent are not random sequences but sentences in some language. And in all languages the various letters appear with a well-known frequency (for example, in English E and T are more frequent than the other letters, while Z is very rare). Or there are particular groups of letters that appear frequently (e.g. THE in English). Or some letters cannot be doubled (e.g. WW never appears in English, while EE and OO do). Therefore, if a letter $y$ appears in a cryptogram with the frequency of the letter $x$ in the language presumably used in the message, the transformation induced by the key is likely to be of $x$ into $y$. With a few tests of this type, and assuming that the message is long enough to allow significant statistics, any cryptogram can be deciphered independently of the number of possible keys.

A genius of the Italian Renaissance, Leon Battista Alberti – a famous architect, but also a mathematician, linguist, philosopher, musician, and archaeologist – deserves credit for understanding this phenomenon and designing an interesting gadget to get around it. Starting from the end of the story, Arthur Scherbius, who in 1918 patented the famous Enigma Machine, used by the Germans to encrypt messages during World War II, declared that he simply extended Alberti's method.

Like previous ones, Alberti's *disk* consisted of two concentric disks, but the way the two alphabets were written and their resulting use were completely new. Figure 6.4 shows one of many possible realizations. We will describe the simplest encryption algorithm for it, even though the disk can be transformed, extended, and used in many other ways. The reader may be tempted to conceive other variations; what matters is to preserve the principle on which the disk is based.

As in the previous cases, the device contains the alphabet for the message on the external disk, from which Alberti removed some scarcely used characters (in the example, conceived for messages written in Latin languages, the characters J, K, X, Y, and W have been omitted). It also contains on the internal disk an arbitrary permutation of the complete alphabet with which the cryptogram is constructed. The characters missing on the external disk are replaced with *special characters*, numeric digits in the example, which are inserted in the message at any position to indicate a key change. For example, those who cipher the message BONUMVES-PERUM can write it as B O N U M 3 V E S P E R U M, obtaining:

> message     B O N U M 3 V E S P E R U M
> cryptogram B L N D G E Q F L C F N P T

Let's see what has happened, referring to Figure 6.4. By agreement between the two partners, the relative position of the two disks is initially the one indicated on the left, with the external A facing the internal F. In a sense, the AF pair is the initial key with which BONUM is encoded as BLNDG. The relative position of the disks is maintained until the arrival of the first special character, 3 in the example, which faces E and indicates that the internal disk must be rotated to bring E to face A (the image to the right in the figure). Hence the extent of the rotation does not depend on the value 3 of the special character, but on its position in the external alphabet. From now on, the key is AE and with this the rest of the message VESPERUM is encoded as QFLCFNPT. The encoding process goes on in the same way by changing the key each time a new special character is encountered.

By frequently inserting special characters, Alberti's cipher is really difficult to attack provided that the permutation used in the inner circle is known only to the two partners. In particular, the frequent change of key makes all attacks based on character statistics in the message language ineffective, because the same character in that message corresponds to many characters in the cryptogram depending on the key used at any particular moment. Alberti's disk then gave rise to the *polyalphabetic ciphers* that, in different versions, were used until the advent of electronics in the twentieth century.

The program ALBERTI to encrypt with this method is shown in Figure 6.5. Two vectors EXTERNAL and INTERNAL of 26 positions each, which we assume have been already uploaded (but otherwise we know how to do it, see Chapter 3), contain in due order the characters of the two discs according to an agreed starting position. For the example in Figure 6.4 we would have EXTERNAL[0] = A and INTERNAL[0] = F, implying that the starting key AF is set. Since subsequent keys are communicated through the message, there is no explicit request in the program to communicate the key that changes from time to time, but the program contains a test on each character of the message to determine whether it is a special character.

Understanding the program is unfortunately more difficult than learning to use the disk. Here is an explanation of the role of the command lines of ALBERTI.

- Let us assume that the disk layout is the one shown in the image to the left in Figure 6.4. The key K is equal to zero.
- The message vector MSG is scanned with the **for**-loop of lines 4–11.
- Lines 5–7 scan the vector EXTERNAL to look for the location $i$ of the character MSG[$h$] which must be encrypted. The position is given by the value of $i$ at the exit of the **while**-loop. This value is then used in lines 8–11.

---

**program** ALBERTI

// encoding a message with Leon Battista Alberti's method

1.  $k \leftarrow 0$;                       // $k$ (the key) equals the counterclockwise rotation of
                                            // the internal disk relative to the external disk

2.  **print** "input the message";

3.  **get** MSG;            // MSG is a vector of 140 characters containing the message

4.  **for** $h = 0$ **to** 139

5.      $i \leftarrow 0$;

6.      **while** MSG $[h] \neq$ EXTERNAL $[i]$   // look for MSG[h] in EXTERNAL

7.          $i \leftarrow i + 1$;

8.      $j \leftarrow (i + k) \bmod 26$;          // here it is MSG $[h] =$ EXTERNAL $[i]$

9.      CRT $[h] \leftarrow$ INTERNAL $[j]$;      // CRT is a vector of 140 characters
                                                 // that will contain the cryptogram

10.     **if** EXTERNAL $[i] \in \{1, 2, 3, 4, 5\}$   // here MSG $[h]$ is a special character

11.         $k \leftarrow (i + k) \bmod 26$;                          // so the key is updated

12. **print** CRT;                                                 // print the cryptogram

---

**Fig. 6.5** Program that executes the encryption of a message contained in a vector MSG via Leon Battista Alberti's method. The cryptogram is built into a vector CRT.

- The key $k$ indicates how much the internal disk rotates counterclockwise if a special character is encountered in the message. With vectors, this is equivalent to putting the characters EXTERNAL $[i]$ and INTERNAL $[j]$ into correspondence, by setting $j = (i + k) \bmod 26$ (lines 8–9), without actually "rotating" the elements of INTERNAL, which would require rewriting the entire vector.
- If MSG $[h]$ is a special character, the key is updated in lines 10–11 *after* the encryption of the character in line 9. Notice that, when the execution of ALBERTI reaches line 9, MSG $[h] =$ EXTERNAL $[i]$.
- By looking at Figure 6.4, if character 3 appears in the message, the internal disk is rotated counterclockwise by 22 positions because EXTERNAL [22] = 3 (left image). In the program the value of $k$ passes from 0 to $(0 + 22) \bmod 26 = 22$, in line 11 (right image).

Once all this is understood, you will be able to attempt to build a deciphering program on your own. Let us now open a window on today's cryptography without pretending to go deep into a mathematically very difficult field.

## 6.4 Today's Ciphers

The Second World War saw a much more extensive and sophisticated use of secret ciphers than in the past, so that important mathematical results were not made public because governments imagined possible uses of them in military communications. And even polyalphabetic ciphers still played a role.

It was common to use the page of a book as a very long key, by changing the page each day according to previous agreements. The method is simple and unexpectedly robust to attacks. Each character of the key (that is, of the selected page) is transformed into the position that the character occupies in the alphabet. For example, in the English alphabet each character is converted into a number from 0 to 25. The sequence of numbers thus obtained is put into correspondence with the sequence of characters of the message, transforming each of them into a character of the cryptogram with a translation module 26 through the alphabet equal to the value of the corresponding character of the key. For example character B of the message would become F if the corresponding character of the key is D = 4. It can be mathematically proved that if instead of using a page of a book, a random sequence of characters is used as a key, changing this key for each message, the cryptogram can not be decrypted. However, even using the pages of a book or other long sequences of characters that can easily be agreed upon by both partners, the method is extremely safe (the challenge is finding the key).

For example, using the opening words of the previous paragraph with the blank spaces removed: "itwascommontouse ..." we would have the key 8 19 22 0 18 4 14 12 12 14 13 19 14 20 18 4 ... and the message BONUMVESPERUM becomes:

|  | | | | | | | | | | | | | |
|---|---|---|---|---|---|---|---|---|---|---|---|---|---|
| message | B | O | N | U | M | V | E | S | P | E | R | U | M |
| key | 8 | 19 | 22 | 0 | 18 | 4 | 14 | 12 | 12 | 14 | 13 | 19 | 14 |
| cryptogram | J | H | J | U | E | Z | S | E | B | S | E | N | A |

Of course, it is very easy, and not very enjoyable, to write a program that implements this transformation and its deciphering, but it is very inconvenient to load, for each message, a different vector containing the key whose length depends on the length of the message. In fact, the key must be changed continuously to prevent an opponent from inferring it by statistical methods if many cryptograms are intercepted. Here too, manual coding is performed much more easily. In any case, we have now a rather secure communication method so that two readers wanting to secretly communicate are encouraged to proceed along this line.

Then, why continue? Could we not be content with this method? The answer is no, because encryption has come into everyday life with such pervasiveness that it makes it unthinkable that all users, especially on the Internet and often without even realizing it, can establish a different secret key stored somewhere to communicate with any other user they will have to deal with. Much less choose a new key for each message exchanged with another user, and just as long as the message itself!

So let us go ahead and give some details as to what is happening today. Many of the cryptographic operations we are dealing with involve using bank cards or credit cards, but encryption is also used to protect correspondence and documents if circumstances so require. There are several protocols, including one known as AES (for Advanced Encription Standard) which would be out of place to describe here except for some basic points. The keys are short, typically a few dozen characters including letters, numbers, and other symbols. The message is divided into blocks as long as the key, which is used to transform a block of the message into a block of the cryptogram. Then the key is automatically transformed to encrypt the next block. Security is based on a *diffusion principle* according to which each character in a block of the cryptogram is a function of *all characters* of both the key, the corresponding block of the message, and the previously encrypted blocks. As you can see, the situation is very different from that of polyalphabetic ciphers. A great novelty compared to the past is that the keys are not set up directly by the users, but by the electronic devices they use to communicate, such as PCs, smartphones, and ATMs. We will see that mathematics, algorithm construction, and coding play a crucial role for this purpose.

## 6.5 Dispositions of Characters

In Section 6.2 we showed that the permutations of $n$ characters are $n!$. However, remember that a permutation contains all the characters exactly once, while cryptographic keys may contain the same characters an arbitrary number of times and may not contain some of them.

This new way of arranging the characters, known in mathematics as *disposition with repetition* or briefly *disposition*, is governed by a different exponential law. Letting $a$ be the number of characters of the alphabet used, the number of dispositions of $n$ characters is $a^n$. In fact for $n = 1$ the dispositions of single characters are $a^1 = a$. For $n = 2$, the two-character dispositions are obtained by placing, in front of each of the $a$ characters, all the characters of the alphabet, for a total of $a \times a = a^2$ dispositions. So for the English alphabet with $a = 26$, we get $26^2 = 676$ dispositions of two characters, namely:

$$AA \ AB \ldots AZ \quad BA \ BB \ldots BZ \ \ldots\ldots \ ZA \ ZB \ldots ZZ$$

For $n = 3$, placing all the characters of the alphabet in front of the preceding dispositions we get $26 \times 676 = 26^3 = 17576$ dispositions, namely:

$$AAA \ AAB \ldots AAZ \ \ldots\ldots\ldots \ ZZZ$$

Generalizing this argument to $n$ characters taken from an alphabet of size $a$, it can be immediately proved that the number of dispositions is $a^n$.

Using the English alphabet, there are more than 17,000 possible three-character dispositions, thereby forming a rich lexicon of possible words in any language (even though, fortunately, languages do not work that way). However, there are sequences of characters built just this way that we use continuously: the numbers, expressed in the usual Indo-Arabic notation, whose alphabet is composed of the ten digits from

0 to 9. Thus, the five digit number constituting the key to open a padlock is chosen from the $10^5$ dispositions between 00000 and 99999.

We now observe that in all electronic devices information is represented with a *binary system* whose alphabet contains only two characters expressed by convention with the digits 0 and 1, called *bits*. For example, each character typed on a keyboard is represented by a group of bits sent from the keyboard to another device in the form of electrical signals each of which assumes one of two values of voltage or current depending on the technology used. The processing then takes place in binary. With four bits, for example, the following $2^4 = 16$ dispositions can be built:

0000 0001 0010 0011 0100 0101 0110 0111

1000 1001 1010 1011 1100 1101 1110 1111

These bit configurations (or binary dispositions) can be interpreted as *binary numbers* with values from 0 (0000) to 15 (1111).[1] With $n$ bits, $2^n$ binary numbers are represented. As we have seen this value grows vertiginously for increasing $n$.

When using a computer, this binary representation is known and directly accessible only to those who program in machine language. High-level languages use alphabetic characters and decimal numbers, but the law of growth is the same, changing the base to which $n$ is raised. In particular, the *value* of binary (or decimal) numbers of $n$ digits ranges from 0 to $2^n - 1$ (or from 0 to $10^n - 1$) and is on average about $2^{n-1}$ (or $10^{n-1}$), an extremely large number. As we will see, the relationship between the *length* (number of digits) $n$ of the representation of a number and its exponential *value* is critical to understanding many important phenomena that characterize the construction of algorithms, not only in cryptography.

The $10^5$ decimal numbers of five digits can be generated in ascending order in a very short time with a program that contains only the command:

**for** $i = 0$ **to** $10^5 - 1$ **print** $i$

with the purpose of opening an electronic padlock by an exhaustive number of attempts. However, if instead of five digits there were 30, even if the program generated a thousand new numbers each nanosecond (i.e. each $10^{-9}$ seconds) the time it would take to generate them all would be about three hundred years.

Generating in pseudocode all binary numbers of $n$ bits for arbitrary $n$, and placing them in an $n$-bit vector N, is harder than we would have expected. It is accomplished in the program BINARY_DISPOSITIONS in Figure 6.6, which generates the bit sequences in the order of increasing binary numbers. The constructed vector $N$ will be useful later on. The program requires some comment.

Adding 1 to a binary number amounts to inserting 1 in the least significant position (i.e., the rightmost) if there is a 0, or scanning the number toward the most significant positions (i.e., leftward) as far as 1s are encountered, changing all these 1s to 0s, and then changing the first 0 encountered to 1. For example, $1010 + 1 =$

---

[1] It is assumed here that everyone knows binary numbers. As in the decimal system, binary numbers use *positional notation*, however, the "weights" of the digits are powers of two. Thus the binary number 1101 indicates the decimal number $13 = 1 \times 2^3 + 1 \times 2^2 + 0 \times 2^1 + 1 \times 2^0$.

---

**program** BINARY_DISPOSITIONS

// dispositions over $n$ bits, constructed in a vector $N$

1.    **for** $i = 0$ **to** $n - 1$

2.         $N[i] \leftarrow 0$;

3.    **print** N                                         // print the first disposition 00...0

4.    $i \leftarrow 0$;

5.    **while** $i \leq n - 1$;

6.         **if** $N[i] = 0$                              // if $i > 0$ we have $N[j] = 0$ for $j < i$

7.              $N[i] \leftarrow 1$;

8.              **print** N;                              // prints the disposition just built

9.              $i \leftarrow 0$;                         // go back to the least significant bit

10.        **else**

11.             $N[i] \leftarrow 0$;                      // the bit 1 in position $i$ is changed to 0

12.             $i \leftarrow i + 1$;                     // go to the next bit

---

**Fig. 6.6** Program for the construction and printing one by one of all the $n$-bit dispositions available in a vector $N$, in the order of increasing binary numbers.

1011, and $1011 + 1 = 1100$. The program BINARY_DISPOSITIONS is designed to do exactly this:

- The initial disposition $00...0$ is built and printed in lines 1–3.
- If there is a 0 in the least significant digit (i.e. $N[0] = 0$) this is changed to 1 and the new configuration is printed in lines 6–8; otherwise all the 1s successively encountered are changed to 0s (lines 10–12), up to where a 0 is found, which is converted to 1, followed by the new print in lines 6–8.
- The program stops for $i = n$ (line 5), having rebuilt the initial disposition $00...0$.

In order to use the program as a binary counter, for example if pulses coming from a detection system must be counted one by one, a command line "**get** pulse" must be added between lines 7 and 8. The program has already built the number next to the last one printed, which in turn will be printed in line 8, and is waiting for the new request.

## 6.6 The Construction of Keys

Let us now imagine an Internet communication for buying some object *online*. The two participants in this transaction do not know each other personally and perhaps they will never interact again. Since the communication contains confidential data, they communicate through a cipher without having any control over it, probably without even knowing how it is done, but relying on the properties of the cipher, of the systems used and of the communication channel. Perhaps they are satisfied to see the abbreviation *https* and a locked padlock icon appearing in their browser's Internet address line, indicating that the network uses an encrypted protocol. But what actually happens?

Each cipher requires a secret key known only to the two partners, who we will call Alice and Bob by cryptographic tradition. However, as we have already explained, the keys for all pairs of users cannot exist beforehand. Therefore, in the first part of their communication, Alice and Bob (or, rather, the devices they use) will have to build a common key that will be forgotten at the end of their interaction. This is like a snake that eats its own tail: the key will be used to communicate safely, but the two users must establish it by communicating safely before being able to use the cipher. Here come into play some mathematical studies born in the 1970s to support the new cryptography that was then emerging. We will try to explain some of these concepts as simply as possible.

In particular, among many others, we mention the American scholars Whitfield Diffie and Martin Hellman. For their studies, the two were awarded the 2015 ACM Turing Award, considered the Nobel prize for computing. In 1976, they designed the key exchange algorithm that we present below and which is still widely used: an algorithm based on a series of *non-encrypted but still safe* interactions between Alice and Bob, referred to as "DH protocol" (from the initials of the authors). The created (secret) key is an integer, which we represent in decimal notation even if the system calculates it in binary. The security of the protocol, that is, the practical certainty that an opponent who intercepts the communication cannot rebuild the key, is based on the relation between the number $n$ of digits of the key and the number of possible keys that is exponential in $n$.

We remind the reader informally that given a function $y = f(x)$, its *inverse function* (if it exists) is $x = g(y)$ such that:

$$g(f(x)) = x \text{ and } f(g(y)) = y, \text{ for each pair of values } x, y.$$

That is, if we calculate $y = f(x)$, and apply $g$ to $y$ so calculated, we find the original value $x$, and vice versa. An elementary example is given by the two funcions addition and subtraction with a constant $c$, one inverse of the other. By putting $f(x) = x + c$ and $g(y) = y - c$, we get:

$$g(f(x)) = g(x + c) = x + c - c = x, \text{ and}$$
$$f(g(y)) = f(y - c) = y - c + c = y.$$

Adding and subtracting is very simple. Even without considering all the particular actions needed (or all the commands executed by a program), we can state that the method we use with paper and pen performs a number of elementary operations proportional to the number $n$ of digits of the two numbers involved because their digits are scanned in pairs and, for each pair, a constant number of operations is performed. This provides an upper bound proportional to $n$ on the computing time required by the algorithm. On the other hand, all the digits of the two numbers must be examined to obtain the final result, so $n$ is also a lower bound and the algorithm is optimal in order of magnitude. That is, we are not saying that the two bounds are expressed by an identical number of operations, rather by the same type of function, and thus the algorithms are optimal.

Let us now play a game among several people to establish a secret key of $n$ digits between a pair of them, Alice and Bob. The basic assumptions are that the algorithm to be used is known to everyone, and everyone can listen to the conversation between Alice and Bob, but only Alice and Bob will get to know the common key being built. The scheme is that of the DH protocol, with a stretch to understand how it works: we assume that the addition of $y = x + c$ is executed in time $n$ with the usual algorithm *but no one* in the community is able to make a subtraction except by trial and error. That is, if the values of $y$ and $c$ are known, to compute the inverse function $x = y - c$ we assume that we have to try all possible values of $x$, starting from $\bar{x} = y$ and gradually decreasing this value until one is found satisfying the relation $\bar{x} + c = y$. Assuming that $y$ consists of $n$ digits, we should perhaps try a number of values for $\bar{x}$ of the order of $10^n$. In computational jargon this operation is said to be "difficult." As we shall see, addition and subtraction are obviously not difficult and thus they are not the two functions used in the DH protocol, but they are useful here to illustrate easily the key-generation process.

Let us simulate the protocol for very small numbers. As we know, security is guaranteed for big $n$, say of 20 decimal digits.

1. **Choose** a value for $c$ known to everyone. For example $c = 5$.
2. Alice **chooses** a random number $a$ as her "secret": $a$ will not be known to anybody else, not even Bob, and is randomly chosen to prevent others from guessing Alice's preferences in choosing the number. Let us assume that $a = 12$.

   Symmetrically, Bob **chooses** a random number $b$ as his "secret." Let us assume that $b = 9$.
3. Alice **calculates** $A = c + a$, and **communicates** $A$ to Bob. We have $A = 17$. Everyone can listen to the communication and knows the value of $A$. However, while Alice has calculated $A$ through an addition that is an "easy" operation, no one else (not even Bob) can retrieve $a$ knowing $A$ and $c$ in a reasonable time, because this requires a subtraction that we are assuming to be a "difficult" operation.

   Symmetrically, Bob **calculates** $B = c + b$, and **communicates** $B$ to Alice. We have $B = 14$. No one (not even Alice) can retrieve $b$ knowing $B$ and $c$ because this would require computing a subtraction.
4. Alice **receives** $B$ from Bob and **calculates** the sum $K_A = B + a$. We have $K_A = 14 + 12 = 26$. Since $B = c + b$ we have $K_A = c + b + a$, which is the common key for Alice and Bob.

   Symmetrically, Bob **receives** $A$ from Alice and **calculates** the sum $K_B = A + b$. We have $K = 17 + 9 = 26$, and since $A = c + a$ we have $K_B = c + a + b = K_A$, which is the common key.

It should be clear that although all the others have heard the communication between Alice and Bob, and know all the protocol data except the secret numbers $a$ and $b$, they will not be able to retrieve Alice and Bob's key without making a subtraction that, by hypothesis, requires exponential time. In fact, they would have to calculate $a = A - c$ and then $K_A = B + a$, where $A, c$ and $B$ are known to everyone.

Clearly, ours is a hypothetical game because actually subtracting is not harder than adding. We must therefore look for a *one-way* function (where "one-way" is a jargon word) that is "easy" to calculate and "difficult" to revert. Searching for these functions has been crucial in modern cryptography studies. We will now describe the one proposed by Diffie and Hellman to build their protocol. For this purpose we ask the reader for a bit of attention, believing that the effort will be sufficiently rewarded by the elegance of the method.

Calculations are performed on integers in modular arithmetic: that is, all results are obtained in modulo $p$, where $p$ is a prime number. The results thus generated are then between 0 and $p - 1$ and the key will be one of them. As you may expect $p$ is very large, say of twenty decimal digits. Among their innumerable properties prime numbers have one that is of interest here: every prime $p$ has at least one *generator* $g < p$, that is, an integer that if elevated to all exponents 1, 2, ..., $p - 1$ with modulo $p$ calculations, still produces as results 1, 2, ..., $p - 1$ but in an order "difficult" to foresee (it is a sort of "random" permutation). For example, $g = 5$ is a generator of $p = 7$ since by doing calculations modulo 7 we have:

$$5^1 = 5, \ 5^2 = 4, \ 5^3 = 6, \ 5^4 = 2, \ 5^5 = 3, \ 5^6 = 1.$$

These modular powers of $g$ have another property that has made it possible to find the one-way function proposed by Diffie and Hellman. Consider an arbitrary pair consisting of a prime and a generator $p, g$. Given a value $y$ of the exponent, calculating $x = g^y \bmod p$ is computationally "easy" but inverting the function, i.e. calculating the value of $y$ given $x$, is computationally "difficult" as far as we know. Note that $y$ is the exponent to give $g$ for obtaining $x$, that is $y$ is the *logarithm of x to the base g*, in this case called a *discrete logarithm* because the calculation is modular and the result is an integer. The computation of $y$ is indicated with the notation $y = \log_g x \bmod p$.

In essence, if $p, g$ and $x$ are known, in order to find the value $y$ that satisfies the equation $y = \log_g x \bmod p$, you have to try all the values of $y$ between 1 and $p - 1$ until arriving at the value $\bar{y}$, such that $x = g^{\bar{y}} \bmod p$. Additionally, this search requires an exponential number of steps in relation to the number of digits of $p$, because if $p$ is for example a 20 digit number its value is $10^{20}$.

Figure 6.7 shows the pseudocode of the DH protocol, structured as the previous game where addition and subtraction are replaced by computing a power and a discrete logarithm, both in modulo $p$. This coding is completely new compared to what has been seen so far, because it is made up of two programs that interact with each other. These programs are identical except in the initial action that decides who starts the connection. An opponent intercepting the transmission gets to know the values of $p, g, A$, and $B$, but retrieving the key $K_A = K_B$ requires knowing $a$ and calculating $K_A$ using $a$ and $B$, or knowing $b$ and calculating $K_B$ using $b$ and $A$. That is, the opponent must be able to calculate $a = \log_g A \bmod p$, or $b = \log_g B \bmod p$: two

**program** DH_ALICE

// Alice chooses a pair $p, g$ known to everyone and communicates it to Bob

1.  **communicate** to Bob: $p, g$;

2.  **wait** from Bob: OK;

3.  **choose** a random number $a$, with $2 \leq a \leq p - 2$;

4.  **compute** $A \leftarrow g^a \bmod p$;

5.  **communicate** to Bob: $A$;

6.  **wait** from Bob: $B$;              // $B = g^b \bmod p$, where $b$ is the secret of Bob

7.  **compute** $K_A \leftarrow B^a \bmod p$;              // we have $K_A = g^{b \times a} \bmod p$

---

**program** DH_BOB

1.  **wait** from Alice: $p, g$;

2.  **communicate** to Alice: OK;

3.  **choose** a random number $b$, with $2 \leq b \leq p - 2$;

4.  **compute** $B \leftarrow g^b \bmod p$;

5.  **communicate** to Alice: $B$;

6.  **wait** from Alice: $A$;              // $A = g^a \bmod p$, where $a$ is the secret of Alice

7.  **compute** $K_B \leftarrow A^b \bmod p$;              // we have $K_B = g^{a \times b} \bmod p$

**Fig. 6.7** Alice and Bob interacting programs to build a key $K_A = K_B$ with the DH protocol, to be later used as the common key in a cipher. The random numbers $a$ and $b$ are, respectively, known only to Alice and Bob. It is assumed that Alice starts the interacting protocol.

operations that require an exponential number of steps in relation to the number of digits of $p$, as already observed several times.

As a final remark, we note that the secrets $a$ and $b$ of Alice and Bob are chosen from integers in the range between 2 and $p - 2$. The values 1 and $p - 1$ are not used because $g^1 \bmod p = g$ and $g^{p-1} \bmod p = 1$ (the latter equality derives from a famous theorem of algebra).

# Chapter 7
# Putting Things in Order

How many times have you tried to play cards with your friends but did not have a new deck of cards available, so you had to be content with recovering a used one from a drawer? Unless you have been involved in gambling, where the perfect state of the cards is a necessary condition to ensure the absence of special marks that could easily identify some of them, any deck of cards in good condition is okay in all games for leisure, *provided that it is complete*. But how can we establish that it is? Or, better, considering the subject of this text, how can we establish this condition as quickly as possible?

Let us first reflect on the practices that are most frequently employed in this situation before embarking on the following algorithmic discussion. Moreover, let us do so from the "computational" point of view by evaluating how fast the proposed methods perform.

Probably the most common approach adopted on vacationers' tables is to count the cards and then verify that their number is equal to the one of a complete deck, namely 54 in the case of French playing cards (including two jokers). It is evident that this *counting* solves the problem only partially, because if the number is smaller than 54 then we can immediately conclude that the deck is incomplete but if the number is greater or equal to 54 we cannot conclude anything about the deck! In fact, it could be the case that the deck includes one or more duplicate cards or, as anyone who plays with French cards knows well, we could have counted the special cards that describe the rules and scores of Bridge. In these cases only an *explicit analysis* of the deck can allow us to establish whether we can use it for playing cards with our friends by discarding the extra cards (if any).

What does it mean to analyze *algorithmically* the cards in the deck? There are several methods; we start with the most common and simplest one. It consists first of partitioning the cards into four groups, according to their suits: hearts ($\heartsuit$), diamonds ($\diamondsuit$), clubs ($\clubsuit$), and spades ($\spadesuit$). This step allows us to also identify, and discard, the two jokers and the cards (if any) showing the scoring in Bridge. Then, we *sort* the cards in each group in ascending "value": 2, ..., 10, J, Q, K, and ace. Finally, we *scan* every sorted group of cards in order to verify its completeness, possibly discovering (thanks to the ordering) duplicates and/or missing cards. Equivalently,

© Springer Nature Switzerland AG 2018

P. Ferragina, F. Luccio, *Computational Thinking*,

https://doi.org/10.1007/978-3-319-97940-3_7

we could *sort* the cards first by value and then by their suits, thereby creating 13 smaller decks.

This description is pretty much *operational* but, unfortunately, misses many details in order to be formally considered an *algorithm*. In fact, while it is crystal clear what it means to "scan" the cards in their order of appearance in a deck, the same cannot be said of the verb "sort." The result of sorting is evident – a sequence of cards ordered according to a given criterion for deciding which one is smaller/larger – but the sequence of steps to be executed in order to produce this sequence is not uniquely defined.

The scientific literature abounds with sorting algorithms characterized by the type of items that can be sorted (such as playing cards, numbers, and words), the criterion underlying their ordering (such as increasing or decreasing), the operations allowed (such as comparisons, swaps between adjacent items, and movement or inversion of blocks of items), the computational resource to optimize (such as number of comparisons, swaps, space occupancy, and communication cost), and possibly many other properties. It is therefore not a coincidence that what is technically called the "sorting problem" is one of the core subjects of the Theory of Algorithms. This problem will be formalized in the next section where we will also introduce two basic algorithms; one is simple and frequently used by cards players and the other is more sophisticated but faster. We will also prove that this second algorithm executes the *minimum number of comparisons in the worst case*, thus resulting *optimal* in the use of this computational resource.

Before digging into the formal issues, let us introduce another sorting method that is very often used by card players and allows us to describe another interesting algorithmic scheme for sorting. It consists of *distributing* the cards over a grid of four rows, corresponding to the four suits of cards, and 13 columns, corresponding to their 13 values. According to the order of the suits and values indicated above, the grid will contain in the first row the cards of suit $\heartsuit$, in the second row the cards of suit $\diamondsuit$, in the third row the cards of suit $\clubsuit$, and, finally, the cards of suit $\spadesuit$ in the fourth row. This way, the card 4$\clubsuit$ will be located in the third column (we are assuming that the ace is the highest card) of the third row, the card 8$\diamondsuit$ will be located in the seventh column of the second row, and so on.

This distribution has formed a grid of 52 *groups* of cards. If a group gets no card or more than one card, we can conclude that we have an incomplete deck. This method involves a *distribution phase*, which is much more complex and costly than the one we described in the previous paragraphs, because here we have to manage 52 groups instead of the previous four or 13. On the other hand, however, the present method requires a simpler analysis of these groups, which consists of just a one-card check, whereas the previous methods needed a sorting-and-scanning phase to check their content.

Which method is *better* depends on several factors that are not so evident to those who are new to algorithms. Let us then introduce and discuss them gradually.

Both methods implement, in different forms, an *algorithmic paradigm* that is very powerful and well-known to experts with the name of *divide et impera* (Latin for *divide and conquer*). It consists of solving the problem at hand, in our case, checking the completeness of a deck of cards — by partitioning it into sub-problems that are equivalent to the original problem but are formulated on a smaller number of items (in our case, a smaller number of playing cards). In fact, the first method partitioned the playing cards into four groups, according to their suit, the second method partitioned the playing cards into 13 groups, according to their value, and the third method partitioned the cards into 52 groups, according to both their suit and value. Hence all three algorithms required some *knowledge* of the items to be sorted: suit, value, or both.

In the rest of this chapter we will provide a *rigorous definition* for such expressions as "better" or "more costly" (by referring to the computational resources: time and space), and "some knowledge required". We will also *formalize algorithmically* the methods we have already sketched, thus showing that the sorting problem is much more complex than expected if we wish to solve it rigorously and efficiently. In fact, the solutions proposed earlier are not optimal, in that they do not execute the minimum possible number of comparisons (between cards). We will show this via a reasoning similar to the one adopted in Chapter 2 where the items compared were coins, a comparison was a weighing step, and the goal was to identify the false coin (if any). This similarity provides further clarification that the algorithmic paradigms presented in this book are general enough to be applied successfully to many contexts beyond the few discussed in these pages. It is the creativity and experience of the algorithm designer that play the crucial role in identifying and applying the most fitting paradigm according to the problem to solve.

We conclude this section by observing that the (classic) algorithms described in the next pages are efficient only if they manage a small number of items. However, the advent of the *Internet of Things* (IoT), and the use of the Web and of various types of social networks, have created the need to design algorithms that are able to efficiently process larger and larger datasets (a.k.a. *Big Data*). In this new context, the evaluation of the efficiency of these algorithms cannot be confined to computing just the "number of comparisons" they execute, but it must consider more sophisticated models and criteria that we will discuss at the end of this chapter.

## 7.1 The Sorting Problem

We have already stated that a problem is computationally interesting if it is formulated on a large input size. This is not the case when playing with French cards, which only number 54. So, in the following, we will forget our illustrative problem and assume that the number of cards is arbitrarily large and denoted with $n$. We will return to the case of a small $n$ at the end of this section.

We also assume that a *total order* among the cards has been defined, denoted with the symbol $\leq$, which means that, for any pair of cards, it is always possible to establish whether they are equal or one is smaller/larger than the other. In our example of French cards this total order may be defined by comparing first the cards' suits (i.e. $\heartsuit, \diamondsuit, \clubsuit, \spadesuit$) and then, in case of equality, comparing the cards' values (i.e.

$2, 3, \ldots, 10, J, Q, K$, and ace). This means that the comparison between the French cards $10\clubsuit$ and $3\spadesuit$ yields $10\clubsuit \leq 3\spadesuit$, because $\clubsuit$ precede $\spadesuit$. As another example, the comparison between $10\clubsuit$ and $3\clubsuit$ gives $3\clubsuit \leq 10\clubsuit$, because they are of the same suit and $3 \leq 10$.

An attentive reader has surely noted that this ordering is the one we used to partition the French cards into four (sorted) groups at the beginning of this chapter. If, instead, we compare first the cards' value and then their suits, then $3\spadesuit \leq 10\clubsuit$ and the final ordered sequence of cards would be the one induced by the second sorting method we proposed previously, namely the one that generated 13 (sorted) groups. The reader may think of any other way of ordering the cards and derive the corresponding sorted sequence. In any case, the key property guaranteed by the sorting algorithms we are going to design below is that they are *independent of the ordering relation* $\leq$, so that they work whichever your favourite method may be.

Now we are ready to state formally the sorting problem by talking generically about the elements to sort (possibly cards).

*PROBLEM. Given a sequence $\mathscr{C}$ of n elements, the goal is to reorganize them in increasing order according to the comparison relation $\leq$.*

The ordered sequence computed by the sorting algorithms is also called the *sorted permutation* of $\mathscr{C}$ because it is obtained by permuting its elements in such a way that the final sequence satisfies the increasing order defined by $\leq$.

To facilitate the writing of the pseudocode we assume that the $n$ elements are stored in a vector $C$ and we indicate with $C[i]$ the element stored at position $i$ in the vector. We also use the notation $C[i : j]$ to denote the portion of $C$ ranging from positions $i$ to $j$ (included), these are $j - i + 1$ elements. Positions are counted from 0, hence the entire vector is indicated with $C[0 : n-1]$. The execution of the algorithms will permute the elements as a consequence of their comparisons until the sorted sequence is obtained, namely, until it holds $C[0] \leq C[1] \leq \cdots \leq C[n-2] \leq C[n-1]$.

We recall that the goal of an algorithm designer is to find algorithms that are *correct*, that is, they compute the sorted sequence whatever the input sequence $\mathscr{C}$; and *fast*, that is, they are able to compute the sorted sequence by executing the smallest number of comparisons between elements. In this definition we are assuming that the *comparison between two elements* is the key operation, and estimating their number provides a reasonable approximation of the overall time taken by the algorithm in practice: this is what we called the *time complexity* of the algorithm. Clearly, the more elements are sorted, the more comparisons are needed, and the larger the time complexity of the algorithm. The latter will be expressed as a function of the number $n$ of input elements which, as we already know, is positive and non-decreasing. Algorithms will be then compared *asymptotically*, that is, we will compare their time complexity functions for increasing $n$.

It is important to note that the algorithms designed in the following pages will be agnostic as to both the type of elements in $C$ and the way the ordering relation $\leq$ is defined among them. These two features determine a twofold opposite effect: on the one hand, the algorithms are flexible enough to be applied in any context, provided that an order $\leq$ is defined among the elements to sort; but, on the other hand, these

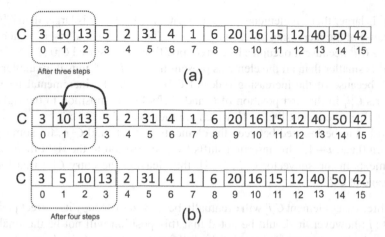

**Fig. 7.1** A running example for the algorithm INSERTION_SORT over a vector $C$ of $n = 16$ integer numbers, i.e. $C = [10,3,13,5,2,31,4,1,6,20,16,15,12,40,50,42]$. Part (a) shows the vector $C[0 : 15]$ after two steps that have sorted the portion $C[0 : 2] = [3,10,13]$; part (b) shows the result of the algorithm applied to the subsequent element $C[3] = 5$ that must be inserted at position $C[1]$ by means of the rightward shift of the elements in $C[1 : 2] = [10,13]$. The final result of this step is the sorted subvector $C[0 : 3] = [3,5,10,13]$.

algorithms may not be the most efficient ones because their execution depends only on the results of a sequence of comparisons that does not exploit any *special features* that the elements in $C$ could possess. For example, if $C$ consists of French cards, then the proposed algorithms will not take advantage of the values and suits of the cards to speed up the sorting process as instead occur in the methods described in the previous section, which distributed cards among groups based on their features. This subtle issue will become clearer in a subsequent section, in which we will propose an algorithm that is faster in sorting *integers*, but its use will be confined only to this type of element!

Our first *comparison-based sorting* algorithm is probably the most used one among card players, perhaps unconsciously, and is scientifically known as *insertion sort*. Its name derives from the way it constructs *incrementally* the sorted sequence by *inserting one after the other* the $n$ elements in their correct sorted position according to the ordering relation $\leq$. Initially, the sorted sequence consists of the single element $C[0]$. The following $i = 1, \ldots, n - 1$ steps create a longer and longer sequence by inserting the element $C[i]$ in its correct position within the (inductively) sorted subvector $C[0 : i - 1]$, which is the output of the previous insertion step. The result is the longer sorted sequence $C[0 : i]$ that, when $i = n - 1$, will provide the finally sorted sequence $\mathscr{C}$. Figure 7.1 shows visually this incremental sorting step.

The incremental insertion of $C[i]$ into the (inductively) sorted subvector $C[0 : i - 1]$ may occur in three different situations:

(a) $C[i]$ is larger than all elements present in $C[0:i-1]$, thus it is larger than $C[i-1]$ because of the increasing order of $C[0:i-1]$. The incremental insertion does not move $C[i]$ because it occupies its correct position in the sorted $C[0:i]$.

(b) $C[i]$ is smaller than all the elements present in $C[0:i-1]$, thus it is smaller than $C[0]$ because of the increasing order of $C[0:i-1]$. The incremental insertion inserts $C[i]$ in the first position of $C$ and shifts by one position to the right the (sorted) elements in $C[0:i-1]$, which are then moved to $C[1:i]$.

(c) $C[i]$ has to be inserted between the elements $C[j-1]$ and $C[j]$, for some $j$ between 0 and $i-1$. This insertion shifts by one position to the right the (sorted) elements in the subvector $C[j:i-1]$, thus leaving the entry $C[j]$ free for the storage of $C[i]$.

In all three cases element $C[i]$ will eventually be moved to occupy its correct position in $C[0:i]$; however, it should be noted that this position will not be the final one because the incremental insertion of the following elements $C[i+1:n-1]$ could perhaps move it. Figure 7.1(b) shows case (c) for the element $C[3] = 5$ that has to be inserted at position 1 within the currently sorted subvector $C[0:2] = [3, 10, 13]$, that is, between the elements $C[0] = 3$ and $C[1] = 10$. This insertion necessitates the rightward shifting of the elements $C[1:2]$ into positions $C[2:3]$, thus freeing the position $C[1]$ where the original element $C[3]$ can now be safely stored. Those who are familiar with the well-known 15-puzzle will find some similarities between the movements of the square tiles there and the movements of the elements in $C$ operated by the algorithm insertion sort.

The pseudocode of INSERTION_SORT, elegant and gracefully succinct, is reported below in Figure 7.2.

```
program INSERTION_SORT(C)
1.    for i = 1 to n − 1
2.        j ← i;
3.        while (j > 0) and (C[j − 1] > C[j])
4.            swap C[j − 1] with C[j];
5.            j ← j − 1;
```

**Fig. 7.2** Program INSERTION_SORT to sort vector $C[0:n-1]$ of $n$ elements on which a comparison relation $\leq$ is defined. As usual between numeric values, the expression $C[j-1] > C[j]$ at line 3 specifies the negation of the relation $C[j-1] \leq C[j]$.

We point out that the rightward shifting of the elements in $C[j, i-1]$ mentioned previously is implemented in the pseudocode in Figure 7.2 with the **while**-loop at lines 3–5. These lines actually merge that shifting with the search for the position $j$ where the element $C[i]$ has to be stored. Specifically, the loop makes use of the iterator $j$ that is initially set to $i$ (line 2), and thus it is $C[j] = C[i]$. At every loop iteration, element $C[j]$ is compared with the preceding one $C[j-1]$ and, if smaller, they are swapped and the process continues onto $C[j-1]$ by decrementing $j$. The swaps continue until one of the two conditions driving the **while**-loop is false: either $j = 0$ or $C[j-1] \leq C[j]$. The first condition corresponds to case (b), namely the one in which $C[i]$ is smaller than all preceding elements, thus the **while**-loop shifts leftward $C[i]$ up to the beginning of the vector $C$. The second condition manages cases (a) and (c) in which $C[i]$ is swapped with some of its previous items until $j$ is its correct position in $C[0 : i-1]$, namely $C[j-1] < C[i] < C[j]$.

It is not difficult to convince yourself about the correctness of INSERTION_SORT: whatever the distribution of the elements within the input vector $C$, the algorithm permutes them in such a way that they are eventually sorted in increasing order according to the relation $\leq$. Mathematically-inspired readers can prove *by induction* that the following statement holds: *"At step $i$, the portion $C[0 : i-1]$ is ordered increasingly according to the relation $\leq$"*. Its proof may be approached as follows:

- the base case corresponds to the situation in which "$i = 1$ and $C[0]$ is a sorted portion"; clearly this holds true because $C[0 : i-1] = C[0]$ consists of one single element which is obviously ordered whatever the relation $\leq$ is;
- the inductive step corresponds to the execution of an iteration $i$ of the **while**-loop: it locates the ordered position of $C[i]$ within the (inductively) sorted portion $C[0 : i-1]$, inserts it there, and thus constructs the ordered $C[0 : i]$.

As far as the time complexity of INSERTION_SORT is concerned, we recall a few basic concepts that were sketched out in previous pages and we wish now to state them in a more precise way. First of all, the time complexity will estimate the number of steps executed by INSERTION_SORT as a function of the number $n$ of elements to be sorted, which is called the *input size* of the problem. This function is non-decreasing because it is natural to expect that the more elements that have to be sorted the more steps that are needed by INSERTION_SORT. We will not try to use a mathematically precise formula to estimate this number, for two main reasons: it would jeopardize the understanding of the main concepts we wish to convey in this book and, the algorithm executes a number of steps that obviously depend on the composition of the vector $C$.

For the former reason, we will focus especially on understanding the *order of magnitude* of the growth of that function; that means, in mathematical terms, we will evaluate whether the function's growth is linear, quadratic, cubic, or of another kind and disregard the lower order terms and the constants that do not influence that growth from an asymptotical point of view. We know that this is a very rough approximation; nevertheless, it has proved over the years to be useful to compare the efficiency of algorithms with sufficient precision. A common *trick* to get that approximation is to count not all steps executed by the algorithm but just the ones involving a specific operation (or some of them) provided that it is (they are) predominant in the computation of the solution of the problem at hand. This is the case of *counting just the comparisons* between elements as they are executed by INSERTION_SORT. In fact, observing the pseudocode in Figure 7.2 we notice that all other operations (i.e. the swap at line 4 and the updates of iterators $i$ and $j$) are executed a number of times that is upper bounded by the number of comparisons. Therefore, we can make an objective estimate of the order of magnitude growth of the time complexity of INSERTION_SORT by just counting the number of comparisons, as indeed the other operations are executed a number of times *proportional* to this one.

Regarding the approximation just discussed, we argue the following. If the vector $C$ is already ordered, INSERTION_SORT will not execute any swap between elements but just one comparison per position $i$ (line 3) that verifies the condition $C[i-1] \leq C[i]$ and thus will not execute the body of the **while**-loop (lines 4–5). Therefore, INSERTION_SORT performs in this case $n-1$ comparisons. This is undoubtedly an advantageous situation for this algorithm whose time complexity is *linear* in the input size $n$ because the function describing (roughly) its number of steps (i.e. comparisons) is linear. Such a time complexity is obviously *optimal* because any other algorithm must examine *at least once* each element of $C$ in order to establish whether it is in a correct position or not. However, if the input vector $C$ is sorted in decreasing order, then INSERTION_SORT needs to shift every element $C[i]$ from its current position to the beginning of the vector (i.e. position 0), thus performing $i$ comparisons (and swaps) in the **while**-loop at lines 3–5. For example, if the input vector is $C[0:2] = [6,4,3]$, iteration $i = 1$ compares and swaps $C[1] = 4$ with $C[0] = 6$ thus creating the new vector $C[0:2] = [4,6,3]$; the next iteration $i = 2$ compares $C[2] = 3$ with both previous elements, because they are smaller, and thus creates the final sorted vector $C[0:2] = [3,4,6]$.

The number of comparisons executed by INSERTION_SORT on that input vector is $1+2 = 3$; in general, if the input vector has size $n$ and is decreasingly ordered, then INSERTION_SORT performs $1+2+3+\ldots+(n-3)+(n-2)+(n-1)$ comparisons to sort it. We have already met this sum in the previous chapter, where it summed the first $n$ integers, concluding that it was equal to $\frac{n(n+1)}{2}$. By applying that formula to the sum of the first $n-1$ integers, we get $\frac{(n-1)n}{2}$. Therefore, for this input configuration the time complexity of INSERTION_SORT grows *quadratically* in $n$, and this constitutes the *worst case* for this algorithm because it performs at any iteration $i$ the maximum number of comparisons to find $C[i]$'s correct position. It goes without saying that this worst case time complexity is much larger than the one we computed for the optimal case. Hence, INSERTION_SORT has an efficiency that suffers from high fluctuations depending on the composition of the input vector $C$.

To generalize, it is not difficult to create an input vector that can be sorted by INSERTION_SORT with at most $kn$ comparisons, where $k < n$ is a given positive integer. It suffices to take the ordered vector $C = [0,1,2,\ldots,n-1]$, and move the $k$ smallest elements to its end in reverse order, thus obtaining $C = [k,k+1,\ldots,n-1,k-1,k-2,\ldots,1,0]$. The execution of INSERTION_SORT over this vector performs one comparison over the first $n-k$ elements, since they are sorted increasingly, and no more than $n$ comparisons for each subsequent element, since they are smaller than all the preceding ones. As a further remark, we note that the optimal input for $C$ can be obtained by setting in that configuration $k = 0$; whereas, the worst input for $C$ can be obtained by setting $k = n-1$. Varying $k$ we can explore different efficiencies for INSERTION_SORT. It turns out to be very fast for small $k$, namely, when the input vector is a little bit disordered. This observation will be crucial when discussing the practical efficiency of the algorithm in the following pages.

As observed in the previous chapters, a good algorithm designer must ask herself at this point: "Is there a more efficient algorithm or can I show a quadratic lower bound for the complexity of the sorting problem?" This latter option would prove that INSERTION_SORT is an optimal algorithm, although it seems a rather remote scenario given its algorithmic structure, which is pretty simple and shows some inefficiencies. For example, every time the element $C[i]$ has to be searched for in the sorted vector $C[0 : i - 1]$, it is compared with (possibly) all previous elements which have already been compared and ordered in the previous steps. This means that the algorithm has already *learned* from its previous steps some information on $C[0 : i - 1]$ that it could exploit to speed up this search. For example, you may consider adopting the algorithm BINARY_SEARCH of Chapter 3 to speed up the identification of position $j$. This is a good intuition but not enough to improve the time complexity of INSERTION_SORT, which also needs the rightward shifting of the elements in $C[j : i - 1]$ to make room for storing $C[i]$ in $C[j]$. This leads us to conclude that a *provably* faster sorter needs a different algorithmic strategy, which is the subject of the next section.

## 7.2 A More Efficient Algorithm

The algorithm we are going to describe improves the time efficiency of INSER-TION_SORT in the worst case by adopting a completely different algorithmic scheme. This hinges on the resolution of a simpler problem, formulated on general sorted sequences of elements (possibly, playing cards).

*PROBLEM. Given two sequences of m elements sorted in increasing order and stored in two vectors $A[0 : m - 1]$ and $B[0 : m - 1]$, the goal is to build the sequence $F[0 : 2m - 1]$ sorted in increasing order and containing all elements of A and B.*

We start from a simple example with $m = 3$, graphically illustrated in Figure 7.3: $A = [1, 5, 7]$ and $B = [2, 3, 4]$. The output vector $F$ will consist of 6 elements sorted increasingly as $[1, 2, 3, 4, 5, 7]$. This configuration of $F$ can be obtained by observing foremost that $F[0]$ should store the smallest element in $A$ and $B$, which can be found as the minimum between $A[0]$ and $B[0]$ since the two sequences are sorted. In Figure 7.3, the compared elements are specified with a downward arrow (step 1): the minimum between the two compared elements is $A[0] = 1$, which is thus stored in $F[0]$. This element is "discarded" from the computation by moving the arrow rightward and then taking into consideration the next element of $A$, i.e. $A[1]$. The algorithm now has to process the rest of $A$, namely $A[1 : 2] = [5, 7]$, and the entire vector $B$, namely $B[0 : 2] = [2, 3, 4]$. This problem is clearly equivalent to the previous one, so that we can proceed as before by comparing the minimum elements of both sequences: in this case, these elements are $A[1] = 5$ and $B[0] = 2$ as indicated at step 2 of Figure 7.3. The minimum is $B[0] = 2$ and it is written in the first available position of $F$, hence $F[1] = 2$. This element is discarded from the computation, which then proceeds onto the sequences $A[1 : 2] = [5, 7]$ and $B[1 : 2] = [3, 4]$. The next two steps

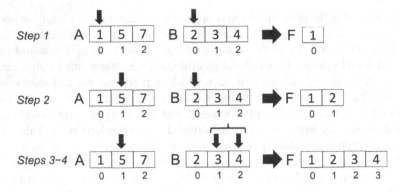

**Fig. 7.3** The first four steps of the algorithm MERGE applied to two increasingly sorted vectors consisting of three elements each. Downward arrows point to the elements that are compared in a step, the moved arrow is the one that points to the minimum compared element. This one is added to the output vector $F$.

(denoted 3 and 4 in Figure 7.3) write $F[2] = B[1] = 3$ and $F[3] = B[2] = 4$ because both elements will be compared with the larger $A[1] = 5$. At the fifth step, the algorithm has processed all elements of $B$ while $A$ still has two elements to be considered (i.e. $[5,7]$). At this point, it suffices to observe that $A$'s elements are larger than all the elements written in $F$ and sorted increasingly, so that they can be appended to $F$ to generate the overall sorted sequence.

The pseudocode of the algorithm is reported in Figure 7.4. Because of its structure, it is called MERGE. Although it should be easy to read, we outline some considerations that should help understand its correctness and structural elegance:

- The three iterators $i, j$, and $k$ are used in the pseudocode to scan rightward the three vectors $A, B$, and $F$. The iterators move according to three **while**-loops. The first loop (lines 2–6) executes the merging of $A$ and $B$ by formalizing in pseudocode the steps of the running example illustrated in Figure 7.3. The other two **while**-loops manage the extreme situations in which either all of $B$'s elements have been discarded (lines 7–8) or all of $A$'s elements have been discarded (lines 9–10). Our running example falls into the first case because MERGE was left only with $A$'s elements (i.e. $A[1:2] = [5,7]$).
- Let us concentrate on the first **while**-loop and assume that the algorithm has to merge $A[i:m-1]$ and $B[j:m-1]$. The **if**-statement present in the first **while**-loop (lines 3–5) compares the two currently minimum values $A[i]$ and $B[j]$, writes the smallest one in $F[k]$, and then advances the corresponding iterator, namely $i$ or $j$, to implement the "discarding step" mentioned in the example. The iterator $k$ is advanced after storing $A[i]$ or $B[j]$ in $F[k]$ (line 6) because it must point to the first available cell of $F$.
- As soon as MERGE discards all elements in vector $A$ (or $B$) and thus $i = m$ (or $j = m$), the boolean condition driving the first **while**-loop becomes false and thus the algorithm proceeds towards the two following **while**-loops (lines 7–10).

```
program MERGE (A, B, F)

// m denotes the number of elements in vectors A and B.
// F is the sorted vector containing elements of A ∪ B.

1.     i ← 0; j ← 0; k ← 0;

2.     while (i < m) and (j < m)

3.         if A[i] ≤ B[j]

4.             F[k] ← A[i]; i ← i + 1;                    // the smaller is A[i]

5.         else F[k] ← B[j]; j ← j + 1;                  // the smaller is B[j]

6.         k ← k + 1;                                    // in any case we advance on F

7.     while (i < m)                                     // copy A[i : m − 1] in F[k : 2m − 1]

8.         F[k] ← A[i]; i ← i + 1; k ← k + 1;

9.     while (j < m)                                     // copy B[j : m − 1] in F[k : 2m − 1]

10.        F[k] ← B[j]; j ← j + 1; k ← k + 1;
```

**Fig. 7.4** Program MERGE creates one sorted sequence $F$ from two sorted sequences $A$ and $B$.

Only one of them is executed, namely the one for which there are still elements to process in $A$ or $B$ that have to be copied into $F$. Referring to the running example, MERGE will execute the first **while**-loop which processes vector $A$ (lines 7–8) and writes $A[1 : 2] = [5, 7]$ in $F$. The second **while**-loop (lines 9–10) will not be executed because all of $B$'s elements have been already discarded and in fact $j = m$.

Having established the correctness of MERGE, we go on to evaluate its time complexity by counting the number of steps it executes to merge vectors $A$ and $B$. There are three kinds of steps: incrementation of an iterator, storage of elements in $F$, and comparison of elements in $A$ and $B$. The first two step counts are easy to derive: iterators move only rightward and for a total of $4m$ steps because $i$ and $j$ move $m$ steps in $A$ and $B$, respectively, and $k$ moves $2m$ steps in $F$. Counting comparisons is a bit more involved but a simple observation also makes this derivation crystal clear: for every comparison, MERGE writes the smaller of the two compared elements in $F$ and then increments $k$. Since $k$ can move only by at most $2m$ steps, this is also an upper bound to the number of possible comparisons executed by MERGE. Therefore, MERGE executes a number of steps which is *asymptotically linear* in $m$, and this cannot be improved because any merging algorithm has to generate the $2m$ elements of vector $F$. MERGE is therefore *optimal* and constitutes the core algorithmic block of a sorting algorithm which is much faster than INSERTION_SORT, and is actually optimal in the worst case. Its name is MERGE_SORT (i.e. sort by merging) and, since its core idea is counterintuitive, we will describe the algorithm gradually, taking advantage of a running example shown in Figure 7.5, where the vector to sort is the same one adopted for INSERTION_SORT in Figure 7.1.

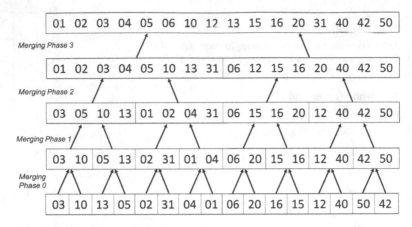

**Fig. 7.5** A running example of algorithm MERGE_SORT over a vector $C$ of $n = 16$ elements, with $C = [3, 10, 13, 5, 2, 31, 4, 1, 6, 20, 16, 15, 12, 40, 50, 42]$. The figure, and hence the execution of the algorithm, has to be read from the bottom to the top.

MERGE_SORT proceeds in phases; they are four in our running example, illustrated from the bottom to the top of Figure 7.5 by specifying the content of the vector $C$. In the initial phase 0, the elements of $C$ are divided into $n = 16$ sequences of $1$ ($= 2^0$ element each. Each of these sequences is sorted (as singletons), thus MERGE_SORT executes the program MERGE over 8 ($= n/2$) pairs of them. This creates 8 ordered sequences of 2 elements each. These 8 sequences form the input to the next phase (phase 1), which merges 4 ($= n/4 = n/2^2$) pairs of ordered sequences consisting of 2 ($= 2^1$) elements each. This creates 4 ordered sequences of 4 ($= 2^2$) elements each, which form the input to the next phase (phase 2). With the help of Figure 7.5, it is not difficult to realize that MERGE processes longer and longer ordered sequences whose length grows as a power of 2, and whose number decreases consequently as a power of 2. This process continues until MERGE is executed over two ordered sequences of $n/2$ elements each (phase 3 in Figure 7.5), thus creating one unique ordered sequence, which is the output of MERGE_SORT. The number of phases is $h = 4$ in our example because $n/2^h = 16/2^4 = 1$. In general, and if $n$ is a power of 2 (i.e. $n = 2^h$), this number can be computed as $h = \log_2 n$ by an argument similar to the one we adopted in Chapter 2 to compute the depth of a decision tree, thanks to the definition and properties of the logarithm function.

The pseudocode of MERGE_SORT is illustrated in Figure 7.6 where, for simplicity of exposition, we assume that $n$ is a power of 2. If this is not the case, we can still apply this pseudocode but we need to extend $C$ by duplicating its maximum element a number of times such that $n$ equals the closest power of 2. At the end of the sorting process, we need to discard from the ordered vector $C$ the additional elements, which are found at its end.

While the logical structure of the program is easy to understand from the wordy description given previously, this is not so for its implementation in the pseudocode

```
program MERGE_SORT (C)
// sort a vector C[0 : 2^h − 1] by using an auxiliary vector F[0 : 2^h − 1]
1.    for r = 1 to h
2.        for s = 0 to 2^{h-r} − 1
3.            a ← s2^r; b ← a + 2^{r-1};
4.            i ← a; j ← b; k ← a;
5.            while (i < a + 2^{r-1}) and (j < b + 2^{r-1})
6.                if C[i] ≤ C[j]
7.                    F[k] ← C[i]; i ← i + 1;
8.                else F[k] ← C[j]; j ← j + 1;
9.                k ← k + 1;
10.           while i < a + 2^{r-1}
11.               F[k] ← C[i]; i ← i + 1; k ← k + 1;
12.           while j < b + 2^{r-1}
13.               F[k] ← C[j]; j ← j + 1; k ← k + 1;
14.           for k = a to a + 2^r − 1
15.               C[k] ← F[k];
```

**Fig. 7.6** MERGE_SORT sorts a vector $C$ of $n = 2^h$ elements by utilizing MERGE as a subroutine.

of Figure 7.6. Therefore, we suggest you simulate its behavior using pen and paper for the vector of Figure 7.5, noting step by step the values assumed by the iterators $r$ and $s$, and taking into account the following:

- The iterator $r$ in the **for**-loop at line 1 represents the index of the merging phase.
- For every phase $r$, the **for**-loop at line 2 driven by iterator $s$ merges $n/2^r = 2^h/2^r = 2^{h-r}$ pairs of sequences that are consecutive in $C$, have length $2^{r-1}$, and start at position $a = s2^r$ and position $b = a + 2^{r-1}$ (line 3).
- Lines 4–13 implement the program MERGE, here specialized to process the two sequences $C[a : a + 2^{r-1} − 1]$ and $C[a + 2^{r-1} : a + 2^r − 1]$.
- The output sequence has length $2 \times 2^{r-1} = 2^r$; it is sorted and stored in $F[a : a + 2^r − 1]$. This portion is then overwritten onto the corresponding portion of the vector $C$ (lines 14–15), previously occupied by the two merged sequences.

The correctness of MERGE_SORT should be clear from the way the computation is structured and the correctness of the program MERGE. The evaluation of its time complexity is manageable if we concentrate on the time complexity of each single phase. We have already observed that MERGE_SORT, in each phase $r$, merges $n/2^r$ pairs of ordered sequences, each of length $2^{r-1}$. Each of these merges takes a time complexity linear in the total length of the merged sequences (see discussion on MERGE), which is $2^{r-1} + 2^{r-1} = 2^r$. Overall, this means a time complexity of each phase $r$ proportional to $(n/2^r) \times 2^r = n$. Multiplying this time complexity by the number of phases, which is $h = \log_2 n$, we derive the total time complexity of MERGE_SORT, which turns out to be a function of the form $n \times h = n \log_2 n$. This function is asymptotically larger than the linear function $n$, but it is asymptotically much smaller than the quadratic function $n^2$. Therefore, MERGE_SORT improves the worst case time complexity of INSERTION_SORT but it is slower than INSERTION_SORT when the input vector $C$ is already sorted, because INSERTION_SORT would "see that" and execute only a linear number of steps, while MERGE_SORT would "not see that" and execute all the $\log_2 n$ phases over all elements of $C$, thus still taking $n \log_2 n$ time. In any case, this is a special input that cannot induce us to consider INSERTION_SORT better than MERGE_SORT.

Another important observation is that the pseudocode in Figure 7.6 is defined for $n = 2^h$. A few paragraphs earlier, we described a variant working for any $n$ based on the duplication of the maximum element a number of times such that $n$ becomes a power of 2. There is, however, a *canonical version* of MERGE_SORT that does not make use of duplicated elements and works for any $n$ by setting $h = \lceil \log_2 n \rceil$. For example, if $n = 13$ the canonical algorithm executes $\lceil \log_2 13 \rceil = 4$ phases, exactly the same number of phases executed by the other variant. The asymptotic time complexity of these two versions is comparable; what differs is their space occupancy, because the canonical version saves space given that $C$ and (in turn) $F$ are not extended.

We conclude this section by noting that the time complexity of MERGE_SORT is still larger than the lower bound $n$ we established a few pages earlier on the time complexity of the sorting problem. However, this *gap* has been reduced with respect to what INSERTION_SORT was able to do. Anyway, we still have a multiplicative factor $\log_2 n$ which grows slowly with the number of elements to sort but still grows enough to consider the upper bound to the time complexity of MERGE_SORT a *non-linear* function. Therefore, we pose again the same question raised at the end of the previous section on INSERTION_SORT: "Is there a more efficient algorithm than MERGE_SORT or can we show a $n \log_2 n$ lower bound for the complexity of the sorting problem?" Surprisingly enough, the second option holds. To prove it, we will develop a sophisticated argument that allows us to state that MERGE_SORT is an optimal algorithm in terms of its time complexity. As a corollary, we can infer that we can sort a sequence *without comparing all pairs of its elements* given that $n \log_2 n \ll n^2$. Something that is absolutely counterintuitive.

## 7.3 A Lower Bound

In Chapter 2 we introduced the concept of a *decision tree* in order to describe as abstractly as possible an algorithm that solves the problem of false-coin detection via a twin-pan balance. Each tree node was *ternary*, because it denoted a weight comparison between two groups of coins with three possible outcomes $(<, =, >)$. Leaves corresponded to the solutions of the problem, namely which coin was false

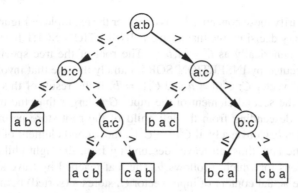

**Fig. 7.7** An example of a binary decision tree for sorting the vector $C = [a,b,c]$. The root-to-leaf paths represent computations executed by the algorithm INSERTION_SORT of Figure 7.2 for every possible input. The path taken by the algorithm for the input $C = [7,2,5]$ and solution $[b,c,a] = [2,5,7]$ is specified in the picture with solid arrows.

(if any) and whether it weighed more or less than the others. Root-to-leaf paths denoted all possible computations performed by the algorithm to find one such solution, driven by the input coins. The longest root-to-leaf path, also called the *depth of the tree*, identified the worst case time complexity of the corresponding algorithm. For that specific problem involving five coins, we showed a ternary tree (algorithm) of depth $\lceil \log_3 11 \rceil = 3$ and, more interestingly, we proved that it was not possible to design a shallower tree and thus a faster algorithm. This allowed us to conclude that the proposed ternary tree (algorithm) was optimal and required three weighs on the twin-pan balance to find the false coin (if any).

This specific argument can be applied blindly to the sorting problem with a few small changes required by its particularities (see Figure 7.7). Here a node of the decision tree specifies the comparison between two elements $a$ and $b$, denoted with $a : b$. The result of that comparison is *binary* – either $a \le b$ or $a > b$ – so that the tree itself is binary. All leaves that descend from the left child of the node $a : b$ store solutions (i.e. permutations of the input sequence $C$) for which $a \le b$, and thus $a$ has to occur before $b$ in the sorted $C$; vice versa, all leaves that descend from the right child of the node $a : b$ store solutions for which $a > b$, and thus $a$ has to occur after $b$ in the sorted $C$. Every leaf $\ell$ stores the permutation of the input sequence $C$, which satisfies all the conditions found in the root-to-leaf path connecting the root to $\ell$.

It should be evident from this description that every binary decision tree abstractly represents a different algorithm for solving the sorting problem on a *given* number of elements $n$. This tree (algorithm) is designed in a way that, for every possible input $C$ of size $n$, has a root-to-leaf path (computation) that reaches the leaf providing the sorted permutation of $C$. A *specific* algorithm corresponds to a *specific family of binary decision trees*: one tree per input size $n$. If we change $n$, we must design a wider and taller decision tree because it must host a larger number of leaves (i.e. sorted permutations) and computations to determine them.

To further clarify these concepts, let us consider the example in Figure 7.7, which illustrates a binary decision tree that abstracts INSERTION_SORT for an input size $n = 3$, denoted generically as $C = [a, b, c]$. The root of the tree specifies the first comparison executed by INSERTION_SORT, namely the one that involves the first two elements of vector $C$: $C[0] = a$ and $C[1] = b$. If the result of this comparison is $C[0] \leq C[1]$, the second element of the input $C$ is larger than the first one and, thus, all leaves descending from the left child of the root store permutations for which $a$ precedes $b$. Conversely, if $C[0] > C[1]$, the second element of $C$ is smaller than the first one and, thus, all leaves descending from the right child of the root store permutations for which $a$ follows $b$. The leaf reached by traversing the tree, according to the actual content of input vector $C$, stores a (sorted) permutation that reflects the outcomes of the comparisons specified by the nodes found on the downward traversed path. The reader can verify that, whatever the input $C$, the decision tree in Figure 7.7 is structured in such a way that it "implements" the algorithm INSERTION_SORT when the input consists of three elements.

There are two main differences between the pseudocode in Figure 7.2 and the decision tree in Figure 7.7. The first one has already been commented on and concerns the *flexibility* of the pseudocode of the algorithm INSERTION_SORT, which works *whatever* the size $n$ of the input vector $C$, whereas the binary decision tree works *only* for inputs of size $n = 3$. If there were four input elements, then the decision tree should be changed to host the 24 possible sorted permutations of the input in its leaves; this is left as an exercise to the reader. We can thus state that an algorithm corresponds to an *(infinite) family of decision trees*, one per possible input size. The reverse is not true because there are binary trees that *do not correspond* to any sorting algorithm, and thus they are not decision trees. Take, for example, a binary tree whose right child of the root is a leaf: this tree cannot abstract a sorting algorithm because one comparison cannot allow us to derive any sorted input!

The second difference is that the decision tree specifies only comparisons and not swaps of elements in $C$, which are needed to effectively sort it. These swaps are *implicitly* encoded in the permutations stored in the tree leaves. However, decision trees can still be used to estimate the time complexity of *comparison-based* sorting algorithms, such as INSERTION_SORT and MERGE_SORT, because comparisons are their predominant operation. We determine a lower bound on this time complexity by computing the *minimum depth* $D(n)$ of all decision trees, thus guaranteeing that any sorting algorithm performs at least one (worst case) computation that takes more than $D(n)$ comparisons. However, how do we estimate this minimum depth for all decision trees solving the sorting problem? There is potentially an infinite number of them...

The reasoning is very elegant and proceeds as follows. The number of solutions for the sorting problem, when the input size is $n$, is given by the number of possible permutations of the $n$ input elements. This number is mathematically indicated with $n! = n \times (n-1) \times (n-2) \times \cdots \times 3 \times 2 \times 1$ (named $n$ factorial), and it was introduced in the previous chapter when talking about ciphers and the number of secret keys. Therefore, the number of leaves in any binary decision tree that "solves" the sorting problem for $n$ elements is $n!$. Any binary tree of depth $h$ has at most $2^h$ leaves so that, in order to have $n!$ leaves, the binary decision tree must reach a depth $h$ such that $2^h \geq n!$. We can solve this inequality in terms of $h$ by applying to both its members the logarithm in base 2 (since it is an increasing function), and thus obtain: $\log_2 2^h \geq \log_2 n!$, which can be simplified to $h \geq \log_2 n!$. We have commented widely on the growth of the *factorial function* in the previous chapter; here it suffices to observe that this function grows asymptotically as $n^n$, so we can conclude that $\log_2 n!$ grows as $\log_2 n^n = n \log_2 n$, where we have applied a known property of logarithms.[1]

Consequently, the depth of any binary tree with $n!$ leaves must grow *at least* as the function $D(n) = n \log_2 n$. The binary trees that match this depth are the ones that show all leaves at the same depth $D(n)$; they are commonly called *balanced binary trees*. If a binary tree admits a leaf at a depth smaller than $D(n)$ then it must also have a leaf at a depth larger than $D(n)$. Consequently, for any decision tree (i.e. sorting algorithm) and for any input size $n$, there is an input that requires at least $D(n) = n \log_2 n$ comparisons to sort those $n$ elements in the worst case. Clearly, there are inputs for which the algorithm may be faster (i.e. their corresponding solutions are stored in leaves at a depth smaller than $D(n)$), but we are interested in the worst case time complexity of algorithms as a measure of their efficiency.

Comparing this lower bound to the time complexity of MERGE_SORT, we can conclude that this algorithm is *asymptotically* optimal, because $n \log_2 n$ comparisons cannot be improved as $n$ gets larger and larger. Nonetheless, it must be noted that there are algorithms that are *better than* MERGE_SORT because they take $n \log_2 n$ comparisons in the worst case *and* they occupy less space (thus avoiding the auxiliary vector $F$, see Figure 7.6). Perhaps more surprisingly, there are algorithms that are yet faster *in practice* even if they use more than $n \log_2 n$ comparisons in the worst case. This is due to their reduced space occupancy, which allows more effective management of the faster and smaller memory levels available in modern computers. One of these algorithms is the very well-known QUICK_SORT, which we will describe in Chapter 11.

In conclusion, while it is true that the asymptotic analysis of the time complexity of the algorithms proposed in these pages provides a *glimpse* of their efficiency in practice, it is also true that many software and hardware features play a role in their actual execution that may change such "predicted" behavior! This imposes on algorithm designers the use of more sophisticated and effective models of computations, which is the next topic.

## 7.4 Sorting Integers

The two pseudocodes presented and analyzed in the previous sections were based on comparing the input elements via the relation $\leq$. The question we address in this section is whether we can design a faster algorithm by exploiting *some knowledge* about the type or features of input elements.

---

[1] In this specific case, we have applied the equality $\log_b x^y = y \log_b x$, which holds independently of the base $b$ of the logarithmic function.

```
program COUNTING_SORT (C)
  1.    for j = 0 to k − 1
  2.        A[j] = 0;
  3.    for i = 0 to n − 1
  4.        A[C[i]] ← A[C[i]] + 1;
  5.    for j = 0 to k − 1
  6.        Write the value j in A[j] consecutive cells of vector C;
```

**Fig. 7.8** Program COUNTING_SORT computes the sorted sequence $C[0 : n − 1]$ by exploiting the fact that the input elements are integers smaller than $k$ and using an auxiliary vector $A[0 : k − 1]$.

We design a simple sorting algorithm that works over *integers smaller than a given value k*. It counts the number of occurrences in $C$ of every possible integer smaller than $k$, then writes down the sorted sequence by exploiting these counts. The pseudocode is reported in Figure 7.8 and is as simple as its description is informal. It consists of three **for**-loops. The first one, in lines 1–2, resets to zero an auxiliary vector $A$, whose role is to store the counts just mentioned. The next **for**-loop scans the input vector $C$ and counts in every entry $A[j]$ the number of occurrences of the integer $j$ in $C$. In the pseudocode, we have $j = C[i]$, for $i = 0, \ldots, n − 1$. The final **for**-loop, in lines 5–6, overwrites the content of vector $C$ by replicating the value $j$ as many times as indicated in the counter $A[j]$, where $j = 0, \ldots, k − 1$.

This algorithm is called COUNTING_SORT because its computation is evidently based on *counting*, rather than on comparing, elements. Its workings recall the algorithm introduced at the beginning of this chapter, which distributed the playing cards on a $4 \times 13$ grid based on their suits and values.

To dig further into the properties of COUNTING_SORT let us run its pseudocode with pen and paper on the vector $C[0 : 3] = [3, 2, 3, 5]$ and take $k = 6$. Lines 1–2 initialize to zero the counting vector $A[0 : 5] = [0, 0, 0, 0, 0, 0]$. Lines 3–4 scan vector $C$ and, at each iteration $i$, increment the number of occurrences of element $C[i]$ currently stored in $A[C[i]]$; for example, the first iteration $i = 0$ increments the counter $A[3]$, because $C[0] = 3$, and thus it gets the value $A[3] + 1 = 0 + 1 = 1$. The next iteration $i = 1$ increments the counter $A[2]$, because $C[1] = 2$, and thus it gets the value $A[2] + 1 = 0 + 1 = 1$. The iteration $i = 2$ increments the counter $A[3]$, because $C[2] = 3$, and thus it gets the value $A[3] + 1 = 1 + 1 = 2$. The final iteration $i = 3$ computes the vector $A = [0, 0, 1, 2, 0, 1]$. The content of $A$ actually informs the algorithm that the first two integers 0 and 1 do not occur in the input vector $C$ (in fact, their counter is zero), that integer 2 occurs once ($A[2] = 1$), that integer 3 occurs twice ($A[3] = 2$), that integer 4 does not occur in $C$ (in fact, $A[4] = 0$), and, finally, that integer 5 occurs once (in fact, $A[5] = 1$). Notice that the sum of all values contained in $A$ is equal to the number $n = 4$ of input elements to sort. After $A$ has been computed, the **for**-loop at lines 5–6 skips writing the values 0 and 1, because their counters are zero, it writes integer 2 once in $C[0]$, integer 3 twice in $C[1:2]$, skips integer 4, and writes integer 5 once in $C[3]$. This obtains the final sorted sequence $C[0:4] = [2,3,3,5]$.

The correctness of COUNTING_SORT is clear: the output sequence is increasingly ordered and contains all input elements with their multiplicity. However, what happens if every input element in $C$ has a *satellite piece of information* associated with it?

This is very common in practice, for example, the integers in $C$ could denote the number of times a product available in a supermarket is purchased each day, and a vector $D$ could be used to record the name of each product plus some other satellite information that describes it. Of course, two different products $i$ and $j$ (hence, $D[i] \neq D[j]$) can be purchased on a given day the same number of times (i.e. $C[i] = C[j]$). Sorting products according to their number of purchases via COUNTING_SORT would "override" $C$, thus severing the connection between product IDs (i.e. vector's positions) and their satellite information. To solve this problem we need to permute $D$ as we permute $C$. This can be done by slightly changing the pseudocode in Figure 7.8. We leave this as an exercise to the reader, because its details are not very interesting from an algorithmic point of view. We concentrate next on the time complexity analysis of the simple COUNTING_SORT algorithm shown in Figure 7.8.

It is immediately clear that the three **for**-loops implementing the algorithm COUNTING_SORT execute a total of $n + 2k$ steps, each consisting of an increment and/or an assignment of values to variables. So that, if $k \leq n$, the time complexity turns out to be $3n$, thus grows linearly with the input size.

The reader must be warned that this result does not contradict the lower bound proved in the previous section, because that one referred to comparison-based sorting algorithms whilst COUNTING_SORT does not execute any comparisons and thus cannot be modeled as a decision tree. This observation allows us to conclude that *plugging some knowledge* in the (sorting) algorithms can significantly speed them up. For example, COUNTING_SORT has a worst case linear time complexity if $k$ is proportional to the input size $n$, which is optimal because all input elements must be examined to produce their sorted permutation.

On the other hand, COUNTING_SORT works only on integers that are *not much larger than* $n$ to have linear time complexity. This may be the case of a supermarket, which offers $n = 1,000$ products, among which the most frequently purchased one is milk with 150 purchases per day. In this situation $k = 151 < 1,000 = n$ so that COUNTING_SORT computes the sorted order in about $n + 2k \simeq 1,300$ steps. Sorting by MERGE_SORT would take about $n \log_2 n = 1,000 \log_2 1,000 \simeq 10,000$ steps; thus, many more than COUNTING_SORT. However, if we consider the number of purchases in a much larger time window, say one year, then it might be the case that milk is purchased 50,000 times and so COUNTING_SORT should set $k = 50,001$ and take $n + 2k \simeq 101,000$ steps. Instead MERGE_SORT would execute the same number of steps as before, because its time complexity depends only on the number $n$ of elements to be sorted, and not on their absolute value. In this case, MERGE_SORT is faster than COUNTING_SORT.

To conclude, many scientists think that algorithm design is an art because it requires a lot of *creativity*. We agree with them, but we also think that this art needs a lot of scientific and technical knowledge in order to allow the "algorithmic artists" to make the *best choice* among the plethora of known algorithms and tools when designing their own algorithmic solutions. This is what we tried to highlight with the supermarket example, which has hopefully shown that missing the deep understanding of algorithmic complexity can impede the choice of the right algorithm in a given situation (e.g. COUNTING_SORT versus MERGE_SORT). The next section will add another bit of "complexity" with the only goal of introducing, at a very high-level (and somewhat superficially), a topic that is getting more and more attention in recent years, even in newspapers, called Big Data (a sort of *buzzword* nowadays), which is here considered within the context of the sorting problem.

## 7.5 Sorting Big Data

Our daily work and personal activities, thanks to the advent of the *Internet of Things*, social networks, and the myriad of apps we use, produce an overwhelming amount of digital information (also called *Big Data*). It has grown so much that in 2010 Google's CEO, Eric Schmidt, famously stated: *"Every two days we create as much information as we did up to 2003, and this is about 5 exabytes* $(= 5 \times 2^{60} \approx 10^{20}$ *bytes)"*. Since his statement, the variety and quantity of the data produced, and the speed at which it is produced, has increased at an even faster pace, so that experts predict for the next few years an annual increase of $4,300\%$ just for the data produced by companies.

On the other hand, it is known that the computing power of modern computers has grown according to Moore's famous law, which foresees a doubling every 18 months. This is clearly an exponential increase which, anyway, is *slower than* the (faster) exponential increase of data available in digital form. This drives our discussion towards two important observations that pay off the effort we have spent in understanding algorithm design and asymptotic analysis of time complexity.

- The asymptotic analysis of the time complexity of algorithms is a very relevant measure nowadays because of the advent of Big Data: it is no longer the job of *theorists* to assume that the input size $n$ keeps increasing.
- The hardware of modern computers has changed so much in recent years that storage memories can no longer be considered as monoliths with uniform and constant access time to the data stored in them. Instead, they are structured in "levels," each with its own features such as access speed, storage capacity, and communication bandwidth, just to mention a few. Nowadays, every computer, or computing device, has from one to three levels of *caches*, which are close to the processor, small in size (on the order of a few megabytes) but very fast in accessing their stored data (on the order of nanoseconds to read/write a few tens of bytes); one memory level called *(D)RAM*, or another kind of internal memory, which is able to store more data (on the order of tens of gigabytes) and access

them slower than caches but still at an interesting speed (on the order of tens of nanoseconds to read/write a few tens of bytes); some *disk memories* (mechanical, solid state disks, or a mix of the two), which enable storage of up to hundreds of terabytes accessible in a few milliseconds (in blocks of kilobytes); and, finally, the *Cloud*, which offers an "unbounded" storage capacity but turns out to be very slow in accessing its stored data (on the order of seconds to read/write blocks of tens of kilobytes).

This level-wise memory structure makes the computational model on which we have based our asymptotic analysis of algorithms unrealistic, because we assumed that the "number of steps" executed by an algorithm is a reasonable estimate of its running time in practice. In fact, this estimate does not take into account the time it takes for every such step to access the large amount of data that modern applications have to process. This time is evidently *very much variable* because it depends on the memory level where the accessed datum is stored. For example, the difference in performance between a cache memory and the Cloud is much larger than one million times in access speed. As a result, researchers have proposed in recent years other more realistic *computational models*; among them we consider the most famous one, probably because of its simplicity, and adopt it to estimate the time complexity of algorithms solving the problem that opened this chapter, namely sorting a (big!) deck of playing cards.

We warn the reader who has the patience and curiosity to read the following pages that they will be dense with sophisticated concepts that introduce some of the most interesting and current challenges of algorithmics. We will try to discuss in an elementary way how issues related to the hardware structure of modern computers affect the design of algorithms and how the latter can point to interesting directions on which to focus hardware engineering developments. This stresses how much the work of algorithmists today is strongly influenced by, and mutually influences, advances in technology, in a kind of continuous and exciting challenge with engineers and physicists who will design new hardware available to the general public.

Let us now dig into the issues that arise when sorting a "big deck" of playing cards. To set up the scene, we assume that the plane on which the cards can be sorted is not large enough to contain all of them, for example it is a beach towel, so that the main part of the deck is transposed onto a large table located at some distance from the beach—for example, under the roof of a lido. This means that if we need a bunch of cards for our sorting problem, we have to move from the beach to the lido in order to go get them. We denote with $P$ the small plane (e.g. the beach towel) that is close to us and easy to access, with $T$ the large table that is far from the beach (e.g. in a lido) and costly to reach, and, finally, with $p$ the (small) number of playing cards that plane $P$ can contain. It goes without saying that when we move to pick some cards from $T$, we will try to get the *most advantage* from our movement and thus take as many cards as possible from $T$ to bring to $P$. However, it is also obvious that the number of cards that we can pick from $T$ cannot be arbitrarily large because we need to carry them and then we have to lay them over $P$. We denote this number with $M \leq p$. For a reason that will be clear in a moment, we will actually

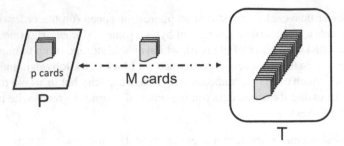

**Fig. 7.9** An image that summarizes pictorially the distribution of the cards between the small plane $P$, of size $p$, and the large table $T$, of unbounded capacity. Playing cards can be moved between $P$ and $T$ in groups of size $M$, with $M \leq p/3$.

impose that $M \leq p/3$. Figure 7.9 depicts pictorially this new scenario and the way playing cards can be accessed and moved in blocks between plane $P$ and table $T$.

It is now natural to ask which method to sort the input cards is the fastest in this new scenario. The algorithm we wish to design (i) can permute and access only a small part of the deck, namely the one that resides over the small plane $P$, and (ii) can move cards between $P$ and $T$ in groups of $M$ cards each. The time complexity of this algorithm should be a function of the cost of these operations, which is clearly larger for the operations of type (ii) than for operations of type (i). Technically speaking, the costly "block movements" are called *I/Os* (i.e. input/output), and in our context they denote the movement of groups of cards between $P$ and $T$.

Formally speaking, this scenario abstracts a computer with two memory levels: $P$ is fast level but with a low storage capacity, similar to the cache or the (D)RAM memory, whereas $T$ is the level that is slow but has a large storage capacity, similar to disks and the Cloud. Accessing data located in the memory level $P$ is much faster than accessing data located in the Cloud $T$ because the *gap in access performance* is of the order of more than one million between these two memory levels (i.e., tens of nanoseconds versus seconds). Therefore, today it is crucial to design algorithms that minimize the number of I/Os because, doing otherwise, one could obtain an algorithm whose running time is so long that it does not complete its computation in a reasonable amount of time even over a medium sized input.

There is a variant of MERGE_SORT that is very effective in this new scenario. Before describing it, we start with an I/O-analysis of the program MERGE in Figure 7.4 and assume that the two decks to merge, namely $A[0:m-1]$ and $B[0:m-1]$, are located on the large table $T$. Since the algorithm can compare only the cards over $P$, it moves them from $T$ as they are needed for the comparisons at line 3. More specifically, it moves not only the two cards compared but also the next $M-1$ cards from each deck in order to take the greatest advantage possible of the costly I/O operation. This *key idea* is implemented by the algorithm as follows. Initially, MERGE will move from $T$ to $P$ the first $M$ cards of decks $A$ and $B$. Plane $P$ can host the $2M$ cards because we assumed that $M \leq p/3$ and thus $2M < p$. MERGE then compares the minima of the two decks as far as these minima are available in $P$. When a block is exhausted, say the one coming from $A$ (the other case is symmetric), then the next block of $M$ cards from $A$ is moved from $T$ to $P$ and the comparisons continue. Every comparison writes the minimum onto vector $F$, which is hosted by table $T$ because it is very long. To avoid one I/O each time a minimum is written in $F$, MERGE writes that minimum temporarily in $P$. When this block of output minima is full, it is moved to table $T$, thus executing one I/O and freeing room in $P$ for another block of minima. We point out that the space for these entries in $F$ is available because the small plane $P$ is occupied by $2M$ cards from $A$ and $B$ and by $M$ cards from $F$: a total occupancy of $3M \leq p$ according to our initial hypothesis on $P$'s size.

Since the two decks $A$ and $B$ consist of $m$ cards each, and one I/O never fetches the same cards from those decks but scans them block-by-block and rightward, the number of I/Os needed to perform the merge is about $2m/M$. The same number of I/Os will be executed to move the blocks of the merged sequence $F$ from $P$ to $T$. Hence, the total number of I/Os executed to merge $A$ and $B$ is proportional to the ratio $m/M$. This function is "linear" in $m$ if we assume that $1/M$ is a "constant of proportionality" that gets smaller as the block of cards that we can move from $P$ and $T$ grows larger. Technically speaking, the parameters $M$ and $p$ are specific features of the hardware we use; they can go from a few tens of bytes to several kilobytes.

From the *blocked* version of MERGE we can design a variant of MERGE_SORT that is I/O-efficient in orchestrating the blocked movements of cards from $T$ to $P$ and vice versa. First of all, we notice that the $p$ cards available on plane $P$ can be sorted *in place* by using any one of the sorting algorithms we have seen in the previous pages. In particular, we use INSERTION_SORT to order $p$ cards in $P$ because this algorithm does not use extra space other than the input vector (unlike MERGE_SORT). We are giving up optimality in the number of steps, but we gain in I/O efficiency, which is the key bottleneck in this new scenario.

The I/O-efficient sorting algorithm proceeds in two main phases:

- the first one uses INSERTION_SORT to create $n/p$ ordered sequences of $p$ elements each;
- the second one uses the blocked version of MERGE to fuse these ordered sequences in pairs, as indicated by the classic scheme of the MERGE_SORT.

The first macro-phase is implemented by moving $p$ cards at a time from table $T$ to plane $P$ and vice versa. Since card movements occur in blocks of $M$ cards each, the algorithm needs $p/M$ block movements to fill the plane $P$; after that, the cards on $P$ are sorted via INSERTION_SORT and then moved from $P$ to $T$ again using $p/M$ block movements. This will have created the first sorted sequence of length $p$. The algorithm will repeat these steps for $n/p$ times, thus processing all $n$ input cards and forming $n/p$ ordered sequences over the large table $T$. The total number of I/Os executed in this first macro-phase equals the number $n/p$ of ordered sequences times the number $p/M$ of I/Os needed to create each of them. Hence the total I/O cost is proportional to $(n/p) \times (p/M) = n/M$.

The second macro-phase is implemented by merging the $n/p$ sequences in pairs via the blocked version of MERGE. In Section 7.2 we proved that MERGE_SORT needs $\log_2 n$ merging levels, each one taking a time complexity that was linear in the number $n$ of elements to merge. In the new scenario, the merging levels are $\log_2(n/p)$ because the number of sequences to merge is $n/p$, instead of $n$. Every merging level processes all input elements in $M$-size blocks, thus requiring $n/M$ I/Os (as we have already proved). Multiplying this cost by the number of merging levels, we get the total number of I/Os required to pairwise merge the $n/p$ ordered sequences, which were the input to the second macro-phase. This cost is proportional to $(n/M) \times \log_2(n/p)$ I/Os.

Overall, this variant of MERGE_SORT takes $(n/M) + (n/M) \times \log_2(n/p)$ I/Os. This formula is interesting because it involves not only the number of cards to be sorted but also the two (hardware) features $M$ and $p$. The interplay among the three parameters allows us to justify mathematically some considerations that, otherwise, would be unsubstantiated. We notice that the larger the plane $P$ is (and thus its size $p$) the smaller the number of sequences formed in the first macro-phase is, thus the smaller in turn the number of I/Os. By a similar argument, we can observe that the larger the block $M$ is, the smaller the number of I/Os is. However, it must be noted that the gain induced in the I/O complexity by the growth of $p$ is smaller than the gain induced by the growth of $M$, because the former parameter appears at the denominator of the argument of a logarithmic term whereas the latter appears at the denominator of a linear term. Hence, the best choice for this algorithm would be to improve $M$ (and thus move more cards at each I/O), rather than enlarging the small plane $P$. Something that can be obtained either by buying more effective storage devices or designing compression algorithms: a topic of a later chapter.

We conclude this section by observing that there are more efficient algorithms, in terms of executed I/Os, still inspired by the algorithmic structure of MERGE_SORT. However, there is no *universally optimal* algorithm; rather, the choice depends on the specific context in which a sorting algorithm is used and the computational resources that have to be optimized during its execution. It is indeed not by chance that the big players on the Web – from Google to Facebook, from Microsoft to Amazon – compete to hire the best algorithmists on the planet at the highest salaries because the design or the selection of the best algorithm for an application can earn these companies millions of euros ... per second!

To stay with our feet on the ground, let us show how the previous I/O-efficient algorithm can be further improved, thus obtaining an I/O-optimal sorter. We invite readers tired of complications to jump directly to the next chapter.

## 7.6 Multi-way Merge (Sort)

Looking at the variant of MERGE_SORT illustrated in the previous section, we notice that its second macro-phase fully exploits the small plane $P$ only when $p = 3M$, but it makes a very inefficient use of that plane when $p$ gets larger than $3M$. In fact, since the merging of the $(n/p)$ ordered sequences operates pairwise, the plane $P$ hosts at any time $2M$ elements of the input sequences $A$ and $B$, and $M$ elements of

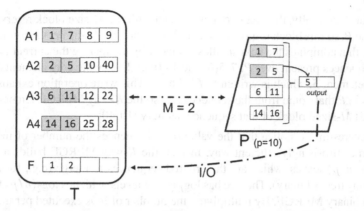

**Fig. 7.10** An image that summarizes the running of the $K$-way MERGE, with $K = 4$, executed over a small plane of size $p = 10$ and a block of size $M = 2$. The four ordered sequences in input, say A1–A4, are stored on the table $T$ and participate in the merging; other ordered sequences could be present on $T$ but they would participate in subsequent $K$-way MERGEs. The figure reports the status of the $K$-way MERGE after three steps that have extracted the first three minima from the four sequences, namely $1, 2$ and $5$, with the first two minima already moved to table $T$.

the output merged sequence $F$. This cannot be improved because (i) $M$ is fixed, as it depends on the features of the used hardware, and (ii) even if we did fetch more blocks from $A$ and $B$ to fill $P$, we would not gain anything because those blocks would be still merged one by one, therefore making their pre-fetching useless.

In order to overcome this limitation, we have to change the second macro-phase in such a way that the merging involves $K \geq 2$ ordered sequences at a time, and hence the name $K$-way MERGE_SORT or, more generally, multi-way MERGE_SORT for the resulting sorting algorithm. Increasing $K$ makes the new merging phase a little bit more complicated, but the algorithmic principle is basically the same as for the case of two merged sequences.

Initially, the algorithm moves from $T$ to $P$ the first $M$ elements of each one of the $K$ sorted sequences we have to merge. We set $K$ so that $KM + M \approx p$ because we wish to keep $P$ as full as possible. Then the $K$-way MERGE must compare $K$ elements, which are the minima of the $K$ sequences we have yet to merge. This $K$-way comparison is obviously more costly than the two-way comparison executed in the classic MERGE, but we have to notice that the elements to compare are located on the fast plane $P$ and thus the comparisons needed to select their minimum are assumed to induce no time cost.

An illustrative example is given in Figure 7.10, in which $K = 4, M = 2$, and the ordered sequences to merge are $A1 = [1, 7, 8, 9], A2 = [2, 5, 10, 40], A3 = [6, 11, 12, 22]$, and $A4 = [14, 16, 25, 28]$. After two merging steps, the algorithm has extracted the smallest two elements from the four input sequences (i.e. $1, 2$). The elements shown in gray on $T$ are the ones already transferred to $P$, whereas the gray elements on $P$ are the ones that have been already extracted by the merging process and stored into the output $F$. Actually, the first two merging steps fill the $M$-size block reserved for $F$ in plane $P$, so this block is moved to table $T$ via one I/O. At the next merging step, the algorithm computes the next smallest element by comparing the current minima of the sequences present over $P$: $7, 5, 6$, and $14$ (they follow the gray elements). The result is element $5$, which is written to $F$'s block. This write operation exhausts the elements in $P$ that come from the sequence $A2$, so the $K$-way MERGE fetches from $T$ the next $M$-sized block of that sequence, namely $[10, 40]$.

It is interesting to notice that the value of $K$ influences the number of merging phases in a surprisingly efficient way. In fact, the $K$-way MERGE builds a $K$-ary tree with $(n/p)$ leaves, which are the ordered sequences to merge (e.g., for $K = 2$ the merging tree is binary). The tree has $\log_K(n/p)$ levels, which is $\log_2(n/p)$ for the case of a binary MERGE. By multiplying the number of I/Os executed per merging level (which is still $n/M$) with the number of merging levels (which is $\log_K(n/p)$), we get the total number of I/Os required by the $K$-way MERGE_SORT to sort $n$ elements: $(n/M) \times \log_K(n/p)$ I/Os. The improvement with respect to the I/O-cost of the binary MERGE_SORT, which is $(n/M) \times \log_2(n/p)$ I/Os, is more effective the larger the number $K$ is, because this value occurs at the base of the logarithm function.[2] It is possible to prove that the $K$-way MERGE_SORT executes an *optimal* number of I/Os in the worst case and thus it cannot be improved by any comparison-based sorting algorithm working in such a two-level memory model. However, this is not so relevant and thus skipped here.

Let us extrapolate a few calculations in order to understand how much faster the new $K$-way sorter that we have just proposed is. For simplicity of exposition, we refer to our problem on playing cards, hence $n = 54$, and compare the two versions of the algorithm: the one with $K = 2$ and the one with $K = 4$. Let us assume that plane $P$ contains $p = 10$ cards and the algorithm can move $M = 2$ cards at each I/O between plane $P$ and table $T$. The first macro-phase, which builds $\lceil n/p \rceil = 54/10 = 6$ ordered sequences via INSERTION_SORT, is the same for both algorithms, and thus it is not accounted for in this discussion. However, the second macro-phase is different: in one case it uses the binary MERGE_SORT and executes $\lceil \log_2(n/p) \rceil = \lceil \log_2 10 \rceil = 4$ scans of the input to create a unique sorted sequence; in the other case, it uses the four-way MERGE_SORT and executes $\lceil \log_4(n/p) \rceil = \lceil \log_4 10 \rceil = 2$ scans of the input.[3] The net result is a speed increase of a factor of 2 when using the four-way MERGE_SORT. This advantage would grow if we could use a larger $K$, which is however imposed by the constraint $KM + M \leq p$, and thus depends on the features of the two-level memory hardware. To have a rough idea of the real value of $K$, we recall that in modern computers it is in the order of millions ($\approx 2^{20}$), so that if we sorted $n \approx 2^{60}$ elements (namely millions of terabytes, i.e. exabytes), the $K$-way MERGE_SORT would take $\log_{2^{20}} 2^{60}$ input scans. Since we know that

---

[2] We recall that between two logarithms with different bases $a, b$ the following equality holds: $\log_a x = (\log_a b) \times (\log_b x)$. This implies that we can write $\log_2(n/p) = (\log_2 K) \times (\log_K(n/p))$. Consequently, the ratio between the I/O complexities of the two-way sorter and the $K$-way sorter is $\log_2 K$ and this grows (slowly) with $K$.

[3] We used the ceiling function because the number of levels must be an integer and this can be computed as the smallest integer that is larger than the argument to which the function is applied.

$\log_a x = \frac{\log_b x}{\log_b a}$, we can write $\log_{2^{20}} 2^{60} = \frac{\log_2 2^{60}}{\log_2 2^{20}} = \frac{60}{20} = 3$, thus just three input scans are enough to sort exabytes of data.

The example just described is one of the best known algorithms for sorting Big Data: it is asymptotically optimal in the "two-level memory" model and is fast enough to be available on our computers (with some technical variations that we skip here). It does a few scans of the input data but each one takes time because it involves Big Data. This fact justifies the interest in producing faster disks, such as solid-state drives, larger RAMs to increase the value of $p$, or compression techniques that virtually increase $p$ and $M$, as we will see in a forthcoming chapter. At this point, the interaction between engineers, physicists, and algorithmists should be clearer: studies and technological advancements by one can influence the results of another in an act of "mutual benefit" and of continuous challenge to bring to the wider public computers and applications that are ever more powerful, and thus capable of efficiently processing the Big Data that nowadays surround us.

# Chapter 8
# "Easy" and "Difficult" Problems

In the previous chapter we reviewed two algorithms to sort the $n$ elements contained in a vector $C[0 : n-1]$: INSERTION_SORT and MERGE_SORT, which belong to the Olympus of classical algorithms. The first one, built according to a simple strategy, has a time complexity proportional to $n^2$; the second one, which is more sophisticated, has a time complexity proportional to $n \log_2 n$, and is thus more efficient than the first.[1]

Let us now suppose that someone gives us a simple algorithm to generate all permutations of a set of $n$ elements (we will do this in the last chapter, though for different reasons). A very lazy designer could then use it to build a new sorting algorithm in a simple way: generate one by one all the permutations of $C$'s elements and, for each of them, scan $C$ to find the permutation in which each element is less than or equal to the next one (i.e. $C[i] \leq C[i+1]$ for $0 \leq i \leq n-2$). In this case the vector is ordered. The algorithm is easy to conceive and horrible at the same time because, as we have seen in Chapter 6, the number of permutations is $n!$ and this value grows exponentially with $n$. So the algorithm would have an exponential time complexity: we will call it FOOLISH_SORT.

From the comparison of the three algorithms we can draw some conclusions. INSERTION_SORT is less efficient than MERGE_SORT but basically they are both acceptable if the number $n$ of data to order is not very large. In fact we recall that their time complexities have been determined "in order of magnitude" and asymptotically, that is, they take into account the type of growth of the two functions but not the "multiplicative coefficients." For example, if the exact numbers of operations executed by the two algorithms were $10n^2$ and $100n\log_2 n$ respectively, INSERTION_SORT would be faster than MERGE_SORT for $n \leq 32$ (in fact we have $10 \times 32^2 = 10,240$ and $100 \times 32 \log_2 32 = 16,000$). In any case, the two algorithms are both acceptable because, for increasing $n$ (i.e. asymptotically), their time complexity is limited by a polynomial in $n$. This is obvious for the function $n^2$, which is already expressed as a polynomial, but it also holds for the function $n\log_2 n$ be-

---

[1] Recall that time complexity always refers to a "worst case" with respect to the distribution of input data. This case for INSERTION_SORT occurs if the data appear in decreasing order, while for MERGE_SORT any initial data distribution leads to the same time complexity.

© Springer Nature Switzerland AG 2018
P. Ferragina, F. Luccio, *Computational Thinking*,
https://doi.org/10.1007/978-3-319-97940-3_8

cause the logarithm grows so slowly that for $n \to \infty$, we have $n \log_2 n < n^{1+\varepsilon}$ for an arbitrarily small value of $\varepsilon$.

The third algorithm, FOOLISH_SORT, is absolutely unacceptable though it can be constructed without any effort when a program that generates all the permutations is available. In fact it has an exponential time complexity and would require centuries of computation on any computer even for very modest values of $n$. Do not forget that *the ease of building an algorithm is by no means related to its efficiency*, and algorithm design must be specifically aimed at the improvement of efficiency.

To conclude, we can usually find different algorithms to solve the same problem, which have a more or less simple formulation but with an exceedingly different time complexity. We must then look for an algorithm that is reasonably efficient and hopefully optimal, but this is not always possible.

A *polynomial time algorithm* is one whose time complexity is polynomial in the input data size, while an *exponential time algorithm* is one whose time complexity is exponential in the input data size. For brevity they are simply called polynomial or exponential algorithms. Algorithmic studies have established a fundamental dichotomy between problems:

- A problem for which a polynomial time algorithm is known, is *easy* (or *tractable*).
- A problem for which only exponential time algorithms exist, or are known, is *difficult* (or *intractable*).

So a problem is said to be easy or difficult in relation to the *time* taken by the best algorithm known to solve it, not to the mental work needed to find a solution. Sorting is an easy problem because it can be resolved in polynomial time, for example by INSERTION_SORT or MERGE_SORT. Building all the permutations of a set is of course a difficult problem because the output has exponential size and therefore requires exponential time to be generated. However, the story is much more complicated than that. We will return to it at the end of this chapter, after discussing as simply as possible some major developments of the studies on algorithmic time complexity, simply referred to as "complexity".

## 8.1 Walking Through a City

Königsberg, literally the "Kings' Mountain," was the name of one of the most important cities in Europe. It was the capital of Eastern Prussia and the River Pregel ran through it. The river surrounded the city center, which was located between the two banks, on the island of Kneiphof. Here stood the splendid cathedral and the famous *Universitas Albertina* where many important scholars studied and taught, from Immanuel Kant to David Hilbert.

Referring to the structure of this town, in 1736, Leonhard Euler published an article that laid the foundation of *graph theory*, yet to be born, and prefigured the creation of *topology*. Writing in Latin, which was the language of science at that time, Euler uses the new wording *geometria situs*, geometry of the place, which is a

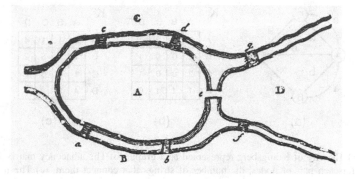

**Fig. 8.1** Sketch of the city of Königsberg with the island of Kneiphof (A) and the seven bridges on the River Pregel (from a famous Euler article of 1736).

branch of mathematics related to geometric entities that is not concerned with their shape or with the distance between them, but just with how they are connected to each other. And here is the problem, actually very simple, from which it started. [2]

It was basically a game that the locals played. The city of Königsberg has the form shown in Figure 8.1, a picture that later appeared in all the texts on the history of mathematics. In the city there are four districts, marked with $A, B, C$, and $D$ ($A$ is Kneiphof), and seven bridges on the Pregel, indicated with $a, b, c, d, e, f$, and $g$. The question was whether it was possible to take a walk through the city and return to the starting point, crossing all the bridges exactly once. Presented with the game Euler posed to himself the general problem of determining whether such a path exists in a city of arbitrary form, with an arbitrary number of rivers, islands, and bridges. The following theorem gives a simple criterion for deciding that question in the positive or negative; we mainly want to prove that this theorem shows that the problem is *easy*. For this purpose, we describe the city in Figure 8.2 (a) as a *graph*, that is as a set of nodes (in this case the districts $A, B, C$, and $D$ are represented by small circles) and a set of arcs connecting them (the bridges $a, b, c, d, e, f$, and $g$, represented by segments of any form). A path that starts from a node and returns to that node traversing all the arcs exactly once is called an *Eulerian cycle* of the graph: as we will see, in the graph of Königsberg such a cycle does not exist and hence the walk is impossible.

The overall result proved by Euler can be expressed in terms of graph theory under two simple conditions that are implicit when dealing with a city:

- There are no arcs joining a node with itself.

---

[2] At the end of World War II, the city was razed to the ground by the Soviet Army and the German population deported to the DDR (better known to us as East Germany). Today, with the name of Kaliningrad, it is part of Russia, and even the river's name has been changed. We recall these very sad facts only in a footnote because we want to continue talking about the Königsberg of the eighteenth century.

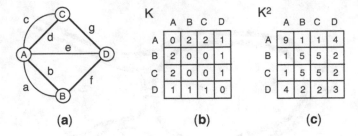

**Fig. 8.2** (a) The city of Königsberg represented as a graph. (b) The adjacency matrix $K$, which indicates, for each pair of nodes, the number of strings that connect them. (c) The matrix $K^2$, which indicates, for each pair of nodes, the number of paths of two arcs that connect them.

- The graph is *connected*, that is, for every pair of nodes there is always a sequence of arcs that connects them.

Still using graph terminology, let the *degree of a node* be the number of arcs incident to it (for example, in the graph of Königsberg node A has a degree of five). We have:

**Theorem** (Euler). *A graph admits an Eulerian cycle if and only if all its nodes have an even degree.*

The necessary condition (*only if*) can be proved immediately, because if a node $X$ has a degree of $g = 1$ you can enter it through the only incident arc but cannot exit without crossing the same arc; and if $X$ has an odd degree $g > 1$ you can enter and exit through $g - 1$ different arcs, but after entering the last time you cannot exit without traversing one of the arcs already used. Therefore, the graph of Königsberg does not contain any Eulerian cycle because all its nodes have an odd degree (and one would have been enough). Proving the sufficient condition (that is, if all the nodes have an even degree there is at least one Eulerian cycle) is much more difficult, and this is really what makes the theorem interesting; we will prove it constructively by designing an algorithm for generating such a cycle. For this purpose we must determine how graphs can be represented on a computer. A standard method uses matrices, whose definition is recalled to start with.

Both in mathematics and in computing a *two-dimensional matrix* is a set of $n_1 \times n_2$ elements where the integers $n_1$ and $n_2$, respectively, indicate the size of the intervals where two indexes $i$ and $j$ can take their values, and one element of the matrix is identified by a pair of values of those indices. In mathematics, the index $i$ varies from 1 to $n_1$, and the index $j$ varies from 1 to $n_2$. In coding, these intervals are generally set from 0 to $n_1 - 1$ and from 0 to $n_2 - 1$, but nothing substantially changes. A matrix $M$ is indicated in coding as $M[0 : n_1 - 1, 0 : n_2 - 1]$, and one of its elements is indicated as $M[i, j]$. Vectors are one-dimensional matrices. While a vector is graphically represented with a sequence of elements, a two-dimensional matrix is represented with a table of $n_1$ rows and $n_2$ columns, although in the memory of a computer these lines are allocated sequentially, one after the other. If $n_1 = n_2$ the matrix is said to be *square*.

A practical method for representing a graph of $n$ nodes in a computer's memory, although it is not the most efficient in some applications, is to associate the integers 0 to $n - 1$ with the node names, and to use a square matrix $n \times n$ called an *adjacency matrix* to represent its arcs. Both the rows and the columns of the matrix correspond to the nodes, and the cell at the intersection between row $i$ and column $j$ contains the number of arcs that connect nodes $i$ and $j$. The adjacency matrix $K$ for the Königsberg problem is shown in Figure 8.2 (b) where, for convenience, the $i$ and $j$ indices of the matrix are replaced by the node names. For example, $K[A,B] = 2$ because the nodes $A$ and $B$ are connected with two arcs. We note immediately that the matrix is symmetrical around the main diagonal because if there are $k$ arcs connecting $i$ and $j$, the value $k$ appears both in [row $i$, column $j$] and in [row $j$, column $i$]. Therefore, it is possible to store only half of the matrix, though this somewhat complicates the program. Note also that the main diagonal of the matrix contains only zeros due to the absence of arcs connecting a node to itself.

Another observation is that, in its common adoption as a mathematical model, a graph establishes whether or not there is a relationship between each pair of nodes (for example, Facebook's friendship graph), so between two nodes $i$ and $j$ only one arc may exist and the matrix contains only ones and zeroes. A graph such as that of Königsberg that may contain multiple arcs between two nodes is generally called a *multigraph* and includes the graph as a particular case. Nothing changes in our discussion if one refers to one or the other model.

Since there are generally pairs of nodes not directly connected by an arc, to move from one node to another we generally consider *paths* consisting of sequences of one or more of arcs. The *length* of a path is measured as the number of arcs it traverses. In the graph of Königsberg there is no arc between nodes $B$ and $C$, but there are five paths of length two that connect them: $ac, ad, bc, bd$, and $fg$. But how can we compute this number? Examining the matrix $K$, we see that node $B$ is connected via two arcs to $A$ and one arc to $D$, as indicated by the entries $K[B,A] = 2$ and $K[B,D] = 1$. Once node $A$ is reached, node $C$ can be directly reached via two other possible arcs since $K[A,C] = 2$. Then following one or the other of these arcs after each of those connecting $B$ to $A$ we find the first $2 \times 2 = 4$ paths of length two listed previously. If instead node $D$ is reached from $B$, then node $C$ can be reached via a single arc because $K[D,C] = 1$, and the fifth path is obtained. We now generalize this reasoning in mathematical terms by using matrix operations.

First, note that an adjacency matrix contains the same number of rows and columns, but in algebra these two parameters can be chosen independently. Given two matrices $A[0 : m - 1, 0 : n - 1]$ and $B[0 : n - 1, 0 : p - 1]$, the first with $m$ rows and $n$ columns and the second with $n$ rows and $p$ columns, define the *matrix product* $A \times B$ as a matrix $C[0 : m - 1, 0 : p - 1]$ whose elements are given by the relation:

$$C[i,j] = \sum_{k=0}^{n-1} (A[i,k] \times B[k,j]) \tag{1}$$

That is, every element $C[i,j]$ of the product matrix is obtained by "combining" the entire row $i$ of $A$ with the entire column $j$ of $B$ as the sum of products between

```
program MATRIX_PRODUCT (A, B, C)

// input: matrices A and B of dimensions m × n and n × p, respectively
// output: matrix C = A × B of dimension m × p

    for i = 0 to m − 1
        for j = 0 to p − 1
        S ← 0;
            for k = 0 to n − 1
                S ← S + A[i, k] × B[k, j];
            C[i, j] ← S;
```

**Fig. 8.3** Program to calculate the product of two matrices.

the $k$-th element of row $i$ and the $k$-th element of the column $j$, for $0 \leq k \leq n - 1$. This sum of products is called the *scalar product* between the row vector $i$ and the column vector $j$. Note that $A \times B$ is defined only if the number of columns of $A$ is equal to the number of rows of $B$, both equal to $n$ in our example.

Relation (1) to calculate the product matrix $C$ is directly implemented in the simple program MATRIX_PRODUCT reported in Figure 8.3, whose functioning should not need any explanation. Regarding its time complexity, note that each scalar product between two vectors takes an amount of time proportional to $n$ (**for**-loop on the index $k$). Since $m \times p$ scalar products are executed (two nested **for**-loops on $i$ and $j$), the time complexity of MATRIX_PRODUCT is proportional to the product $m \times n \times p$, which is *cubic* if these three values are comparable to each other.

As already mentioned, to work on a graph of $n$ nodes using a computer, we indicate the nodes with integers from 0 to $n - 1$ and represent the graph with its adjacency matrix $M$ of dimensions $n \times n$, where node $k$ corresponds to row and column $k$, and each cell $M[i, j]$ contains the number of arcs that connect the nodes $i$ and $j$. Note also that the square $M^2$ of a matrix $M$ is constructed as a particular instance of a matrix product, namely $M^2 = M \times M$, where the numbers of rows and columns are all equal. So even the matrix $M^2$ has dimensions $n \times n$ and each element $M^2[i, j]$ is obtained as the scalar product between the row of $M$ corresponding to node $i$ and the column of $M$ corresponding to node $j$.

Figure 8.2(c) shows the square $K^2$ of the Königsberg matrix, where rows and columns are again indicated with the node names. For example, the scalar product of row $B$ and column $C$ of $K$ produces the result: $2 \times 2 + 0 \times 0 + 0 \times 0 + 1 \times 1 = 5$ which appears in $K^2[B, C]$. This is exactly the number of paths of length two between $B$ and $C$ computed previously, when reasoning on the graph in Figure 8.2(a). The reader can immediately verify that such a reasoning is mathematically interpretable as the scalar product between row $B$ and column $C$ of matrix $K$. The matrix $K^2$, therefore, indicates the number of paths of length two, for each pair of nodes of $K$. Obviously, $K^2$ is also symmetrical with respect to the main diagonal whose elements, however, may differ from zero. In fact there may exist a path of length two leading from a node

```
program CONNECTED(M)

// M: adjacency matrix for a graph of n nodes
// R: vector of n cells to record the nodes reachable from 0

1.     R[0] ← 0; s ← 0; f ← 0;
2.     while s ≤ f                        // f points to the last occupied cell of R
3.         i ← R[s];                      // i is a node to be considered
4.         foreach (M[i,j] > 0, 1 ≤ j ≤ n − 1)   // i.e. for each element > 0 in row i
5.             if j not-in R[0 : f]       // if node j is not among those already in R
6.                 f ← f + 1; R[f] ← j;                   // we record j in R[f]
7.                 if f = n − 1           // if all nodes have been inserted in R
8.                     print "the graph is connected";
9.                     stop;
10.        s ← s + 1;
11.    print "the graph is not connected";
```

**Fig. 8.4** Using a *breadth-first* search to decide whether a graph with adjacency matrix $M$ is connected.

to itself, as shown by the element $K^2[A,A] = 9$ which indicates that there are nine paths of two arcs beginning and ending at $A$, namely $aa, bb, ab, ba, cc, dd, cd, dc$, and $ee$. An extension of this reasoning, which we invite you to undertake by yourself, leads to stating a general property that will be particularly significant in the next chapter, talking about search engines:

**Property 1.** *The matrix obtained as the $\ell$-th power of the adjacency matrix of a graph, for $\ell \geq 1$, contains the number of paths of length $\ell$ for all the pairs of nodes.*

Initially, that is for $\ell = 1$, the starting adjacency matrix $M$ specifies single arcs, thus paths of length one.

We can now argue algorithmically on Euler's theorem and therefore build an Eulerian cycle in a graph, if it exists. First, we check that the graph is connected (otherwise an Eulerian cycle cannot exist), using the program CONNECTED in Figure 8.4. This program inserts in a vector $R[0 : n - 1]$ the nodes that can be reached from node 0 and checks that at the end $R$ contains all the nodes of the input graph. CONNECTED actually implements a *breadth-first* search (or search "in amplitude") of the graph. It is written with some license in the pseudocode to make it more understandable. In particular, the program contains the new commands **foreach** and **not-in**, requiring that all elements of a set be examined and determining whether an element belongs to the set, respectively. These commands are usually not directly available in coding (but Python has them); nonetheless, they can be simply emulated with a **for-** or **while**-loop.

To understand how the program works, note that it starts from node 0 in $R[0]$ and makes use of two indexes $s$ and $f$ pointing to cells of $R$: $s$ points to the cell containing the current node from which other nodes reachable with an arc are sought, and $f$ points to the last cell of $R$ where a node has been inserted. So the portion $R[s : f]$ contains all nodes that still have to be explored in their adjacent nodes to advance the breadth-first search. Technically speaking, this set of nodes is called the *frontier* of the graph search.

Index $s$ is used in the **while**-loop of rows 2–10, in which the **foreach** command examines the nodes adjacent to the node $i = R[s]$: the nodes $j$ for which $M[i, j] >$ 0. Each of these nodes not already present in $R$ (as checked in line 5) is entered into $R$ (line 6). If this operation reaches the cell $R[n-1]$, the algorithm terminates successfully (lines 7–9) since all the nodes have been reached and inserted into $R$. Otherwise, the index $s$ is incremented by 1 (line 10) and, if $s$ is still $\leq f$, the **while**-loop is repeated for the new node $R[s]$; if instead $s$ exceeds the value of $f$, the **while**-loop terminates and the algorithm ends with failure (line 11) since no other nodes can be reached and those that have been reached are less than $n$.

An upper bound to the time complexity of the algorithm is easily estimated by noting that, if the computation ends at lines 8–9, all the rows $i$ of the matrix have been examined in the **foreach**-loop (line 4) and this operation was repeated $n$ times in the **while**-loop (line 2), for a total of $n^2$ operations; in addition, examining the elements $j$ contained in each cell of $M$ may require up to $n$ operations in the implicit cycle relative to the command **not-in** (line 5). Therefore, the total number of operations is at most $n^3$. Time complexity could be more accurately evaluated and the algorithm itself could be improved substantially, but at the moment we are interested in showing that the graph's connectedness can be checked in polynomial time.

Once the graph's connectedness has been established, we can determine whether an Eulerian cycle exists by verifying whether all the nodes have an even degree. This is done with the program DEGREES in Figure 8.5, which also outputs a vector $D[0 : n-1]$ where the node's degrees are inserted if they are even. The program scans the adjacency matrix row by row (**for**-loop with iterator $i$) summing up all the arc numbers specified in row $i$ (**for**-loop with iterator $j$) to compute the degree $g$ of node $i$. The first time a node with an odd degree is found, the program stops, signaling this condition. If this never happens, then all nodes have an even degree, which are stored in vector $D$, where $D[i]$ is the degree of node $i$. The algorithm executes the maximum number of operations when the entire matrix is examined, so its time complexity is proportional to $n^2$ because that is the number of cells examined, and the time taken for each check is constant.

To conclude, we can say, based on Euler's theorem, that the problem of determining whether a graph contains an Eulerian cycle can be solved by running the two programs CONNECTED and DEGREES for a total time proportional to $n^3$ in the worst case (note that the complexity of CONNECTED prevails). Therefore, this is an *easy* problem, but the two programs do not show what such a cycle is. For this purpose we have to design an algorithm for *building* an Eulerian cycle, which is valid for any connected graph with all nodes having an even degree. The algorithm will provide a proof of the *sufficient condition* specified in the "if" part of

```
program DEGREES (M)

// M: adjacency matrix of a graph of n nodes
// D: vector storing the node degrees that are even

    for i = 0 to n − 1
        g ← 0;                              // g will indicate the degree of node i
        for j = 0 to n − 1
            g ← g + M[i, j];                // computing the degree g of node i
        if g is odd
            print "The graph contains a node with an odd degree";
            stop;
        else D[i] ← g;
    print "All graph nodes have an even degree";
```

**Fig. 8.5** Checking whether all the nodes of a graph with adjacency matrix $M$ have even degrees.

Euler's theorem. This is a type of proof different from the ones we are accustomed to because it has a "constructive" character.

We only describe the proposed algorithm, called EULERIAN_CYCLE, because its coding is not simple. Interested readers should be able to code it and analyze it by themselves, taking into account the following points:

- Let $n$ and $m$ be the number of nodes and the number of arcs of the graph. We note at this point that in graphs that do not admit more than one arc between each pair of nodes we have $m \leq n(n-1)/2$, and that equality occurs if the graph is *complete*, that is, there is an arc connecting each pair of nodes. In fact, the term $n(n-1)$ depends on the fact that each of the $n$ nodes is connected with an arc to all the other $n-1$ nodes, and this number is divided by two because each arc was counted twice for each pair of nodes (e.g. the arc connecting nodes A and B was counted as A-B and B-A). Instead, in multigraphs like that of Königsberg where there may be more arcs connecting the same pair of nodes, $m$ is independent of $n$ and may be far greater than it. Then, while the time complexity of the previous algorithms depended only on $n$ for any graph, it will now depend crucially on $m$ because all the arcs must be inserted in the Eulerian cycle. Since each node has an even degree $\geq 2$, the total number of arcs incident to all nodes is at least $2n$ and we have $m \geq 2n/2 = n$ because, as before, each arc was counted twice. Therefore, time complexity will now be expressed as a function of $m$.
- A cycle in a graph, that is, a path that begins and ends at the same node (although it may not contain all the nodes of the graph), will be expressed as the ordered sequence of the nodes encountered, with the intent that the last node is connected to the first one with an arc that forms part of the cycle. An Eulerian cycle may contain the same node $N$ several times if its degree is at least four, but it cannot traverse the same arc twice. For example, in the graph in Figure 8.6 the sequence

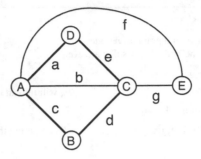

**Fig. 8.6** A graph that contains the Eulerian cycle $ACEABCD$ (that returns to A). As it will be explained below, this graph does not contain a Hamiltonian cycle.

of nodes $E, A$ and $C$ indicates a cycle beginning and ending at $E$, and traversing the arcs $f$, $b$, and $g$. The sequence $ACEABCD$ indicates the cycle beginning and ending at $A$, and traversing the arcs $b, g, f, c, d, e$, and $a$, where the nodes $A$ and $C$ with a degree of four appear twice: specifically, this is an Eulerian cycle because it contains all the arcs.

- The algorithm EULERIAN_CYCLE constructs a path in the graph *marking* each of its arcs as traversed, so that they will not be traversed again later. Unmarked arcs are said to be *free*. The path begins with any node, say $N_1$, and develops according to a node sequence $N_1 N_2 N_3 \cdots$ by choosing from every node $N_i$ a free arc that leads to $N_{i+1}$, marking this new arc as traversed, and continuing until a node $N_{k+1}$ is encountered that has no incident-free arc. As we now show, this implies that $N_1 = N_{k+1}$, that is $N_1 N_2 \ldots N_k$ is a cycle, albeit not necessarily an Eulerian cycle since some arcs of the graph may not be contained in it. Denote this cycle by $\gamma$.

- To prove that $N_1 = N_{k+1}$ note that at the beginning of the construction the arc leading from $N_1$ to $N_2$ is marked, then the number of free arcs incident to $N_1$ becomes odd. For each subsequent node of the path both the incoming arc and the outgoing arc are marked, so the number of free arcs incident to any of these nodes becomes zero if the degree of the node was two (and the node itself will be no longer encountered), or becomes an even number if the degree was four, six etc.. In this case, the node will possibly be encountered again in the path, and its degree will be decreased by two for each crossing. Node $N_1$ may also be encountered several times if its degree is at least four, but it is the only node with an odd number of incident-free arcs that can become zero when it is reached by another node, then node $N_{k+1}$ must coincide with $N_1$.

- Note also that the number of arcs in a cycle (that is, the ones marked) is equal to the number of nodes in the sequence representing the cycle. So, if in the cycle $N_1 N_2 \ldots N_k$ we have $k = m$, the number of its arcs equals the total number of arcs of the graph, then the cycle is Eulerian and the algorithm terminates. Otherwise, there must be at least one node $N_i$ in the cycle that still has incident-free arcs and the algorithm extends $\gamma$ including these arcs. Two cases may occur:

1. if one or more nodes do not appear in the cycle $\gamma$, at least one node $N_i$ of $\gamma$ must have incident-free arcs because the nodes not in $\gamma$ must be reachable from the nodes in $\gamma$, given that the graph is connected;
2. if all the nodes of the graph appear in $\gamma$, the $m - k$ free arcs not belonging to $\gamma$ must be incident to some nodes of $\gamma$, say $N_i$ is one of them.

In both cases node $N_i$ must have an even number of incident-free arcs because it has a total even number of incident arcs by Euler's Theorem and an even number of marked incident arcs in the cycle $\gamma$. Then extend the current cycle $\gamma$ as follows:

a. consider the subgraph $G'$ containing all the free arcs of $G$ and the nodes to which these arcs are incident. Note that $N_i$, and possibly other nodes of $G'$, are nodes of the cycle $\gamma$;
b. build a new cycle $\gamma'$ in $G'$ that starts and ends at node $N_i$ and, then, merge $\gamma$ and $\gamma'$ to form one longer cycle. To this end $\gamma$ is traversed starting from $N_i$ instead of $N_1$, that is, it is rewritten as a sequence $S = N_i N_{i+1} \ldots N_k N_1 \ldots N_{i-1}$, and the longer cycle is obtained by concatenating $S$ with the sequence $S'$ of the nodes of $\gamma'$, where $S'$ also starts at $N_i$ and ends at a node adjacent to $N_i$. Now, let $\gamma$ denote this longer cycle;
c. if all the arcs in $G$ are marked then $\gamma$ is an Eulerian cycle for $G$, otherwise repeat steps a. and b. to further extend the current cycle.

In the example in Figure 8.6, once the cycle $EAC$ has been built it cannot be further extended because the two arcs $f$ and $g$ incident at $E$ were marked. The cycle is then rewritten as $ACE$, and is extended from $A$ through the free arcs $c$, $d$, $e$, and $a$, thus obtaining the Eulerian cycle $ACEABCD$.

To estimate the complexity of the algorithm, we note first that the resulting Eulerian cycle is represented by a sequence of nodes of length $m$ (as the number of graph arcs). Therefore, $m$ is a lower bound to the number of required operations as the sequence must be built. We also have $m \geq n - 1$ (which may result in $m \gg n$) otherwise the graph would not be connected; therefore, $m$ will be the essential reference parameter in evaluating the time complexity. Now, if the first cycle found that $N_1 N_2 \ldots N_k$ is the solution (i.e., $k = m$), the algorithm has a time complexity proportional to $m$, otherwise it depends crucially on how the cycle is restructured to extend it and how many times this restructuring is performed. The simplest solution, though possibly not the most efficient one, is to scan every cycle in search of a node that has free arcs, and rewrite the cycle starting from this node as indicated previously. Since each cycle is up to $m$ long, this scanning requires up to $m$ steps. Since the total number of cycles that can be extended in this way until the final cycle is built is also at most $m$ (this happens if only one node is added at each restructuring phase), the time complexity of the algorithm in the worst case is proportional to $m^2$. Therefore, the problem of *building* an Eulerian cycle is easy, too.

The above discussion originated from the problem of the bridges of Königsberg. We now consider a problem that appeared more than a century later: it appears very similar to the previous one, but its computational nature is exceedingly different. In

1859, William Rowan Hamilton proposed a mathematical game physically realized with a wooden dodecahedron whose twenty vertices were associated with different city names. The goal of the game was to move along the edges of the polyhedron to visit all the cities exactly once and return to the original one. In this initial setting the game was associated with a specific example, like the original problem of the bridges of Königsberg. However, we propose a general version in terms of graph theory, as the vertices and the edges of a polyhedron can be, respectively, associated with the nodes and the arcs of a graph.

Given a graph $H$, we wonder whether it contains a *Hamiltonian cycle*, that is, a cycle that traverses all the nodes of $H$ exactly once. In a sense this is the "dual" of Euler's problem, formulated on nodes instead of edges, but its computational nature is completely different. As yet no one has found a reasonably simple criterion to answer the question, and not even an algorithm to build such a cycle, if it even exists, without basically trying to build cycles in all possible ways. In 1971, however, a fundamental mathematical result made it possible to clarify the terms of the question, as we will see in the next section. Before we go ahead, however, let us try to become better acquainted with the problem.

A reasonable criterion for studying the existence of a Hamiltonian cycle must of course be applicable to any graph. In the absence of such a criterion, some examples might be easy to answer, especially if they do contain the cycle, but for others it would be very difficult. In the graph of Königsberg in Figure 8.2(a) the existence of the Hamiltonian cycle $ACDB$ is immediately apparent. In the graph of Figure 8.6 such a cycle does not exist, but to establish this requires some reasoning even if the graph is very small.

As mentioned already, the problem can be solved on an arbitrary graph with an *enumerative* algorithm that builds a Hamiltonian cycle in all possible ways. We describe it in words.

- Let $H$ be an arbitrary graph, and let $N_1, N_2, \ldots, N_n$ be its nodes.
- As in the case of the Eulerian cycle, a condition for the existence of a Hamiltonian cycle is that graph $H$ is connected. This, as we know, can be decided in polynomial time with the algorithm CONNECTED.
- As for the algorithm FOOLISH_SORT, let we assume to have access to a simple algorithm PERMUTATIONS that builds one by one all the permutations of an arbitrary set of $h$ elements. As we know, its time complexity is exponential in $h$ since all the $h!$ permutations are generated.
- To build a Hamiltonian cycle start from any node, say $N_1$. Apply the algorithm PERMUTATIONS to the set $\{N_2, N_3, \ldots, N_n\}$ and concatenate with $N_1$ the permutations thus obtained. This generates, one by one, all the permutations of the nodes of $H$ starting with $N_1$. Denote with $N'_1, N'_2, \ldots, N'_n$ any one of these $(n-1)!$ permutations ($N'_1$ is always equal to $N_1$).
- Scan each one of the permutations to check whether there is an arc connecting each node $N'_i$ with $N'_{i+1}$ for $i = 1, 2, \ldots, n-1$. If such an arc does not exist, the scan stops and the next permutation is considered. If there are arcs up to the one connecting $N'_{n-1}$ with $N'_n$, check whether there is also an arc connecting $N'_n$

with $N_1'$. If this arc exists, the permutation corresponds to a Hamiltonian cycle; otherwise consider the next permutation. If no permutation generates a cycle, the graph does not contain a Hamiltonian cycle.

Obviously this program has exponential time complexity because, apart from the time to scan each permutation, the total number of permutations is $(n-1)!$ and all of them must be examined in the worst case (that is, if the Hamiltonian path coincides with the last permutation considered, or it does not exist).

It can be observed at this point that the proposed method solves a more general problem than the one at hand because it is designed to construct a Hamiltonian cycle rather than simply decree it to exist. In reality no algorithm *essentially* more efficient (i.e. polynomial) is known to merely answer the question of the existence of the cycle. Therefore the problem of deciding the existence of a Hamiltonian cycle is *difficult*. However, we in fact know much more, as we will now see.

## 8.2 P=NP?

The question contained in the title of this section, obviously incomprehensible to nonexperts in computational complexity, is at the heart of one of the most fascinating open problems in a field that extends from the theory of computation to mathematical logic, and has implications in many sectors. Before we enter into a discussion on it, albeit superficially, let us say that in the year 2000 an important American scientific institution, the Clay Mathematics Institute, defined the seven major mathematical problems that the previous millennium had left open and established a prize of $1,000,000 for the solution of each one of them. Ours is among these "millennium problems". Therefore, it is worth knowing at least what it is about, especially because it has not been solved yet and the $1,000,000 is still available.

First, **P** and **NP** are two classes of problems and the acronyms relate to the time complexity of the respective computing algorithms. The discussion is formally limited to *decision problems*, namely the ones that investigate the validity of a statement, but as we will see, this is not an important limitation. In particular:

- **P** is the class of decision problems for which there is a *solution algorithm* whose time complexity is polynomial in the input size.

- **NP** is the class of decision problems for which there is a *verification algorithm* (that is, one that verifies the legitimacy of a proposed solution) whose time complexity is polynomial in the input size.[3]

---

[3] **P** stands for "polynomial". **NP** stands for "nondeterministic polynomial" referring to a nondeterministic model of computation on which this class was originally defined. Going deeper into this subject would be out of place here. It must be pointed out, however, that **NP** does not stand for "not polynomial" as is sometimes erroneously stated; even though, as we shall see, this confusion may be somewhat justified.

An example to start with is given by the problems of the Eulerian cycle and the Hamiltonian cycle in their decision form, that is, given an arbitrary graph of $n$ nodes and $m$ arcs, decide whether there is a cycle with the required property. Denoting the two problems in decision form with $P_E$ and $P_H$, respectively, we have:

1. $P_E \in \mathbf{P}$, a notation indicating that the Eulerian cycle problem belongs to the class $\mathbf{P}$; that is, the existence of an Eulerian cycle can be decided in polynomial time.

2. $P_H \in \mathbf{NP}$, a notation indicating that the Hamiltonian cycle problem belongs to the class $\mathbf{NP}$; that is, verifying that a given cycle is Hamiltonian can be done in polynomial time.

Assertion 1 can be proved simply by recalling that there is a polynomial-time algorithm to find an Eulerian cycle, if it present, which therefore implicitly answers the question about its existence.

Assertion 2 can also be proved very simply, but this requires a somewhat subtle logical discussion. If the graph contains a Hamiltonian cycle, this can be described with a sequence of $n$ distinct nodes $N'_1, \dots, N'_n$. Given such a sequence, it can be *verified* in a time proportional to $n$ that it constitutes a Hamiltonian cycle by checking that an arc exists between each pair of nodes $N'_i, N'_{i+1}$ for $0 \le i \le n-1$, plus an arc between $N'_n$ and $N'_1$. Therefore, a polynomial-time verification algorithm for $P_H$ exists, as required by the definition of the class $\mathbf{NP}$.

All this may sound like a joke: to verify the legitimacy of a solution it is essential that it is available, but nothing is said about how to find it. If we could determine the solution in polynomial time, the problem would belong to the class $\mathbf{P}$. If, instead, determining it requires exponential time, we would not be reasonably able to find it and somebody else should provide it, for it to be verified. To understand the meaning of what we are saying, we have to made a few observations, starting from long ago.

In the Stone Age, people did not know how to use metals. It took hundreds of thousands of years to develop a technique to build new and useful artifacts, melting certain minerals at very high temperatures and cooling them in suitable molds. Once a technique for metal melting and casting was known, it was "easy" to apply it and then to verify its functioning; but inventing this technique had been "difficult." Similarly, proving a mathematical assertion can be very difficult (sometimes it has taken centuries), but verifying the correctness of its proof once known is much easier. This, essentially, is the concept that the classes $\mathbf{P}$ and $\mathbf{NP}$ formally capture.

These remarks, however naïve, make it possible to highlight another aspect of the discussion. While it is easy to verify the melting process of metals, it can be very difficult to decide that other substances cannot melt because this would require verifying the failure of all possible melting procedures. If we go back to our original problem, checking that a sequence of nodes $N'_1, \dots, N'_n$ corresponds to a Hamiltonian cycle of a graph can be done in polynomial time, but verifying that such a cycle does not exist would require examining all the $n!$ permutations of its nodes. Therefore, the problem of deciding the *nonexistence* of a Hamiltonian cycle is not even verifiable in polynomial time. Surprisingly, we are at an even higher level of difficulty, and many problems we cannot go through here share this condition.

Leaving behind these logical subtleties, we now enter into the concrete world of computer use, to recognize that the distinction between the two classes **P** and **NP** has an important practical meaning. For many problems, no attack strategy to solve them in polynomial time has been found over the years, if not essentially carrying out an exponential enumeration of possible cases and verifying whether one of them constitutes a solution. Generally they are not decision problems, such as $P_E$ or $P_H$, but require a more articulated solution such as the specification of a cycle, if it exists; or a solution that optimizes a suitable parameter such as a particular "cost" of a cycle. Some problems of this type will now be shown. However, first we note that in 1971 two scholars, Stephen Cook in Canada and Leonid Levin in Russia, framed these problems within a rigorous mathematical theory, resulting in the division between **P** and **NP**.

The main result of Cook and Levin is too complicated to be explained here, but the resulting theory may be surprising. As far as we know today, there are many problems in **NP** that we are able to solve only in exponential time, but that can be *reduced* to one another, in the sense that if there was a polynomial algorithm to solve one of them, the same algorithm could be extended in polynomial time to solve all the others. Here is a brief list of these problems that arise in different fields.

1. Graphs: Determine whether an arbitrary graph contains a Hamiltonian cycle.
2. Molecular biology: Given a set of DNA fragments, determine whether there is an unknown DNA sequence of given length that contains all these fragments.
3. Industry: Determine whether a set of sheet metal pieces of different shapes can be cropped out of the same sheet by placing them on it without overlapping.
4. Timetables: Given a set of classes of one or more hours to be taught in a school, and a set of available classrooms, determine whether the classes can be deployed among the classrooms so that teaching terminates within a given time limit.
5. Algebra: Determine whether a second-degree equation in two variables $x, y$ with integer coefficients has a solution (among the infinite ones) where $x$ and $y$ are both integers (for a first-degree equation the problem is in **P**).

It is known how to solve all these problems only by trying out a number of possible solutions, which is exponential in the input size. However, it can easily be seen that verifying the correctness of a proposed solution takes polynomial time for each of them, as required in the definition of the class **NP**. These problems, and many others related to them, are called **NP-complete** and are the "most difficult" among the ones of the class **NP**. If a polynomial algorithm was found to solve one of them, all the problems in **NP** would be transferred to the class **P**.

We finally add that the class **NP** also contains some problems that are solved in exponential time but are "less difficult" than the **NP-complete** problems, in the sense that a polynomial algorithm for their solution could not be extended to solve the **NP-complete** ones. Some of them are at the base of important cryptographic codes currently in use, which could be attacked if a polynomial algorithm were discovered to solve them, without any impact on the theory of *NP-completeness*.

It is now time to discuss the usefulness of limiting the theory to decision problems while in general it is necessary to figure out a problem's solution rather than
simply ascertaining its existence. The point is that the theory of complexity makes it
possible to prove that the hard core of the problems in **NP** is the test of the existence
of a solution. Once this existence has been established, the precise determination of
a solution itself can usually be obtained in polynomial time. For the five problems
listed above—to *find* a Hamiltonian cycle, to *identify* a proper DNA sequence, to
*place* a set of pieces on a larger sheet of metal, to *print* the schedule of classes, and
to *determine* the integer values of $x$ and $y$—it is not substantially more difficult than
establishing their existence.

After these tedious premises, let us now return to the $\$1,000,000$ problem. The
polynomial time resolution of a problem in **P** constitutes a proof of existence of the
solution (if any) whose validity it implicitly verified. That is, the solution of any
problem in **P** can be verified in polynomial time and we have $\mathbf{P} \subseteq \mathbf{NP}$. However,
no one has yet proved whether equality does not hold, that is, whether **NP** is larger
than **P** and therefore contains problems that cannot be solved in polynomial time.
The question, therefore, is:

$$\mathbf{P} = \mathbf{NP}?$$

In all likelihood, the answer is negative because despite an impressive number of
studies on the subject a polynomial-time algorithm to solve all problems in **NP**, that
is, to solve one of the **NP-complete** problems, has not been found. Essentially all
scholars are convinced that the classes **P** and **NP-complete** are disjoint, with the
consequence that $\mathbf{P} \neq \mathbf{NP}$. The proof, however, does not exist yet.

# Chapter 9
# Search Engines

It has been a little more than 25 years since the internauts first had the opportunity to *search* for documents of interest to them on the newly created Web (1991) by specifying a sequence of *keywords*. The context was very different from the present one: there were just a few internauts and the Web consisted of only a few million well-maintained and reliable documents (aka *pages*) belonging to governmental or university sites. The search engines of the era, whose names such as Wanderer and Aliweb are now forgotten, were based on extremely elementary algorithms for searching for the user-specified keywords through *meta-information* that the authors of the pages had associated to them. The search proceeded on the words contained in the archived pages using a linear scan similar to that described in Chapter 3: this was possible due to the limited number of pages existing on the Web at that time and the queries sent to the search engine.

The sudden growth of the Web made this approach ineffective and new search engines were born, with perhaps more familiar names, including AltaVista, Lycos, Excite, and Yahoo!. These engines boosted the potential of the users' searches through the textual content of the pages and introduced for the first time a set of criteria for *sorting* the results of a search. In fact, the growth of the Web had resulted in a consequent increase in the number of possible responses and it was no longer reasonable to assume that a user could examine them all. So the concept of the *relevance of the results* emerged, which at that time was measured with reference to the *frequency* on each page of the keywords in the query.

The results were excellent as long as the documents available on the Web were of high quality. However, as both use of the Web in the business sphere and knowledge of how search engines worked spread, many users, especially companies, began to build pages in such a way as to influence search results (a practice now known as *spamming*). The technique used was to include numerous words in the Web page that had little or nothing to do with its content but were related to other frequent queries by users, written in the same color as the page's background so that the reader could not see them – but the search engine did! For example, the author of a page about cooking products could artfully insert in the page many words related to trips to Thailand and make the font the same color as the page's background

© Springer Nature Switzerland AG 2018

P. Ferragina, F. Luccio, *Computational Thinking*,
https://doi.org/10.1007/978-3-319-97940-3_9

(typically, white). This way the words added were not visible to the human reader but the search engine found them in its content and then associated them to that page, so that the page was returned to the internauts who searched for "Thailand trips." Additionally, if the words "travel" and "Thailand" were repeated many times in the page, the search engine would evaluate them as extremely relevant to that page and then return it among the first results of the search. This heavily penalized the performance of these search engines, making them often unusable for queries that contained frequent words of interest to Web users. Countermeasures, therefore, became necessary.

## 9.1 From Words to Hyperlinks

As soon as it was established that the content of Web pages alone was insufficient to determine their relevance to users' queries, studies to make the Web more useful then turned to the ties between pages. Since the Web is a *network of pages* defined by pointers between them (called *hyperlinks*), it became clear that the properties of this network should also be used to improve the mechanism for evaluating the relevance of the pages.

The 1997–1998 biennium marked the beginning of the third generation of search engines and coincided with Google's birth, with its famous *PageRank* algorithm crucially based on the interconnections between Web pages. This generation of engines, to which for example Ask Jeeves, Yahoo!, and Bing also belong, dominated the Web search scenario during the following decade. In the first version of Google, the relevance of a page depended on its content, as in AltaVista, but also on what other pages contained about it. These wordings referring to other pages, called *"anchor-texts"*, are those associated with hyperlinks and are usually colored in blue or underlined in Web pages. Figure 9.1 shows an example where the pages $P1$ and $P2$, containing two hyperlinks with anchor-texts "el pibe oro" and "mano de dios," point to the page $P$, related to the famous soccer player Diego Armando Maradona. The first one shows a nickname of the player and the second one indicates a sporting event in which Maradona was the protagonist in the 1986 Football World Cup. Such anchor-texts were (and are) used to enrich the contents of page $P$, so that if a user searches for "pibe oro" (even without specifying "el" and "de" because search engines work on single words) page $P$ will be found. The more anchor-texts pointing to $P$ contain the words "pibe" and "oro," the more these words will be correct and relevant in describing the content of $P$ and will therefore have an impact in determining the relevance of $P$ to the query "pibe oro."

Furthermore, another mechanism of relevance was added, even more significant for that era. This was the calculation of the "rank" of each page $P$, called *PageRank* $\mathscr{R}(P)$, which did not depend on the query but captured the relevance of the page within the Web network as a function of the number and of the relevance of the pages pointing to it. This is a *recursive definition* as we will better explain in Chapter 11. It is surprisingly well-based mathematically and far more complex than the simple

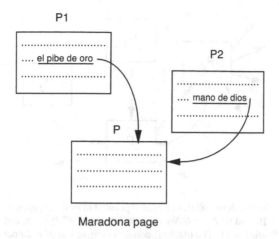

Maradona page

**Fig. 9.1** An example of two hyperlinks and their anchor-texts, between the pages $P1$ and $P2$ and the page $P$ referring to the famous soccer player Diego Armando Maradona.

count of the hyperlinks pointing to that page. The greater the value of $\mathscr{R}(P)$, the more relevant the page is in the context of the Web. Since its debut, PageRank has proven to be one of the most important and persistent measures used to determine the relevance of a "node" of the Web, a social network, or a network in general: be it a user, a restaurant, a tweet, or just a Web page. The concept has evolved over the years, but its original definition and properties are still valid and we refer to them here. Letting $\mathscr{H}(Q)$ indicate the number of hyperlinks from a page $Q$ to other pages, the value of $\mathscr{R}(P)$ is essentially calculated as:

$$\mathscr{R}(P) = \sum_{i=1}^{k} \mathscr{R}(P_i)/\mathscr{H}(P_i) \tag{1}$$

where $P_1, P_2, \ldots, P_k$ are the pages pointing to $P$.

The meaning of formula (1) is illustrated in Figure 9.2, and should be clear. The higher the relevance of the pages pointing to a page $P$, the more relevant $P$ is. However, the relevance of the pointing pages is "weighed" by the number of hyperlinks that originate from them, decreasing linearly if this number increases. In the example of Figure 9.2, page $P_1$ is assumed to have a rank of nine and points to three other pages, so its contribution to the rank of each one of them is $9/3 = 3$. Page $P_2$ is assumed to have a rank of ten but points to five other pages, so its contribution to the rank of each of them is $10/5 = 2$. Page $P_3$ is assumed to have a rank of six, smaller than the rank of the others, but points only to $P$, thus contributing with the full value of six to the rank of $P$.

Beyond intuition, the mathematical meaning of $\mathscr{R}(P)$ is the probability that a random walk on the Web graph ends at page $P$. Surprisingly, this is obtained by the algorithm with which PageRank is computed, which we will now mention. The basic formula (1) has been enriched with other terms to make sure that there is a path connecting any pair of nodes of the graph, and to guarantee certain properties

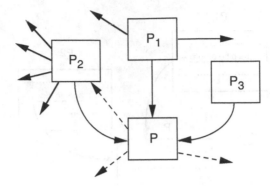

**Fig. 9.2** Computing the PageRank $\mathscr{R}(P)$ of a page $P$ pointed to by three pages $P_1, P_2$, and $P_3$, where $\mathscr{R}(P_1) = 9$, $\mathscr{R}(P_2) = 10$, and $\mathscr{R}(P_3) = 6$. We have $\mathscr{H}(P_1) = 3$, $\mathscr{H}(P_2) = 5$, and $\mathscr{H}(P_3) = 1$, then $\mathscr{R}(P) = 9/3 + 10/5 + 6/1 = 11$. The (dashed) pointers coming out of $P$ do not directly affect its PageRank but do affect the computation for the pages pointed to by $P$, as for example $P_2$.

that we cannot discuss here but are fundamental to ensuring that the resulting value of $\mathscr{R}(P)$ is independent of the starting point of the random walk. In any case, the basic calculations remain the same.

Denoting by $P_0, P_1, \ldots, P_{n-1}$ all the pages collected by the search engine (therefore, $n$ is a huge number), a vector $R[0:n-1]$ is defined where each element $R[i]$ contains the values of $\mathscr{R}(P_i)$ once the computation is completed. In Chapter 8 we have seen that a graph of $n$ nodes can be represented by an adjacency matrix $M[0:n-1,0:n-1]$ where each element $M[i,j]$ has a value of one if there is an arc from node $i$ to node $j$, and has a value of zero otherwise. We have also seen that the successive powers $M^k$ of that matrix represent the number of $k$-long paths in the graph, so that the element $M^k[i,j]$ indicates the number of paths of length $k$ from node $i$ to node $j$. Again, from Chapter 8 we know that the multiplication between a vector of $n$ elements (that is, a $1 \times n$ matrix) and a $n \times n$ matrix, produces a new vector of $n$ elements.

The PageRank computation is based on these considerations by using the adjacency matrix $W$ of the Web graph. One *speciality* of the Web graph, with respect to the graphs we have previously discussed, is that it is *directed* because its arcs can be traversed only in one direction and the matrix may be not symmetrical around the diagonal. In fact, if a page $P_i$ points to another page $P_j$ this does not mean that there is also a pointer in the opposite direction. However, nothing changes in the matrix computation, which proceeds as follows. Start from a set of arbitrary values of PageRank for all the Web pages, inserted in a vector $R$. These values constitute its initial configuration $R_0$. Take the adjacency matrix $W$ of the Web graph, where each element $W[i,j]$ is divided by the number $\mathscr{H}(P_i)$ of arcs leaving the page $P_i$, as required for calculating the PageRank of the pages pointed by $P_i$. Then proceed by iterations according to the following sequence of vector-matrix multiplications:

$$R_1 = R_0 \times W, \quad R_2 = R_1 \times W, \quad \ldots\ldots, \quad R_k = R_{k-1} \times W \qquad (2)$$

where the vector $R_k$ contains the PageRank values of all the pages, computed on paths of length $k$ in the Web graph. In fact we have $R_2 = R_0 \times W^2$, etc., up to $R_k = R_0 \times W^k$. We cannot enter here into the details of a theoretical justification of this calculation that is perfectly consistent with a probabilistic model, where the values in the vector $R_k$ for larger and larger values of $k$ tend to express the probabilities of reaching each of the corresponding nodes of the graph following a random path of any length, and tend to those values regardless of the initial choice $R_0$.[1]

First of all, how can such a calculation be made? Based on the information given in Chapter 8, you should be able to write your own simple program that computes $R \times W$ and iterate it $k$ times, for a small value of $n$. In fact, if the Web graph contains hundreds of billions of pages, then this computation can be done only by powerful search engine companies with giant parallel systems, where each one of a large number of computers processes a small section of the array $W$. It is easier instead to address a legitimate doubt about the inaccuracy of the result after a finite number $k$ of iterations, since, according to the theory, to get a precise result $k$ must tend to infinity. However, in our case we do not claim to have accurate PageRank values but only to be able to compare them for determining a significant *relative relevance* of the pages. Therefore, the iterations stop when the order of relevance of the pages is reasonably stabilized, usually within a hundred iterations.

In conclusion, the third generation of search engines combined the textual information contained in the Web page and in the anchor-texts of the hyperlinks pointing to it with general information on the structure of the Web graph. This approach was so effective in answering user queries that second-generation search engines disappeared within a short time, starting with AltaVista.

## 9.2 Fourth Generation

The third generation of search engines delivered extraordinary results to which users soon became accustomed, while leaving many insiders almost stunned by such overwhelming progress. However, as is often the case in the world of the Web, the mechanisms for determining page relevance were quickly threatened by new *spamming* techniques, the most famous of which was named *Google bombing*.

A famous example, which took place in December 2003, is the "miserable failure" query that led Google to return, as the first result, the home page of the former U.S. President George W. Bush. The idea had been to automatically create millions of Web pages containing hyperlinks to the presidential page, with the wording "miserable failure" as an anchor-text. The Google engine thus added those words to George W. Bush's page, and since numerous hyperlinks so labeled pointed to it, the page was considered relevant for the miserable failure query.

Today, it would be much easier to create this sort of spamming thanks to social networks and how easy they make it to copy links between posts. Google and the

---

[1] Strictly speaking this is assured if the matrix $W$ satisfies certain properties that we mentioned above and are way too complicated to be discussed here.

other search engines have made up for these attacks to their relevance mechanism (and seek to do so daily), in order to ensure a substantial correctness of the results whatever the user-specified keywords may be. However, there is a flourishing activity by SEO (*search engine optimization*) companies to build sets of Web pages connected via hyperlinks labeled with appropriate anchor-texts, with the ultimate goal of increasing the PageRank of a specific page, thus making it "go up" in the list of results of the queries on specific keywords. These are usually commercial pages for which this action tends to increase the number of visitors and thus the sales of their products.

We are living in the age of fourth generation search engines, in which there is a world-class engagement of the two giant protagonists, Bing and Google, plus Baidu in China and Yandex in Russia, and a multitude of others that act on specific contents (products, publications, users, maps, etc.), or purport to do "semantic" searches (Blekko, DuckDuckGo, etc.) by interpreting users' questions and carrying an in-depth analysis of document content. This latest generation is marked by an improvement in the efficiency and effectiveness of the technology made available to the users and by an expansion of the data on which a search can be done: not just Web pages but also news stories, social network contents, encyclopedias (Wikipedia, Britannica, etc.), airplane and train timetables, sporting events, files of different formats (pdf, xls, doc, etc.), multimedia, and much more. The search engines *index* many document sources with the primary goal of *understanding and satisfying the information needs* that lie behind the few words in the user's query. So, today, a search engine responds to a query by also displaying maps, news, weather forecasts, or dictionary definitions.

However, how difficult is it to "understand" a query? Almost all Web users specify about two words to characterize an information request and then expect the search engine to find the most relevant results among the thousands of billions of available documents of variable nature and composition. However, the relevance of a document is a subjective judgment of the user, and may also change over time as it depends on the user's knowledge of the subject specified and on his or her specific interest when formulating the query. The question "red bull" could mean an interest in "Formula 1" or in animal skins or in beverages. For this reason, search engines nowadays pay great attention to identifying the user's profile (that is, interests) from her earlier queries, to display the answers that supposedly interest her the most. However, the profile may also be misleading if an animal skins importer decides to inquire about Formula 1 that day. Thus, search engines, which are not fortune tellers, diversify their more relevant results in order to cover as much as possible the information needs that might hide behind queries that are difficult and/or *polysemic* (that is, with multiple meanings).

It seems impossible that the algorithmic techniques that drive search engines today are the result of only 25 years of research. These software programs have become so sophisticated in all their parts that, according to some, they can be considered as the most complex human artifacts in history. The algorithmic challenge is still evolving, because the amount of information available on the Web is already so large that it cannot be stored permanently in the existing *data centers* and must be filtered, compressed, and indexed for the retrieval of its parts.

Of the many concerns we face regarding the use of the Web, perhaps the most subtle one recalls Socrates' warning that writing imparts readers "*not truth, but only the semblance of truth; they will be hearers of many things and will have learned nothing; they will appear to be omniscient and will generally know nothing*".[2] For those using the Internet, this danger is much more serious today. However, in this book we will not discuss the use of search engines and the implications that this may have on accessing useful, relevant, and correct information. Rather, we will only describe a search engine's structure and the operation of some of its software modules. In particular, we will study in detail how search engines build an index of the stored documents, describing several interesting algorithmic solutions that are used in practice. To this end, we will explore the problem of searching for an element in a vector, already encountered in Chapter 3 in which linear scanning and binary search were introduced. We will also see that these two techniques, albeit very simple, provide a basis for the sophisticated query solvers that run every time an information is searched for on the Web. You may not achieve "true wisdom" on search engine functioning, but you will gain some useful knowledge to become a more savvy Web explorer.

## 9.3 The Structure

A search engine consists of five main interacting modules, as shown in Figure 9.3. These modules can be grouped into two classes based on their functions and inputs: those that work on documents extracted from the Web (the Crawler, the Analyzer, and the Indexer), and those that work on user queries (the Query Resolver and the Ranker). Often this subdivision is defined as the *back end* and the *front end* of the search engine, respectively, where the words *back* and *front* refer to their relation with the user's query.

Going a bit further into detail, the *Crawler* (also called *Spider* because the Web is a "cobweb" of documents) is the module that collects documents from the Web according to a policy for visiting the network that depends on the search engine, and is necessary as Web users constantly and dynamically create new documents or modify existing ones. The documents so identified are stored in an archive to be used as the potential results of user queries. Documents not in this archive are unknown to the search engine, and although they may be relevant to a query, they cannot be found and therefore returned as results. In fact, it would be unthinkable that a search engine explored even a part of the Web for each query because it would take hours or days for each of them, and it would not be possible to examine all of the pages because of their huge number.

---

[2] Plato, *Phaedrus*. Translation by Benjamin Jowett, C. Scribner's Sons (1871)

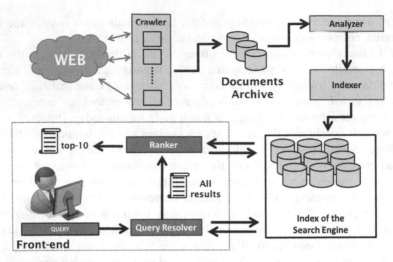

**Fig. 9.3** The simplified structure of a search engine with its five main software modules.

The Crawler's activity must then be repeated at a certain frequency depending on the characteristics of the stored page. Social pages, for example, must be downloaded by the Crawler more often than those of newspapers, and the latter more often than the main page of an institution or a company. Clearly, the ratio between visit frequency and number of pages visited is an important parameter for the efficiency of a search engine because it captures the relationship between how recently the data have been made available and how rich and varied they are, as a function of the computational resources used (the crawling time and the space occupied by the index). However, this parameter cannot be defined manually; it is determined automatically by modern search engines for each of the billions of documents indexed, using sophisticated techniques that we cannot deal with in this text.

The documents captured by the Crawler are the input on which the *Analyzer* works. This module determines the formatting, language, structure, hyperlinks, anchor-texts, and contents of the parsed document. This information is then used by the *Indexer* module that builds a data structure called an *index*, which allows the *front end* of the search engine to quickly find the documents containing the keywords specified in user queries. The index also contains a multitude of information reflecting the use of a page made by the users, for example, the number of times they click on it, the time they spend on it while navigating, etc. Google declared a few years ago that its index was occupying more than 100,000 terabytes (remember that 1 terabyte equals $10^{12}$ bytes). Since the goal is to provide the user with a Web index that is as complete and frequently updated as possible, both the Analyzer and the Indexer are run each time the documents archive is modified.

Consider now the *front end* modules that deal with solving a user query formulated as a sequence of keywords. The *Query Resolver* module is first activated, to retrieve from the index all the documents containing the words in the query. As already mentioned, the first generation of search engines only indexed a few documents so all the results could be examined by the user. Today, this is impossible because a single query can return thousands or even millions of results, so the engine must automatically select the most relevant ones for each query.

This task is assigned to the *Ranker* module that performs the selection by *ordering* the results according to a set of sophisticated criteria that vary from engine to engine and are still largely kept secret. Certainly some of these criteria are related to the frequency of the query keywords in the pages returned as results (as it was in AltaVista). Others are related to the page relevance generated within the Web (as for PageRank). Yet others depend on the number of clicks and on the time users stay on a page, and so on. Modern search engines claim to use more than 200 criteria to characterize a Web document and determine its relevance. This task is extremely tough because recent statistics show that more than 80% of user queries are made up of at most two words and the average is about 2.5 words per query. This is not just due to the users' laziness when writing queries, but also to the difficulty of finding the right keywords to express their information needs. This explains the ongoing search for algorithms that can *automatically* understand the true needs concealed behind the users' short queries, as well as the *semantics* (i.e. the meaning) of pages and documents on the Web.

We end our description of the five modules here, inviting the reader interested in a more in-depth study to refer to the scientific literature, or to the many documents available on the Web. In the following we focus on the Query Resolver module by addressing the apparently simple and well-known mathematical problem known as *set intersection*. To this end, we adopt the approach of the previous chapters to discover that this problem, if formulated in computational terms, is very interesting and admits algorithmic solutions that are absolutely non-trivial. The analysis of the time complexity of these solutions will prove that they are very efficient, as it should be to allow a search engine to respond daily to the queries of millions of users in a few milliseconds each.

## 9.4 How to Solve a Query

In describing the Query Resolver module, we have said that its task is to find *all the documents* in the search engine's index that contain *all the keywords* in the user's query. We now describe some efficient algorithms to solve this problem through a mathematical abstraction, which must first define what a query is and how the data structure containing the index is made.

Let a query $Q$ consist of the keywords $p_1, p_2, \ldots, p_q$, so that they are $q$ in number. For example, if the query consists of the keywords tower and Pisa, we will have $q = 2$, $p_1 = $ tower, and $p_2 = $ Pisa.

The search engine's index consists of many parts, but as far as we are concerned in this section it will be composed of a *dictionary* of words (sequences of characters) extracted from documents collected by the Crawler, and of *one list per dictionary word*, each containing the specification of the sequence of documents that contain that word. Since each Web document is identified by a universal address called the URI (Universal Resource Identifier), and this is potentially a very long string of characters that is expensive to store, search engines represent documents by positive integers, called docID, each associated to a URI. For example the Web page of The New York Times (www.nytimes.com/index.html) may be assigned docID = 570, the Web page of the Department of Computer Science at the University of Pisa (www.di.unipi.it/index.html) may be assigned docID = 2015, and so on. For each docID search engines also store the positions where a word appears in that document: this requires an even greater space for storing the index, but extremely advanced compression techniques make it possible to reduce it sufficiently. In the following we will simply show docID lists without specifying the word positions.

The data structure containing the dictionary and the lists is called an *inverted list* because the order in which the entries are listed is not built with the documents first followed by the words in them, but is in the alphabetic order of the words followed by the lists of documents that contain them. The reader will rediscover in this ordering what we have already discussed in Chapter 7 on card games and their sorting by suit and value, or vice versa.

For simplicity, we represent the dictionary and the lists with vectors. Specifically, we denote with $\mathscr{D}$ the vector containing the dictionary words sorted alphabetically, and with $L_p$ the vector containing the list of docIDs where the word $p$ occurs. So, we will have as many vectors $L_p$ as dictionary words, and each of these vectors will have a different length depending on the number of documents in the index that contain the word $p$. Figure 9.4 shows an example of an inverted list on which we will develop our algorithms: for the word $p$ = abacus, the vector $L_p$ = $[4, 23, 56, 77, 176]$ contains the docIDs of the Web pages containing abacus.

| Dictionary | List of docIDs |
|------------|----------------|
| abacus     | $4, 23, 56, 77, 176$ |
| ack        | $137, 199, 428, 733$ |
| b12        | $55, 56, 1011, 5001, 7142$ |
| baptistery | $1, 5, 7, 15, 16, 18, 23, 38$ |
| cat        | $35, 46, 51, 501$ |
| ...        | ... |
| pisa       | $1, 3, 9, 144, 210$ |
| rome       | $2, 6, 7, 10, 15, 81, 82, 93, 94, 101, 105, 107$ |
| ...        | ... |
| tower      | $9, 11, 15, 21, 27, 89, 101, 150, 500, 800, 811$ |
| ...        | ... |

**Fig. 9.4** An example of an inverted list. The portion of dictionary shown contains only a few words in alphabetic order, in lower case letters. The list of documents where a word is present is associated to the word, and is stored by docID in increasing order. The correspondence between the docID and the URI address of each document is stored in another table not shown in the figure.

To build a Query Resolver, the first step is to decide how to search the keywords $p_1, p_2, \cdots p_q$ of a query in the dictionary $\mathcal{D}$. The dictionary is ordered so as to make it possible to search its items quickly and to create sophisticated compression techniques that reduce the space occupied by the dictionary (see Chapter 10). For the dictionary search we described the techniques of linear scanning and binary search (see Chapter 3). The former has a time complexity that is linear in the dictionary dimension; the latter has a much smaller logarithmic time complexity in the same dimension. Since the dictionary $\mathcal{D}$ contains the words that appear in the indexed documents, we could expect it to contain only some tens of thousands of words as in a dictionary of any natural language. However, in a search engine the concept of a "word" is much more general as we can search for the commercial code of an appliance, a telephone number, or the acronym of a project. Therefore, the dictionary is very broad and may contain hundreds of millions of "words," so that searching for $p_i$ by linear scanning is impractical. Binary search is much faster and we know that it is optimal in the number of comparisons, so the first step of the Query Resolver can be done efficiently with this search, although there are more efficient algorithmic techniques that are too sophisticated to be explained in this text.

Given that every keyword of the query $Q$ appears in the dictionary, otherwise no result would be returned, the Query Resolver's next step is to find the indexed documents that contain all the keywords $p_1, p_2, \ldots, p_q$.[3] To do this, the module needs to solve the following problem efficiently, which is the algorithmic heart of the first phase of the query resolution.

*PROBLEM. Given q sets of positive integers (our `docIDs`) represented with the vectors $L_{p_1}, L_{p_2}, \ldots, L_{p_q}$, find the integers that appear in all these sets, that is, the integers belonging to the intersection $L_{p_1} \cap L_{p_2} \cap \ldots \cap L_{p_q}$.*

Mathematically, this is a well-defined problem known as set intersection. Less obvious is its efficient resolution, which is the "computational variant" implicitly required in the problem. Let us focus our attention on a query with two keywords (so $q = 2$) referring to the example $Q = $ tower Pisa to illustrate how the following algorithms work. The first algorithm that comes to mind to construct the intersection between the two sets $L_{\text{tower}}$ and $L_{\text{pisa}}$ is to compare each element (`docID`) of the first vector with all the elements of the second, printing those that appear in both vectors. The pseudocode of this first algorithm called INTERSECTION1 is given in Figure 9.5. Its correctness is obvious, so we immediately go through the analysis of its time complexity.

Let $m$ and $n$ denote the lengths of the two lists. Since we perform $n \times m$ comparisons of element pairs and the same number of increments of the iterators $i$ and $j$, while the print operations are fewer, the function $n \times m$ captures the time complexity of the algorithm. Therefore, the algorithm is very slow, as is apparent from a simple calculation. Among the documents indexed by Google, the word tower appears in about 200 million of them, and the word pisa appears in approxi-

---

[3] Again we are simplifying because modern search engines also return documents that contain only a subset of the keywords $p_i$, provided that it is sufficiently large. We will discuss this case later.

```
program INTERSECTION1 (A, B)
// The vectors A and B contain n and m elements, respectively
1.     for i = 0 to n − 1
2.         for j = 0 to m − 1
3.             if A[i] = B[j]
4.                 print A[i];
```

**Fig. 9.5** The program INTERSECTION1 to print the elements of the intersection between two sets of integers contained in vectors $A$ and $B$. The search of the common elements is performed by comparing each element of $A$ (**for**-loop in line 1) with all the elements of $B$ (**for**-loop in line 2), and verifying their equality (line 3).

mately 70 million of them. With algorithm INTERSECTION1 the number of comparisons would be $n \times m \approx 200 \times 10^6 \times 70 \times 10^6 = 14 \times 10^{15}$, which would take about $14 \times 10^{15}/10^9 = 14 \times 10^6$ seconds on a computer running a billion (or $10^9$) operations per second. In other words, about 162 days!

The inefficiency of the algorithm INTERSECTION1 is due to the fact that it compares *every* element of a list with *all* the elements of the other list by scanning the second list as many times as there are elements in the first one. However, if one of the lists is sorted, and in particular the longer of the two, its scanning can be replaced with a binary search as shown in algorithm INTERSECTION2 in Figure 9.6, where we assume that $m \le n$ (the case $m > n$ is symmetric and works by swapping the role of the two lists).

```
program INTERSECTION2 (A, B)
// Vector B[0 : m − 1] is shorter than vector A[0 : n − 1], and A is ordered
1.     for k = 0 to m − 1
2.         i ← 0; j ← n − 1;
3.         while i ≤ j
4.             c ← ⌊(i + j)/2⌋;
5.                 if (B[k] = A[c]) print B[k]; break;
6.             else
7.                 if (B[k] < A[c]) j ← c − 1;
8.                 else i ← c + 1;
```

**Fig. 9.6** The program INTERSECTION2 prints all the elements of the vector $B$ that are also contained in the vector $A$. The search for each element $B[k]$ in $A$ is done in lines 2–8 applying BINARY_SEARCH (see Figure 3.2 of Chapter 3). The vector $B$ does not have to be ordered because all of its elements are examined sequentially. The **break** command makes the program exit from the **while**-loop.

In this algorithm each element of the shorter list $B$ is searched for in the longer list $A$ via a binary search. This requires $m \log_2 n$ comparisons: a noticeable improvement in order of magnitude over the previous algorithm INTERSECTION1 since the dependency on $n$ is reduced exponentially from $n$ to $\log_2 n$. Note that searching for the elements of the longer list $A$ in the shorter list $B$ would be less advantageous. For the query $Q = \texttt{tower Pisa}$, the algorithm INTERSECTION2 performs a number of comparisons that grows as $m \log_2 n \approx (70 \times 10^6) \log_2 (200 \times 10^6) \approx 196 \times 10^7$ comparisons, which executed on the computer of the previous example would take $196 \times 10^7 / 10^9 = 1.96$ seconds. So INTERSECTION2 is significantly faster than INTERSECTION1 but still far from the performance of modern search engines, which take a few milliseconds to answer the query.

We can improve INTERSECTION2 if we are able to take advantage, when searching for $B[k]$ in $A$, of the results of the comparisons executed during the search of the previous element $B[k-1]$. This is exactly what the new algorithm INTERSECTION3 of Figure 9.7 does. Its algorithmic structure is similar to that of the algorithm MERGE introduced in Chapter 7 in the context of MERGE_SORT, with one substantial difference: INTERSECTION3 prints only the shared elements, and the scanning of $A$ and $B$ is interrupted as soon as the algorithm has finished examining one of them (hence the use of one **while**-loop instead of the three loops contained in MERGE). We are ready to prove the correctness of INTERSECTION3 and to calculate its time complexity. Note that both vectors must now be ordered.

- *Correctness.* Assume that, in a generic step, the algorithm has already individuated and printed, one after the other, the elements of the intersection of the first $i-1$ elements of $A$ with the first $j-1$ elements of $B$. That is, the algorithm has found the elements common to the sub-vectors $A[0 : i-1]$ and $B[0 : j-1]$.
  This is clearly true at the beginning of the computation, where $i = j = 0$. In fact, the sub-vectors $A[0 : i-1], B[0 : j-1]$ are empty, and thus their intersection is empty, and the algorithm (correctly) did not print anything. In the generic step, there are two cases. If $A[i] \neq B[j]$ the iterator of the smaller element of the two is increased by one (lines 4 or 6): this element cannot appear in the other vector as this vector is ordered and hence the following elements are greater . If instead $A[i] = B[j]$, a common element is found and printed (line 7), and then discarded from the subsequent comparisons (line 8).
- *Complexity.* The worst case is found with an argument similar to that used in Chapter 7 for the algorithm MERGE. The iterators $i$ and $j$ scan the vectors without ever going back. Each comparison between two elements causes at least one of the iterators to progress by one step and the algorithm stops when an iterator reaches the end of its vector (i.e. the **while**-condition at line 2 becomes false). Then the number of elements examined, and consequently the number of their comparisons, is at most $n + m$. This is a function that represents the time complexity of INTERSECTION3 in the worst case, which occurs if both vectors are scanned to the very end without finding equal elements (in this case line 8 never applies and the iterators are always increased separately).

---

**program** INTERSECTION3 (A,B)

// ordered vectors $A[0:n-1]$ and $B[0:m-1]$

1.    $i \leftarrow 0; j \leftarrow 0;$

2.    **while** $(i < n)$ **and** $(j < m)$

3.        **if** $A[i] < B[j]$

4.            $i \leftarrow i+1;$

5.        **else if** $A[i] > B[j]$

6.                $j \leftarrow j+1;$

7.            **else print** $A[i];$                      // in fact, here $A[i] = B[j]$

8.                $i \leftarrow i+1; j \leftarrow j+1;$

---

**Fig. 9.7** The program INTERSECTION3. Like the previous ones, this program prints the common items of the two vectors $A$ and $B$, but is usually faster. Both vectors $A$ and $B$ must be ordered.

Referring to the example in Figure 9.4, the algorithm INTERSECTION3 operates on the two vectors $L_{\texttt{tower}} = [9, 11, 15, 21, 27, 89, 101, 150, 500, 800, 811]$ and $L_{\texttt{pisa}} = [1, 3, 9, 144, 210]$. The first comparison is done between the elements 9 and 1 at the head of the lists, establishing that the second one is smaller and must therefore be discarded by advancing the search in $L_{\texttt{pisa}}$. The same thing happens in the next comparison between 9 and 3, where the element 3 is discarded, advancing again in $L_{\texttt{pisa}}$. The third step compares two equal elements (i.e. 9 and 9), thus this shared element is printed and the advancement occurs in both vectors. Recalling the previous estimate of the number of entries in the Google index for $L_{\texttt{tower}}$ and $L_{\texttt{pisa}}$, we conclude that the number of steps performed by INTERSECTION3 is at most $n + m \approx (70 \times 10^6) + (200 \times 10^6) = 270 \times 10^6$. Therefore, the computer in this example would require $270 \times 10^6 / 10^9 = 0.27$ seconds for computing $L_{\texttt{tower}} \cap L_{\texttt{pisa}}$. This shows that the new algorithm is more efficient than the previous ones and its performance is very close to that one of the algorithms used in modern search engines. In fact, INTERSECTION3 is very close to the algorithmic structure of current solutions.

To conclude, two observations are in order. The first concerns a comparison of the complexity of the last two algorithms. The approximate calculations done on the basis of the length of the two vectors $L_{\texttt{tower}}$ and $L_{\texttt{pisa}}$ indicated that INTERSECTION3 is the best algorithm among those proposed, but this conclusion is only partially correct. The time complexities of INTERSECTION2 and INTERSECTION3, respectively, grow as $T_2(n,m) = m \log_2 n$ and $T_3(n,m) = n + m$. If $n \approx m$ then $T_3(n,m) < T_2(n,m)$, as occurs in the previous example. However, if $m$ is much smaller than $n$, then $T_2(n,m)$ is much smaller than $T_3(n,m)$ and the binary search-based algorithm is much more efficient in this case. Consequently, neither of the two algorithms is better than the other in all cases, so the choice between them depends on the length of the lists whose intersection is being computed.

The second observation concerns queries consisting of more than two keywords. The algorithm for this case deeply resembles the structure of INTERSECTION3 except it uses $q > 2$ iterators and compares the $q$ pointed elements in the lists $L_{p_1}, L_{p_2}, \ldots, L_{p_q}$ at every step. With an argument similar to that used for the case $q = 2$, it can be proved that this algorithm is correct, that is, it finds all (and only) the elements present in all the $q$ lists; and its worst case time complexity equals the total length of the $q$ lists. This algorithmic scheme is particularly interesting as it can be adapted to design a *soft* variant of the Query Resolver module that returns a document if it contains at least $k$ keywords, where $k$ may be smaller (but not too much smaller) than $q$. The algorithm checks at each step whether there are at least $k$ lists with an equal currently-compared element, which is printed in this case. The time complexity does not change, but the effectiveness of the method strongly increases. For example, there may be relevant documents where words have spelling errors (e.g. toer instead of tower) that would not be found if all the keywords of the query had to be present in the answer; or, the common case of the absence in the document of non-significant keywords such as articles or prepositions (e.g. "the tower" in the query but only "tower" in the document).

## 9.5 Still an Improvement

As can be expected, search engines use algorithms more sophisticated than the ones presented in the previous section, although they are based on the same principles. To delve deeper into the subject we ask the reader for a little bit of additional attention, which will be paid back with the in-depth knowledge of how a real Query Resolver works. However, if you feel satisfied with what has been explained so far you may skip this section.

As already mentioned, the algorithm INTERSECTION3 is very efficient if the two vectors are about the same length, and in this case few comparisons are used to determine whether the element $B[j]$ appears, or not, in the residual vector $A[i : n-1]$. The worst case is if $B[j]$ is greater than $A[n-1]$ so that the algorithm scans the entire vector $A$ to find that $B[j]$ does not appear in it. And in fact, if $A$ is much longer than $B$, that is $n \gg m$, INTERSECTION2 is faster than INTERSECTION3, as seen previously. In this case, to improve INTERSECTION3 we need a more efficient method to determine whether $B[j]$ appears in $A[i : n-1]$. Now, since $A[i : n-1]$ is ordered we could use a binary search on it. However, that would not be enough because the length $n - i$ of this vector portion could still be very large compared to the position of $B[j]$ in $A[i : n-1]$. This would make binary search more costly than a simple scan of $A[i : n-1]$.

The solution, which optimally manages the case of $B[j]$ close to the beginning of $A[i : n-1]$ or at the end of it, is very elegant. It is based on an algorithm which quickly estimates the portion of $A[i : n-1]$ that can contain $B[j]$, and then applies binary search on that portion to check its actual presence. The algorithm is called

DOUBLING due to the way it operates. We will describe it only in words since its pseudocode is not simple and would divert attention from the nature of the method.

So let us start with the ordered vectors $A$ and $B$. DOUBLING proceeds by scanning the shorter vector, say $B[0 : m-1]$. At step $j$ the algorithm checks for the presence of $B[j]$ in $A$ keeping track of the comparisons previously executed in $A$ for searching the elements of $B[0 : j-1]$. In fact, the algorithm is aware of the position $i$ where the search in $A$ of the previous element $B[j-1]$ has been interrupted; therefore, $B[j]$ must be searched for in $A[i : n-1]$. To this end, the algorithm compares $B[j]$ with $A[i]$ and then proceeds according to three alternatives.

- If $B[j] = A[i]$ this element is printed and the process advances by one position both in $A$ and $B$.

- If $B[j] < A[i]$ (hence $B[j]$ does not appear in $A[i : n-1]$, being smaller than all of its elements), then $B[j]$ is discarded and the algorithm proceeds to examine $B[j+1]$, incrementing the value of $j$ without changing the value of $i$.

- If $B[j] > A[i]$ (then $B[j]$, if present, appears in $A[i : n-1]$ after position $i$), $B[j]$ is compared with the elements of $A$ that are at a power of two distance from $A[i]$, that is $A[i+2^h]$ for $h = 0,1,2,\ldots$ until one of the following conditions holds:

  - the position $i+2^h$ falls within $A$ (i.e., $i+2^h \leq n-1$) and $B[j] = A[i+2^h]$. Then $B[j]$ is present in $A$ and is printed. If $i+2^h < n-1$ the search goes on for $B[j+1]$ in the remaining part of $A$;

  - the position $i+2^h$ falls within $A$ (i.e., $i+2^h \leq n-1$ as before) but $B[j] < A[i+2^h]$. Then $B[j]$, if present, is in the portion $A[i+2^{h-1}+1 : i+2^h-1]$ since in the previous step we found that $B[j] > A[i+2^{h-1}]$. At this point, the algorithm checks for the presence of $B[j]$ in that portion of $A$ by a binary search on it in at most $\log_2(2^{h-1}-1) < h$ comparisons;

  - the position $i+2^h$ falls outside $A$ (i.e., $i+2^h > n-1$) and $B[j] > A[n-1]$ (i.e., $B[j]$ is larger than the last element of $A$). Then $B[j]$ does not appear in $A$ and the algorithm terminates since all the elements in the remaining portion $B[j+1 : m-1]$ are larger than $A[n-1]$ and therefore do not belong to the intersection;

  - the position $i+2^h$ falls outside $A$ (i.e., $i+2^h > n-1$ as before) and $B[j] = A[n-1]$. Then $B[j]$ appears in the last cell of $A$ and is printed, and the algorithm terminates as in the previous case;

  - the position $i+2^h$ falls outside $A$ (i.e., $i+2^h > n-1$ as before) and $B[j] < A[n-1]$. The algorithm checks for the presence of $B[j]$ by a binary search in the portion $A[i : n-2]$ taking at most $\log_2(n-i-1) < h$ comparisons.

An example should help in understanding the previous algorithm better. Let us consider again the lists $L_{tower}$ and $L_{pisa}$ in Figure 9.4. After scanning the shortest list $L_{pisa}$ up to its third element 9 that is found in the first position of $L_{tower}$, the algorithm DOUBLING continues to look for the next element 144 in the remaining portion of $L_{tower}$, that is $[11, 15, 21, 27, 89, 101, 150, 500, 800, 811]$. To this end the algorithm compares 144 with 11 and, as it is greater, continues with jumps of a power of two in length from the position $i$ of 11, comparing 144 with

15 in position $i + 2^0$, with 21 in position $i + 2^1$, with 89 in position $i + 2^2$, and with 800 in position $i + 2^3$. At this point, we have $144 < 800$ and the binary search is executed on $[101, 150, 500]$ since $89 < 144 < 800$.

Then the algorithm DOUBLING may continue scanning $B$ and searching for the next element $B[j+1]$ in $A$. In the itemization above, we have illustrated several cases that might have occurred during the search of $B[j]$; however, whichever was the case that applied to $B[j]$, we can surely state that $B[j] > A[i + 2^{h-1}]$. In the example, $B[j] = 144 > A[i + 2^{h-1}] = A[i + 2^2] = 89$. Now, since the vector $B$ is assumed to be ordered increasingly, we have $B[j+1] > B[j]$ and so we can search the former starting from $A[i + 2^{h-1} + 1]$. Referring again to our example, the search for the next element 210 that follows 144 in $L_{\text{pisa}}$ can then be executed in the portion of $L_{\text{tower}}$ that follows 89, namely $[101, 150, 500, 800, 811]$. Computationally this means that in the search for 210 the elements $[11, 15, 21, 27, 89]$ can be skipped without examining them.

We can therefore deduce that the algorithm DOUBLING executes $h$ comparisons on the element $B[j]$ and discards $2^{h-1}$ elements from $A$ because the binary search is executed on the portion $A[i + 2^{h-1} + 1 : i + 2^h - 1]$. This is a very advantageous exponential relation which has a strong positive impact on the time complexity of the algorithm. To the point that it can be proved, though it would be too complicated to do so here, that the number of steps executed by DOUBLING can be described with a function of the form $m(1 + \log_2(n/m))$. This is a somewhat surprising function whose value is always smaller than $m \log_2 n$ (the complexity of INTERSEC-TION2) and also smaller than $n + m$ (the complexity of INTERSECTION3). The first inequality is obvious; the second is obtained by verifying algebraically that $n > m \log_2(n/m)$.

## 9.6  A Concluding Remark

The algorithms described so far constitute only the first part of the *front end* of a search engine, which must be followed by an ordering, for relevance, of the documents obtained by list intersection. This is a problem, as already pointed out, that is algorithmically very difficult and not yet solved satisfactorily. Discussing this point would lead us to talk about trigonometry, analysis of functions, multi-dimensional spaces, and other mathematical concepts apparently "distant" from the reality of these software tools. The subject is fascinating but at the same time too complex to be discussed further in these pages.

Nowadays search engines are considered to be still in their infancy, although they have already evolved substantially and their (quite) sophisticated algorithms can be used with ease. This ease of use hides their algorithmic complexity so well that search engines are often seen as elementary tools that can be easily designed and implemented. We hope that these pages have provided evidence that this statement is unfounded.

# Chapter 10
# Data Compression

The advent of Big Data and the Internet of Things has revived a strong interest, both in academia and industry, in the compression of large datasets. This is because of its three main benefits:

- it reduces the amount of space needed to store data, thus *virtually* increasing the size of a computer's memory;
- it reduces the time needed to transfer data between computers, thus *virtually* increasing the bandwidth of the network over which these data are transmitted; and
- it may speed up the execution of algorithms because their working dataset may fit into memory levels that are faster to access but smaller in size, such as the (various levels of) caches available in modern computers and computing devices.

The input to a data compressor is a finite sequence of characters from an arbitrary alphabet: this sequence is often called *text* and it is denoted with $T[0:n-1]$; the alphabet is denoted with the Greek letter $\Sigma$ and the number of distinct alphabet characters with the notation $|\Sigma|$. Compressing the text $T$ means to *change its representation* from a sequence of characters of $\Sigma$ to a binary sequence $T_C$ that is hopefully more succinct than the original text, and for which an algorithm exists that can reconstruct $T$ from $T_C$ approximately. The first condition, on succinctness, aims at decreasing the amount of space occupied (as well as the time taken, due to the considerations above). The second condition, on the re-constructibility of $T$, aims at guaranteeing the practical utility of the compression transform according to the context in which it is used. In fact if $T$ is a linguistic text, then it is mandatory (a) for its compression to occur *without any loss* and (b) that $T$ can be reconstructed *exactly* from $T_C$. Compressors of this type are called *lossless*. If $T$ is instead a multimedia file, then we can admit *some loss* in its reconstructed text but the differences must be sufficiently small that the human eye or ear cannot perceive them (as is the case in the compressed formats MP3, JPEG, MPEG, etc.). This loss is fully compensated by the reduction gained in space occupancy by the compressed $T_C$, which is much more significant than operating via a lossless transform. Compressors of this type are called *lossy*.

© Springer Nature Switzerland AG 2018
P. Ferragina, F. Luccio, *Computational Thinking*,
https://doi.org/10.1007/978-3-319-97940-3_10

In the rest of this chapter we will concentrate only on lossless compressors and we will construct the examples by defining each text $T$ with the 26 letters of the English alphabet. In practice, there are many possible *encodings* for the characters of $\Sigma$. A typical example is the classic ASCII code, which uses eight bits per character thus allowing the encoding of an alphabet that consists of $256 = 2^8$ characters (namely, lowercase and uppercase letters, punctuation marks, and some special symbols). Another example is the more recent UNICODE, which uses up to 24 bits per character thus allowing the encoding of millions of distinct characters; indeed, it is currently used within most writing systems, such as the ones adopted in mathematics, chemistry, biology, cartography, the Braille alphabet, ideograms, emoji, etc. In the rest of this chapter we will assume that the 26 possible letters of the input text $T$ are each encoded with five bits which will suffice to represent $2^5 = 32 > 26$ different binary configurations (see Chapter 6). More precisely, we encode the letter A with the smallest binary sequence $00000$ (corresponding to the number 0) and we use the subsequent binary sequences over five bits to represent the following letters up to the letter Z, which will get the encoding $11001$ (corresponding to the number 25 since we count from 0).

The algorithm that transforms the original text $T$ into the compressed one $T_C$ is called the *compressor* or just the *coder*. The algorithm that implements the *inverse transformation* from $T_C$ to $T$ is called the *decompressor* or the *decoder*. The quality of these algorithms is evaluated in terms of (at least) two computational measures: the *efficiency* in time of the compression and decompression processes (i.e. speed), and the *effectiveness* in space of the compressed output (i.e. succinctness). The latter is computed as the ratio between the length $|T_C|$ of the compressed text and the length $|T|$ of the original input text, both expressed in bits. The value $|T_C|/|T|$ is called the *compression ratio* and captures the *gain* in storage space achieved by representing $T$ via the compressed sequence $T_C$. Typically, $|T_C| < |T|$ and thus this value is smaller than 1, yielding a space reduction that is larger and larger as this value gets closer to 0. The other case $|T_C| \geq |T|$ occurs when the "compressed" file is longer than the (uncompressed) input text $T$, so that the compression is useless. In that case the compression ratio is larger than (or equal to) 1. This is a rare, but possible, event that may be due to either the use of a bad compressor or the attempt to compress an *incompressible* text.

In order to clarify further these definitions, let us consider the following example. Take the text $T = \text{AABABA}$ consisting of six letters and let us encode each of them with five bits, as specified previously. The length of $T$ is then $6 \times 5 = 30$ bits. A compressor can trivially take advantage of $T$'s composition, consisting of only two distinct letters, and substitute the letter A with the bit 0 and the letter B with the bit 1. This generates the encoded text $001010$ whose compression ratio is $6/30 = 1/5 = 0.2$. In other words, the proposed encoding transforms every five bits of the original text (i.e. one letter) into one single bit. The decompressor can reconstruct the original text $T$ from the binary sequence $001010$ by deploying the knowledge of the encoding A $\rightarrow$ 0 and B $\rightarrow$ 1. Specifically, the compressed file $T_C$ consists of two parts: a *preamble*, which describes the *inverse* transformation 0 $\rightarrow$ A and 1 $\rightarrow$ B, and a *body*, which contains the sequence of bits encoding all the letters in

$T$. The decompressor works as follows: it reads the inverse transformation from the preamble, then it decodes the body by substituting each occurrence of the bit 0 with the letter A and each occurrence of the bit 1 with the letter B. We should point out that in the previous calculation of the compression ratio, and in all the following ones, we will not account for the space taken by the preamble, both because we wish to simplify calculations and because the alphabet is typically small enough that the preamble is negligibly short compared to the body.

The previous compressor is trivial because it deploys only the fact that the number of distinct letters of $T$ is two and thus one bit is enough to distinguish between them. In general, however, the input text $T$ has many more distinct letters and, therefore, requires more sophisticated compression techniques to squeeze its content. The most famous of these compressors will be the subject of this chapter.

The birth of the theory of data compression dates back to the middle of the last century, thanks to the groundbreaking results published by the brilliant scientist Claude Shannon. After 70 years of research, our understanding of data compression is so wide and deep that it is getting harder and harder for a software engineer to choose the best compressor for any given application's needs. To simplify, data compressors can be grouped into three main algorithmic families: *statistical compressors*, *dictionary-based compressors*, and *sort-based compressors*. We will examine each family without going into much detail by choosing a description level that will allow us to offer some algorithmic considerations about the efficiency and effectiveness of these algorithms and the challenges behind their design.

In order to describe the workings of these algorithms we will refer to the following (Italian) text $T = $ LA BELLA BALLA, which consists of four distinct letters (i.e. $\{A, B, E, L\}$) for a total length of 12 letters. We chose a slightly repetitive text on purpose because this will allow us to highlight the issues pertaining the use of the three families of compressors mentioned previously. However, this repetitiveness is not unnatural in practice because the files that we compress daily are much longer and include some structure that derives from their linguistic nature, or from the format used to encode them. If we do not consider the spaces in $T$, and encode its letters in ASCII, this would take $8 \times 12 = 96$ bits. If, instead, we were to adopt a simple compressor inspired by the one we used a few pages earlier, which assigns a code of two bits per letter (given that there are four distinct ones) such as A $\rightarrow$ 00, B $\rightarrow$ 01, E $\rightarrow$ 10, and L $\rightarrow$ 11, then the encoding of $T$ would need only $2 \times 12 = 24$ bits. The compression ratio is then equal to $24/96 = 1/4 = 0.25$ where, as observed previously, we have not accounted for the length of the preamble in estimating $T_C$'s length.

This compression ratio is good, but often the simple *re-encoding* of letters with a *fixed length code* of $(\log_2 |\Sigma|)$ bits achieves a very poor compression ratio that can be, nonetheless, significantly improved by deploying two main features of real texts:

- The *frequency of the letters* in real texts is often not uniform. In our example, the letter A occurs five times, B occurs twice, E occurs once, and L occurs six times. The *statistical compressors*, described in the next section, will take into account the frequency of the letters to assign *variable-length* binary codes that deploy the following *golden rule* of data compression: letters that appear frequently must be assigned short binary codes, whereas rare letters can be assigned longer binary codes. The reason underlying this rule is pretty easy to deduce from the previous example: since L occurs more frequently than B, it is *better* in terms of space occupancy to assign it a binary code shorter than that assigned to B.

- The *frequency of groups of letters* in real texts may be not uniform. This could be exploited by compressors to squeeze the *very regular* text AAABBB more than any other text consisting of three occurrences of A and three occurrences of B: something that would be impossible to capture if the compressor made use only of the frequency of the individual letters A and B. The effectiveness of this approach must also compensate for the increased sophistication of the compression algorithm required to efficiently count the frequencies of (perhaps many) groups of letters and store a longer preamble in $T_C$ because of the larger number of these groups. This could nullify the advantage of a shortened body. The two compression families based on dictionaries and on sorting that we will describe in the subsequent sections cope efficiently and effectively with repetitive blocks of letters of variable length, which is the state-of-the-art in the modern design of compressors.

## 10.1  Statistical Compressors

These compressors encode one letter (or one group of letters) at a time by outputting, for each of them, a *sequence of bits* whose length depends on the frequency of that letter (or of that group of letters) in the input text $T$. For example if the text to be compressed is the one of the previous example, namely $T = $ LABELLABALLA (where we have removed the spaces between the words for the sake of simplicity), then a statistical compressor could compute the following encoding: A $\rightarrow$ 01, B $\rightarrow$ 001, E $\rightarrow$ 000, and L $\rightarrow$ 1. Notice that this encoding follows the golden rule mentioned in the previous section because the code of the letter L is shorter than the code of the rarer letter B, whereas the letters B and E are both assigned a code of three bits each given that they have almost the same frequency in $T$. The body of the corresponding compressed text $T_C$ is then 1 01 001 000 1 1 01 001 01 1 1 01, where spaces are shown for better visualization of each letter code. It has a length of 22 bits, which is shorter than the 24 bits taken by the previous compressor, that assigned fixed-length codes to each letter.

Although this code assigns a *variable-length sequence of bits* to each individual letter, it is still *uniquely decodable* in the sense that it is possible to recognize the code of each single letter in $T_C$ without any ambiguity during its rightward scanning. This property derives from the fact that the proposed code is *prefix free*, namely, the codes of each pair of letters differ by at least one bit. In our example, the code 01 of A and the code 000 of B differ in the second bit when left-aligned; similarly, the

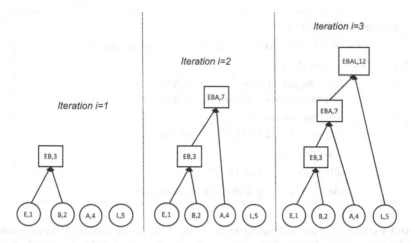

**Fig. 10.1** The evolution of the tree $\mathcal{T}$ during the execution of the Huffman algorithm on the text $T = \text{LABELLABALLA}$.

code 1 of L and the code 01 of A differ in the first bit. This can be verified for every pair of letter codes in our previous example.

At this point it is natural to ask how we have derived this efficient code and whether it is possible to design a better code that encodes $T$ in fewer than 22 bits. The answers to these questions were both provided by David A. Huffman in 1952, when he was a student at the Massachusetts Institute of Technology (MIT). His algorithm, whose pseudocode is shown in Figure 10.2, is a milestone in Data Compression; therefore, we will dedicate the rest of this section to describing it.

The algorithm constructs a binary tree $\mathcal{T}$ starting from its leaves that represent the distinct letters occurring in the text $T$. In our example (see Figure 10.1), the tree is built over four leaves that are labeled with the letters A, B, E, L and their number of occurrences in $T$. For example, the leaf corresponding to the letter A also contains the number 4 because A occurs four times in $T$. In general, a leaf $u$ is labeled with a pair $\langle \Sigma[u], F[u] \rangle$ where $\Sigma[u]$ is the letter associated with $u$ and $F[u]$ is its frequency in $T$; hence, the leaf corresponding to the letter A is labeled with the pair $\langle \text{A}, 4 \rangle$.

In order to complete the construction of the binary tree $\mathcal{T}$, the Huffman algorithm creates a set $\mathcal{S}$ that consists initially of the pairs $\langle \Sigma[u], F[u] \rangle$ labeling all of its $|\Sigma|$ leaves (in our example $|\Sigma| = 4$, line 1 of the pseudocode of Figure 10.2). Then, the algorithm executes a **for**-loop (lines 2–6) that consists of two main parts: the first one updates the set $\mathcal{S}$ (lines 3–6), while the second one updates the tree $\mathcal{T}$ correspondingly (line 7). More precisely, in the first part, the algorithm chooses in $\mathcal{S}$ the two pairs (and thus the two nodes) with the minimum frequency: in the first iteration of our running example these pairs correspond to the two leaves $u = \langle \text{E}, 1 \rangle$ and $v = \langle \text{B}, 2 \rangle$, which have a total frequency of three. This choice leads the algorithm to create a new node $w$ labeled $\Sigma[w] = \text{EB}$, obtained by concatenating the letters labeling $u$ and $v$, and the frequency $F[w] = F[\text{E}] + F[\text{B}] = 1 + 2 = 3$, obtained

**program** HUFFMAN $(\Sigma, F)$

1.    $\mathscr{S} \leftarrow$ set of pairs associated with the $|\Sigma|$ leaves of the tree $\mathscr{T}$;

2.    **for** $i \leftarrow 1$ **to** $|\Sigma| - 1$

3.       choose the pair of nodes $u, v \in \mathscr{S}$ such that
         the frequencies $F[u]$ and $F[v]$ minimum in $\mathscr{S}$;

4.       create the node $w$ with
         $\Sigma[w] \leftarrow \Sigma[u] \cdot \Sigma[v], F[w] \leftarrow F[u] + F[v]$;

5.       cancel the pairs of $u, v$ from $\mathscr{S}$;

6.       add the pair $\langle \Sigma[w], F[w] \rangle$ to $\mathscr{S}$;

7.       insert in $\mathscr{T}$ the node $w$ as parent of the nodes $u, v$;

**Fig. 10.2** Pseudocode of the Huffman algorithm to statistically compress a text $T$. For each node $u$ of the binary tree $\mathscr{T}$ we denote with $\Sigma[u]$ the sequence of letters associated with $u$, which consists of a single letter if $u$ is a leaf, and we denote with $F[u]$ the total frequency in the text $T$ of the letters in $\Sigma[u]$. The notation $\Sigma[u] \cdot \Sigma[v]$ denotes the concatenation of these two sequences of letters.

by summing the frequency of the chosen nodes (line 4). The pairs corresponding to the nodes $u$ and $v$ are then removed from the set $\mathscr{S}$ (line 5), and the new pair $\langle \text{EB}, 3 \rangle$ associated with node $w$ is added to $\mathscr{S}$ (line 6). This completes the update of $\mathscr{S}$ that, as a result of the first iteration, will consist of three pairs: $\langle \text{EB}, 3 \rangle$, $\langle \text{A}, 4 \rangle$, and $\langle \text{L}, 5 \rangle$. It is clear that in the subsequent iterations the set $\mathscr{S}$ will include pairs whose first component consists of a *sequence of letters* and whose second component consists of the *total frequency* in $T$ of those letters.

In the second part of the **for**-loop (line 7), the algorithm updates the structure of the tree $\mathscr{T}$ by inserting the node $w$ as the parent of the two nodes $u$ and $v$. This completes the first iteration of the **for**-loop whose resulting tree is illustrated in the leftmost part of Figure 10.1. We notice that the three pairs present in $\mathscr{S}$ label the three nodes of tree $\mathscr{T}$ that do not yet have a parent.

At this point, the Huffman algorithm repeats the **for**-loop for another iteration by selecting the new pair of nodes with the minimum frequency. In our example, these are the nodes labeled $\langle \text{EB}, 3 \rangle$ and $\langle \text{A}, 4 \rangle$. Then it deletes these two nodes from $\mathscr{S}$ and it creates a new node in $\mathscr{T}$ which is labeled with the pair $\langle \text{EBA}, 7 \rangle$ obtained by "merging" the labels and summing the frequencies of the two selected pairs. This node becomes the parent of $\langle \text{EB}, 3 \rangle$ and $\langle \text{A}, 4 \rangle$. The tree resulting from this second iteration of the **for**-loop is illustrated in the central part of Figure 10.1. The set $\mathscr{S}$ consists now of two pairs $\langle \text{EBA}, 7 \rangle$ and $\langle \text{L}, 5 \rangle$ and, again, these nodes are the ones missing the parent in $\mathscr{T}$.

The third, and last, iteration of the **for**-loop selects the two remaining pairs in $\mathscr{S}$ and "merges" them into the pair $\langle \text{EBAL}, 12 \rangle$ that becomes the label of the root of the final tree $\mathscr{T}$ (shown in the rightmost part of Figure 10.1). The number of iterations executed by the Huffman algorithm is equal to $|\Sigma| - 1 = 4 - 1 = 3$, because at every iteration it cancels two pairs from set $\mathscr{S}$ and adds one pair to it, thus reducing the

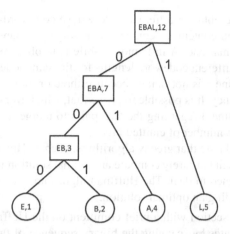

**Fig. 10.3** The tree $\mathcal{T}$ created by the Huffman algorithm applied to the text $T = $ LABELLABALLA. The tree arcs are labeled with the bits 0 (left arc) and 1 (right arc), and the Huffman code for a letter is derived by concatenating the sequence of bits encountered over the path that connects the root of $\mathcal{T}$ with the leaf corresponding to that letter.

cardinality of $\mathcal{S}$ by one unit. There are three iterations ($= |\Sigma| - 1$) and not four because the algorithm stops when $\mathcal{S}$ consists of just one node, namely the root of $\mathcal{T}$. The algorithmic scheme implemented by the Huffman algorithm is known as *greedy* because it selects at each iteration the pair of nodes that *(greedily) minimize* an objective function equal to the sum of the frequencies of the selected nodes.

It is easy to derive a uniquely decodable code from the binary tree $\mathcal{T}$. Label each tree arc with one bit, conventionally 0 for the left arc outgoing from a node and 1 for the right arc. The Huffman code for a letter is then constructed as the sequence of bits that label the arcs lying on the downward path connecting the root of $\mathcal{T}$ with the leaf labeled with that letter. Referring to the Huffman tree in Figure 10.3, we derive the following code: E $\to 000$, B $\to 001$, A $\to 01$, and L $\to 1$. This code is exactly the one that we proposed at the beginning of this section.

A few observations are in order at this point. The first observation is that the Huffman code is *prefix free* because each pair of leaves descends from a distinct path, and thus their corresponding letters are assigned binary codes that differ by at least one bit. The second observation is that the length of the codewords assigned to the letters of $\Sigma$ is the *optimal* one for the text $T$, in the sense that any other code that encoded the letters of $\Sigma$ via binary sequences would result in a compressed body not shorter than 22 bits. The proof of this optimality property is too sophisticated to be reported in this book. Here we are content to give an intuition of why this property holds: the Huffman code fully respects the golden rule of data compression because the letters with the smallest frequencies occur deeper in the tree $\mathcal{T}$ given that they are selected earlier in the tree construction process (line 3); thus they descend from longer tree paths and are assigned to longer codewords. The third observation is that, if we change the assignment of bits to tree arcs, by exchanging the role of left/right arcs and bits $0/1$, we obtain a different code whose codewords preserve the same length but change their content. Of course, the quality of the new code is unchanged so it is again an optimal one. A little more subtle is to observe that optimal codes may exist that have different codeword lengths for the same letters. This case occurs when the choice at line 3 is not unique because three or more pairs exist that have the same total frequency. It is possible to prove that, whichever choice the Huffman algorithm makes in line 3 regarding the two pairs to merge, the final code will be always optimal in the number of emitted bits.

Finally, we should note that greedy algorithms, such as Huffman's, are typically very simple and elegant but rarely compute an optimal solution for the problem with which they are designed to deal. The Huffman algorithm is a perfect example of a greedy algorithm finding an optimal solution.

We conclude this section with a brief comment on the Huffman decompression algorithm. This operates by scanning the binary sequence of the compressed body and using each bit to navigate the arcs of the tree $\mathcal{T}$ starting from its root. In our example in Figure 10.3 the compressed body is $1010010001101001011101$, so the first bit examined is $1$ and it makes the decompressor take the right arc outgoing from the root of $\mathcal{T}$, thus reaching the leaf labeled with the letter L. This letter is output as the first letter of the decompressed text, and the process is repeated over the remaining bits restarting the tree navigation from the root. Now the decompressor reads the next two bits $01$ and percolates the left arc going from the root to the node labeled $\langle \text{EBA}, 7 \rangle$, and then the right arc reaching the leaf labeled with the letter A. This letter is output as the second letter of the decompressed text, and the process is repeated again over the remaining bits restarting each time from the tree's root. It is easy to notice that every bit read from the compressed sequence determines the visit of one arc in the tree $\mathcal{T}$, so that the overall number of arc percolations is *linear* in the length of the compressed text, and thus it is computationally optimal because in any case we have to reconstruct $T$ by reading $T_C$.

We caution the reader not to be induced by this optimality to conclude that the proposed algorithm is efficient in practice. The complexity evaluation has been done on the number of bits read and thus it does not take into consideration the fact that the navigation driven by the bits of $T_C$ could occur over a large tree spread over various memory levels of larger and larger size but slower and slower access speed. Consequently, as we have already observed in the section on "Big Data" in Chapter 7, the number of bits read and arcs percolated provides only a *very rough* approximation of the time taken by the decompressor to reconstruct $T$. Therefore, it would be more proper to adopt the two-level memory model described in that section that accounts every navigation operation as a slow cache or I/O-miss. The proposed decompressor executes a linear number of I/O-misses, which is slow. There are variants of the Huffman algorithm that reduce significantly the number of I/O-misses by properly laying down the tree in the memory levels, but they are too sophisticated in their algorithmic ideas to be even sketched out in this book.

In the next sections we describe two compressors that prove to be more efficient and effective than the Huffman algorithm, both in the compression and decompression phases, while still being elegant and simple in their design. These compressors introduce a new algorithmic scheme that is the one now underlying the design of modern compressors. First, they transform the text $T$ into a new *text $T'$*, possibly defined over a different alphabet, which is *more compressible* than the original $T$. Next, they use the Huffman algorithm or any other efficient statistical compressor to encode $T'$ in a succinct way. The key algorithmic challenge here is to design a transformation from $T$ to $T'$ that is *invertible* ($T'$ must be decompressible), efficiently computable (the [de]compressor should be fast), and effective in obtaining a body $T'_C$ that is more succinct than $T_C$ (the compression ratio should be smaller than it would be using the Huffman algorithm directly over $T$). This design has many possible implementations. We will describe the most well-known ones that actually are the state-of-the-art in many applicative settings.

## 10.2 Dictionary-Based Compressors

We have previously observed that, in the presence of texts with *structured and long regularities*, such as in the text $T =$ AAABBB, a statistical compressor based on the frequencies of individual letters fails to discover and exploit them because the two letters A and B have the same frequency. As a result, the achieved compression ratio would be the same as for a *scrambled* text that contains the same number of *A*s and *B*s. An elegant solution to this problem was proposed at the end of the 1970s by two researchers – Abraham Lempel and Jacob Ziv – who introduced a compression scheme that was *mainly syntactic*. Today, this solution is at the algorithmic core of most of the compressors in use, from gzip, pkzip, and lzma, just to cite a few, up to the compressors recently introduced by Google, such as Snappy and Brotli. The key algorithmic idea underlying the so called *LZ-compressors* (from the initials of the inventors) is simple and elegant, but the proof of their compression ratio's optimality is complicated and thus we do not report it here. The compressor designed by Lempel and Ziv operates in two phases:

1. The first phase transforms the text $T$ into a sequence of pairs, denoted with $\mathscr{C}$; each pair represents a sequence of letters (*substring*) occurring in $T$;
2. the second phase squeezes $\mathscr{C}$ by applying a statistical compressor (which may be Huffman's) to the values assumed by its pairs' components.

In this section we will concentrate only on the first phase, which mimics a sort of *cut-and-paste process*, and we will illustrate its working in Figure 10.4 on our exemplar text $T =$ LABELLABALLA. The pseudocode is reported in Figure 10.5.

The algorithm divides the text $T =$ LABELLABALLA into a series of substrings L-A-B-E-L-LAB-A-LLA, here separated by dashes to facilitate their identification by the reader. Each substring consists either of a single letter, when it first occurs in $T$ (lines 4–6), or of a sequence of $\ell \geq 1$ letters that have previously repeated in the text $T$ (lines 7–10). In the first case, the single letter $T[i]$ is encoded as the pair $\langle 0, T[i] \rangle$: this occurs, for example, in the first four iterations illustrated in Figure 10.4, which generate the pairs $\langle 0, \text{L} \rangle$, $\langle 0, \text{A} \rangle$, $\langle 0, \text{B} \rangle$ and $\langle 0, \text{E} \rangle$. In the second

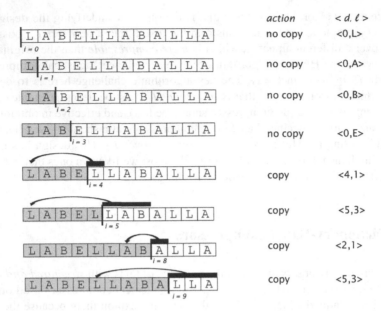

**Fig. 10.4** Transforming the text $T = $ LABELLABALLA into a sequence of pairs $\mathscr{C}$ representing either the first occurrence of a single letter (first component set to 0) or the copy of a text substring (first component set to a value larger than 0). The arrows show where the text substring is copied from within $T$. A copied substring may consist of a single letter.

case, in which the letter $T[i]$ and possibly some of its following letters have previously occurred in $T$, the algorithm generates the pair $\langle d, \ell \rangle$, which identifies the repetition of the substring $T[i : i + \ell - 1]$ at distance $d$ from the currently examined letter $T[i]$. In Figure 10.4 the fifth letter L of $T$ appears for the second time and thus it is represented with the pair $\langle 4, 1 \rangle$, which identifies a substring of length 1 that can be copied from a position which is 4 letters back in $T$ (shown by an arrow in the figure). This case could be also encoded as $\langle 0, L \rangle$ without changing the number of pairs in $\mathscr{C}$, but hereafter we use the copy operation whenever possible.

In order to minimize the number of pairs that are output, the Lempel-Ziv algorithm searches at each iteration of the **while**-loop for the *longest* repeated substring (line 3). The reader can verify the correctness of the running example reported in Figure 10.4 and the property that no other *parsing* of $T$ is possible that outputs a smaller number of pairs. Here we are dealing with another *greedy algorithm* that is optimal with respect to another objective function; in this case, the number of output pairs for the input text $T$.

It is not so easy to provide an efficient implementation of line 3. Therefore, we limit ourselves to presenting a simple solution and commenting on its efficiency to provide an idea of the main difficulties involved in its design. It consists of scanning $T$ backward from position $i$, and computing at each previous position $j$ the longest common substring starting at positions $i$ and $j$; namely, it computes the largest value

---

**program** LZ_Encoding $(T)$

1.     $i \leftarrow 0, \mathscr{C} \leftarrow \emptyset$;

2.     **while** $(i < n)$

3.         Find the longest string $T[i, i+\ell-1]$ that repeats before position $i$ in $T$;

4.         **if** $(\ell = 0)$            // $T[i]$ occurs for the first time here

5.             Append to $\mathscr{C}$ the pair $\langle 0, T[i] \rangle$;

6.             $i \leftarrow i+1$;

7.         **else**              // it is a repeated copy of length $\ell > 0$

8.             Let $T[j, j+\ell-1]$ be a copy of $T[i, i+\ell-1]$, with $j < i$;

9.             Append to $\mathscr{C}$ the pair $\langle i-j, \ell \rangle$;

10.            $i \leftarrow i+\ell$;

11.     Statistically compress the first component of $\mathscr{C}$'s pairs;

12.     Statistically compress the second component of $\mathscr{C}$'s pairs;

---

**Fig. 10.5** Pseudocode of the Lempel-Ziv algorithm to transform the text $T$ into a sequence of pairs, denoted by $\mathscr{C}$, and its subsequent statistical compression, possibly via the Huffman algorithm.

$\ell_j$ such that $T[i : i+\ell_j - 1] = T[j : j+\ell_j - 1]$. This requires a character-by-character comparison; hence, the time complexity is proportional to $\ell_j$. After inspecting all positions $j < i$, the algorithm computes the maximum among all lengths $\ell_j$; this gives the value $\ell = \max_{j<i} \ell_j$ indicated in line 3 of the pseudocode in Figure 10.5.

This algorithm is slow because it executes two nested loops – the external one over the iterator $i$ and the internal one over the iterator $j < i$ – which examine about $n^2$ pairs of positions $i, j$, and for each such pair it takes $\ell_j < n$ steps to compute the longest match $T[i : i+\ell_j - 1] = T[j : j+\ell_j - 1]$. This yields a number of steps that grows *cubically* with the length of $T$ to be compressed, and hence is too slow even for texts of just a few megabytes. Some speed can be gained by limiting the backward scanning of $j$ to a *bounded window* of positions, say $W$, and thus setting $\ell = \max_{i-W \le j < i} \ell_j$. This is exactly the choice made by the well-known compressor gzip, in which $W$ is set from tens to hundreds of thousands of characters. The size of $W$ induces a trade-off between time efficiency and compression effectiveness: on the one hand, it *speeds up* the implementation of line 3 in the pseudocode in Figure 10.5 by reducing the time efficiency to a quadratic complexity; but, on the other hand, it could *increase* the number of pairs in $\mathscr{C}$ and thus the space occupied by the compressed text because the algorithm could miss some longer copies that might occur outside of the window examined.

Looking at our example in Figure 10.4 we notice that, by limiting the search to a window of size $W = 4$, the algorithm would miss the pair $\langle 5, 3 \rangle$ which denotes a copy of the substring LAB at a distance of five. As a result, this substring would be parsed into three substrings L-A-B, which would be encoded as the pairs: $\langle 1, 1 \rangle$, $\langle 0, A \rangle$ and $\langle 0, B \rangle$. The same issue would occur for the last pair $\langle 5, 3 \rangle$ referring to

```
program LZ_decoding (𝒞)
1.      i ← 0;
2.      while 𝒞 ≠ ∅
3.          Let ⟨a, b⟩ be the first pair of 𝒞;
4.          if (a = 0)                              // it is the first occurrence of letter b
5.              T[i] ← b, i ← i + 1;
6.          else                    // it is a copy of the b-long substring at distance a
7.              for k ← 0 to b − 1
8.                  T[i + k] ← T[i − a + k];
9.              i ← i + b;
```

**Fig. 10.6** Pseudocode of the Lempel-Ziv decompression algorithm that transforms the sequence of pairs $\mathscr{C}$ back to the original text $T$.

the substring LLA that would be thus parsed as the pairs: $\langle 4, 1 \rangle$, $\langle 1, 1 \rangle$ and $\langle 3, 1 \rangle$. In general, a small variation in the window size can induce a large change in the length of $\mathscr{C}$, depending on the frequency and distribution of the substring copies in $T$.

It is easy to design the *backward transformation* that reconstructs the original text $T$ from the compressed file $T_C$. The transform first adopts a proper statistical decompressor to derive $\mathscr{C}$'s pairs from the binary sequence $T_C$, then it substitutes each pair with its corresponding substring. This means that it writes the letter $b$, if the pair to be decoded has the form $\langle 0, b \rangle$ (lines 4–5 of the pseudocode in Figure 10.6), or writes the substring $T[i - a, i - a + b - 1]$, if the pair to be decoded has the form $\langle a, b \rangle$ with $a > 0$ denoting the distance of the copy and $b$ denoting now its length. A crucial observation relates to the special case in which the length $b$ of the copied substring is larger than the distance $a$ from which the copy must be executed. This actually means that the two substrings, the copy-source and the copy-destination, involved in the cut-and-paste process overlap each other. This situation occurs in some special cases, which nonetheless are not very rare in practice. To exemplify, let us consider the simple text $T = $ AAAA which is parsed by the Lempel-Ziv algorithm into the substrings A–AAA thus originating the sequence of pairs $\mathscr{C} = \langle 0, A \rangle \langle 1, 3 \rangle$. The second pair has a copy distance $a = 1$ that is smaller than the length $b = 3$ of the copied substring, and indeed the copy-source $T[0:2]$ overlaps the copied substring $T[1:3]$. Nevertheless lines 7–8 in Figure 10.6 operate correctly because the copy of $T[0:2]$ into $T[1:3]$ is not executed in *one shot* but one letter at a time, so that, when the letter $T[i - a + j]$ is copied into $T[i + j]$, the former letter is available because it has occurred before and thus has already been decompressed.

We conclude the present section with some further considerations about the effectiveness of the compression phase and the efficiency of the decompression phase designed by Lempel and Ziv more than 30 years ago. If the text does not present long repeated substrings, the algorithm achieves a *poor* compression ratio. This occurs either for short texts or for some "pathological" cases in which the source outputting $T$ is one that does not operate by cut-and-paste operations, as seems to be the case in nature with the creation of DNA sequences. The other issue that we wish to briefly address here concerns the presence of *more than one longest copy* of the string $T[i : i + \ell - 1]$ before position $i$ in $T$: when this occurs line 3 would have more than one choice in selecting the string to copy. Typically, the choice falls on the copy *closest* to position $i$, and thus the one at the smallest distance from $T[i]$. This choice is dictated by the observation that the closer the substring to copy is, the more likely it is to find that copy in the fastest cache of the computer, given that it has been examined just a few positions earlier, thus gaining in compression and decompression speeds. However, this takes into account only the speed and not the compression ratio as it could generate different (small) distances that could unfavorably impact the statistical compression executed in line 11 of the pseudocode in Figure 10.5. Consequently, it is not surprising that Google's most recent compressor, named `Brotli`, proposes a very sophisticated and efficient implementation of this elegant compression scheme, which is nowadays adopted in most Web browsers and servers. These issues make the design of efficient and effective LZ-based compressors very difficult and are still an active area of research.

## 10.3 Sort-Based Compressors

The third family of compression algorithms we deal with in this chapter is based on a transform of the input text $T[0 : n - 1]$ into another text $L[0 : n - 1]$, which is a *permutation* of $T$ satisfying the property of being *more compressible* than $T$ by means of the use of known, simple, and fast compressors. This novel approach was publicly disclosed by Mike Burrows and David Wheeler in 1994. However, according to anecdotes, Wheeler had actually discovered this transform many years earlier, when he was a professor at the University of Cambridge and Burrows' Ph.D. adviser, and had proposed it to the latter as his thesis topic! Given the name of its inventors, this transform is universally known as the *Burrows-Wheeler Transform* or, briefly, BWT.

This transform (permutation) is rather surprising in the way it is computed and the properties it guarantees. In this section we will describe all of its features, starting with the *direct BWT*, which transforms the text $T$ into the permuted text $L$, then the *inverse BWT* that reconstructs $T$ from $L$. To be precise, BWT is not a compressor in itself, because the two strings $T$ and $L$ have the same length. However, in the following pages we will attempt to convince the reader that the transformed string $L$ is *highly compressible*. We will do this by means of proper examples and observations that will obviate the need to provide formal and difficult mathematical proofs.

When we talk about the high compressibility of $L$ we refer to the combination of BWT and a series of simple, fast, and effective compressors. This pipeline of transforms and encoders constitutes the well-known software `bzip`, available within all

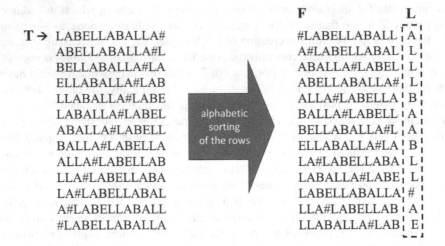

**Fig. 10.7** Burrows-Wheeler transform of the text $T = $ LABELLABALLA. The matrix on the right is obtained from the one on the left by sorting alphabetically its rows, where it is assumed that the symbol # is the first one in the alphabet $\Sigma$. The transformed string $L = $ BWT($T$) is given by the last column of the sorted matrix, identified in the figure with a dashed rectangle.

Linux distributions, which generates compressed files with the extension bz and achieves compression ratios typically smaller than those achieved by gzip.

An example of the computation of the direct-BWT is illustrated in Figure 10.7 by adopting the running exemplar text $T = $ LABELLABALLA. On the left side of the figure we find a square matrix, $M$, in which the first row is the text $T$ extended with the special symbol # assumed to be the first character in alphabetic order: i.e., the first row is LABELLABALLA#. The second row is obtained by *cyclically rotating to the left* the first row: this means, moving the first letter L to the end of the first row after the special symbol #, thus originating the string ABELLABALLA#L. The left-cyclic rotation is applied to each following row, thus creating the matrix $M$, whose size is $(n+1) \times (n+1)$ because of the addition of the special symbol # to the text $T$ that has length $n$.

The matrix $M$ satisfies two interesting and useful properties that the reader can easily verify in Figure 10.7:

(i) every row of the matrix $M$ is formed by all the letters of the string $T$#, because every row is a cyclic rotation of that string;
(ii) every column of the matrix $M$ is formed by all the letters of $T$# because through every column passes every row with a "distinct" letter given its cyclic rotation.

The BWT of the text $T$ is obtained by sorting alphabetically the rows of the matrix $M$, and then taking the last column of the sorted matrix. In the example in Figure 10.7, the result of BWT is the string $L = $ ALLLBAABLL#AE, which is the last column of the matrix shown on the right side of the figure. We notice that $L$ contains *all and only* the letters of $T\#$ because it is one of its permutations (property (ii)); the first column of the sorted matrix, denoted with $F$, is the alphabetically sorted permutation of *all and only* the letters of $T\#$ and thus it is a permutation of $L$: $F = \#\texttt{AAAABBELLLLL}$. In the rest of this section we will explicitly refer to $F$ and $L$ because the algorithms computing or exploiting BWT strongly hinge on them.

In terms of time efficiency, we notice that BWT's computation requires a sorting step executed over $(n+1)$ rows of $(n+1)$ letters each. In Chapter 7 we dealt widely with the problem of sorting $z$ items and proposed the MERGE_SORT algorithm, which requires $z \log_2 z$ comparisons in the worst case to sort them. In the case of BWT, it is $z = n+1$, because we have to sort $(n+1)$ rows, so that MERGE_SORT computes the sorted matrix by executing $(n+1) \log_2(n+1)$ comparisons between pairs of rows. Since each row-comparison involves no more than $(n+1)$ letter comparisons, MERGE_SORT executes at most $(n+1)^2 \log_2(n+1)$ *single letter* comparisons to compute the sorted matrix. Therefore, the time cost is more than quadratic in the length of the original text $T$. To this time inefficiency we should add a more significant (quadratic) space inefficiency due to the construction and use of the matrix $M$, which makes the previous algorithm inapplicable to a real context even for short texts; for example, the BWT of a 1 Megabyte text ($= 2^{20}$ byte) would need a space of 1 Terabyte ($= (2^{20})^2 = 2^{40}$ byte) to be computed.

In fact, the algorithms used in the available implementations of the BWT do not pass through the *explicit* construction of the matrix $M$ but use more sophisticated data structures that keep it *implicit*, and thus are more succinct in space and faster in time. In order to keep our exposition simple, we cannot go into the technical details of these solutions, which are rather complex. Here we mention only that these data structures are used also as the core algorithmic components of search engines over genomic sequences and, in general, of many bioinformatics applications.

Let us now concentrate on the inverse BWT-transform, whose pseudocode is reported in Figure 10.8. It is a hermetic algorithm, probably the most sophisticated and elegant algorithm we report in this book. However, we believe that the effort required to understand this algorithm is fully justified and will greatly repay the reader who attempts it. This algorithm uses two iterators: $i$ moves backward over text $T$ starting from its last position $n-1$ (line 1), and $r$ moves over the string $L$ driven by the need to find the letter $L[r]$ to write in $T[i]$.

Line 1 initially sets $r = 0$ and $i = n-1$, so $r$ points correctly to the first row of the sorted matrix, which is equal to $\#T = \#\texttt{LABELLABALLA}$ (see Figure 10.7): this way, $L[0] = T[n-1] = \texttt{A}$. Line 2 builds a vector $C$ indexed (for simplicity of exposition) by the letters of $T\#$ so that, in our example, we have $C[\texttt{E}] = 7$ because the first occurrence of the letter $\texttt{E}$ is at position 7 of vector $F$ (recall that this means the eighth row of the matrix because we assume that vector and matrix positions are counted from zero). Then the algorithm computes the string $F$ by sorting alphabetically $L$'s letters (according to property (ii)). In our running example this sorting gets $F = \#\texttt{AAAABBELLLLL}$, so that the algorithm can easily derive the vector $C$ by scanning $F$ and setting $C[\#] = 0$, $C[A] = 1$, $C[B] = 5$, $C[E] = 7$ and $C[L] = 8$.

Given the strings $L, F$ and the vector $C$, the **while**-loop at lines 3–6 reconstructs *backward* the text $T$ (line 4) by decreasing the iterator $i$ from the value $n-1$ (which

---

**program** INVERSE_BWT $(L)$

1.    $i \leftarrow n - 1; r \leftarrow 0;$

2.    **for** $(\sigma \in \Sigma)$

        $C[\sigma] \leftarrow$ position of the first occurrence of the letter $\sigma$ in $F$;

3.    **while** $(i \geq 0)$

4.        $T[i] \leftarrow L[r];$

5.        $i \leftarrow i - 1;$

6.        $r \leftarrow C[L[r]] + \texttt{Rank}(L, r) - 1;$

---

**Fig. 10.8** Pseudocode of the algorithm that reconstructs the original text $T$ from its BWT $L$. The function $\texttt{Rank}(L, r)$ computes the number of occurrences of the letter $L[r]$ within the prefix string $L[0 : r]$. Remember that $F$ is the first column of the matrix $M$ sorted alphabetically.

is the position of the last letter in $T$, line 5). It then moves the iterator $r$ according to a peculiar property that ties the letters in $L$ with the letters in $F$ given that both strings are permutations of $T\#$, and thus consist of the same letters with the same multiplicities (property (ii)). Referring to our running example in Figure 10.9 we notice that the third occurrence of the letter A in $F$ (i.e. $F[3]$) and the third occurrence of the letter A in $L$ (i.e. $L[6]$) are the "same" letter of the text $T$; in fact, they both correspond to its second letter $T[1] = $ A. More precisely, the letter $F[3]$ is the first letter of the fourth row of the sorted matrix, namely the string ABELLABALLA#L, and, given that every row is a cyclic left-rotation of $T\#$, the letter $F[3] = $ A precedes in $T$ the substring BELLABALLA and follows the letter $L[3] = $ L in $T$. The "same" letter A occurs at the end of the seventh row of the sorted matrix, which equals the string BELLABALLA#LA, and we have that $L[6] = $ A is the letter that precedes the string BELLABALLA in $T$. We can therefore conclude that $F[3] = L[6] = $ A. As a further example shown in Figure 10.9, let us look at the first occurrence of the letter B in $F$ (i.e. $F[5]$) that is the "same" letter as the first occurrence of the letter B in $L$ (i.e. $L[4]$): this is the letter B that precedes the substring ALLA and follows the substring LABELLA in the text $T$, as the reader can verify by left-rotating cyclically the sixth and the fifth rows of the sorted matrix.

These two examples allow us to derive a *key property* of BWT:

(iii) The $j$-th occurrence of the letter $\sigma$ in the string $F$ equals the $j$-th occurrence of the same letter in string $L$. The value $j$ is called the rank of $\sigma$ in $F$ and in $L$.

    This property states that two occurrences of the same letter *preserve their relative order* in both strings, as one can infer from the previous example: the third A in $F$ equals the third A in $L$; the first B in $F$ equals the first B in $L$ (see Figure 10.9). On the other hand, distinct letters may *exchange* their order when considering their occurrences in $F$ and in $L$: this is the case for the letters A and B in the previous examples in which the letter $F[3] = $ A precedes the letter $F[5] = $ B in string $F$ (by

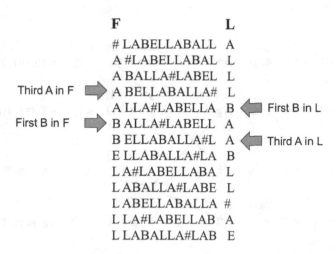

**Fig. 10.9** Two examples of correspondence between one letter of $L$ and the same letter of $F$.

the way, this is obvious because $F$ is alphabetically sorted), but the same letters are exchanged in string $L$ as $L[4] = $ B precedes $L[6] = $ A.

In order to keep the reading sufficiently simple, we leave out the formal proof of this property and encourage the reader to verify its correctness over all the other letters of $T$ using the example in Figure 10.9. Property (iii) is very important from an operational point of view because it provides a simple method to *jump* from a letter in string $L$ to the "same" letter in string $F$ without needing the matrix $M$, and instead using only the vector $C$ and the function rank, which accesses string $L$ as detailed in line 6 of the pseudocode in Figure 10.8.

For completeness we report in Figure 10.10 a detailed simulation of the first five lines executed by the algorithm INVERSE_BWT. Basically, this algorithm performs two main operations: the first one jumps from a letter in $L$, i.e. $L[r]$, to the same letter in $F$, i.e. $F[r']$ (property (iii)); the second operation selects the next letter $L[r]$ as the one that ends the row $r'$ (property (i)), and this letter is written into $T[i]$. The arrows in Figure 10.10 pictorially illustrate both operations: we use solid and right-to-left arrows for the first type of operation (i.e. $F[r'] \leftarrow L[r]$), and we use dashed and left-to-right arrows for the second type of operation (i.e. $F[r'] \rightarrow L[r'] = $ the new $L[r]$). Therefore, lines 4–6 allow the algorithm to jump from row $r$ to row $r'$ and write $L[r']$ into $T[i]$ thus correctly setting the letter that precedes $T[i+1] = L[r]$. The iterator $i$ is then decremented thus reconstructing $T$ from right to left (i.e. from position $n-1$ up to position 0).

Let us exemplify the description of the pseudocode by illustrating the first two iterations of the **while**-loop for the running example in Figure 10.10.

- Initially, $i = n - 1 = 11$ and $r = 0$ (i.e. top-right of Figure 10.10).

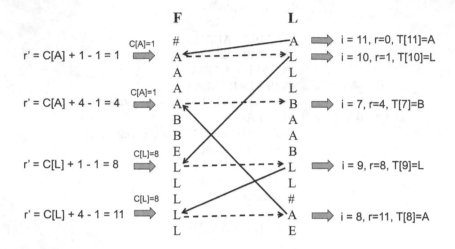

**Fig. 10.10** Simulation of the algorithm INVERSE_BWT($L$) for the first five iterations: on the right are shown the values of $i$ and $r$ assumed in the **while**-loop, and the assignment $T[i] = L[r]$ (line 4); on the left are indicated the new values $r'$ assumed by $r$ at line 6, to be used in the next iteration of the **while**-loop. Vector $C$ and string $F$ can be derived from string $L$ which is an input parameter of the algorithm. Notice the *jumps* from $L$ to $F$ (solid arrows) and from $F$ to $L$ (dashed arrows) that pictorially describe the way the algorithm updates the iterator $r$ and assigns $T[i] = L[r]$.

- The algorithm enters the body of the **while**-loop and executes line 4 by setting $T[11] = L[0] = $ A, which is correctly the last letter of $T$.
- Line 5 decrements the iterator $i$ by assigning to it the value $11 - 1 = 10$.
- Line 6 computes the new row $r' = C[$A$] + \text{Rank}(L, 0) - 1 = 1 + 1 - 1 = 1$. As we did earlier, we distinguish, for simplicity of description, between the new row $r'$ and the current row $r$ (whereas line 6 uses just $r$, which is updated in a single step). So, as stated previously, the first letter $F[r'] = F[1] = $ A of the new row $r' = 1$ is equal to the last letter $L[r] = L[0] = $ A of the current row $r = 0$. In fact that is the first occurrence of the letter A in $L$ and in $F$ (property (iii)).

• In the next iteration of the **while**-loop, $i = 10 \geq 0$ and $r = r' = 1$, so the body (lines 4–6) is executed.

- Line 4 sets $T[10] = L[1] = $ L, which is the penultimate letter of the text $T$.
- Line 5 decrements the iterator $i$ by setting $i = 10 - 1 = 9$.
- Line 6 computes the new row $r' = C[$L$] + \text{Rank}(L, 1) - 1 = 8 + 1 - 1 = 8$. Notice that $F[r'] = F[8] = $ L and the sequence of equalities $F[r'] = F[8] = L[1] = L[r]$ holds because that is the first occurrence of the letter L in $L$ and in $F$ (property (iii)).

• The reconstruction of $T$ continues backward until the **while**-loop gets to $i = 0$. At that point $r = 3$ because the fourth row contains as its last letter the first one of the text $T$, so line 4 assigns correctly $T[0] = L[3] = $ L and line 5 sets $i = -1$ thus making the algorithm exit the **while**-loop and stop!

Before concluding this section let us briefly comment on the correctness of line 6 in mapping the letters of $L$ to the same letters of $F$. We have already noted, for the example in Figure 10.9, that the third occurrence of the letter A in $L$ (i.e. $L[6]$) equals the third occurrence of the letter A in $F$ (i.e. $F[3]$). Line 6 derives the mapping $L[6] \to F[3]$ by summing two quantities that we call base and rank of A, defined as follows:

- The base of letter A is the position of the first occurrence of that letter in string $F$, and this equals the number of occurrences of letters in $T\#$ that are alphabetically smaller than A (and therefore occur before A in $F$). This value is immediately available in $C[$A$]$ because it has been computed in line 2 of the pseudocode of INVERSE_BWT($L$). In the running example the base of A is 1 because it is preceded only by the special symbol #.
- The rank of letter $L[6] = $ A is the number of occurrences of that letter in $L[0:6]$. This value is computed by the function rank($L, 6$) and it is 3 because A occurs three times in $L[0:6]$.

Given the base ($= 1$) and the rank ($= 3$) of $L[6] = $ A, we can compute the row that starts with that same letter by *summing* the two quantities: $1 + 3 = 4$ and subtracting $1$ ($= 4 - 1 = 3$) because the vector's positions are counted from zero. In fact, we get to the fourth row where $F[3] = L[6] = $ A.

Let us develop another example by taking the letter $L[4] = $ B in Figure 10.8. This letter has a base equal to 5 (because $T$ contains one occurrence of # and four occurrences of A) and rank($B, 4$) $= 1$ (because B occurs only once in $L[0:4]$). Applying the formula of line 6 we compute the value $5 + 1 - 1 = 5$ which is the correct position of the letter $L[4] = $ B in string $F$, as illustrated in the figure.

Line 6 of INVERSE_BWT actually works for any other letter in string $L$, as the reader can verify by looking at the other letters of the text in Figure 10.8.

## 10.4 Concluding Remarks

The greater compressibility of string $L$ compared to string $T$, which we claimed at the beginning of this chapter, is not evident from our examples. The intuition that this claim holds true, which is all we can provide in order to keep this text simple, derives from an observation that is obvious in linguistic texts but can be extended to many other file types created or accessed daily by Web users.

In a linguistic text the occurrence of a letter "depends" on the letters that precede it, or follow it, in the text. For example the letter H is surely followed in an Italian text by a vowel and preceded by G, C, A, or a space; similarly, in English the letter H is probably followed by a vowel and preceded only by T, W, or a few other letters. If instead of a single letter we consider the bigram TH then, in English, the letters following it are most probably vowels. If the following letter is, say, E, then the bigram TH is technically called *the preceding context* of that occurrence of E, and the bigram HE is called *the following context* of that occurrence of T. The *longer* the context, the fewer the *distinct* letters that can follow or precede that context in a linguistic text.

As a result, if we compute the BWT of a linguistic text, the rows of the sorted matrix that start with HE will be adjacent and they will have at the end (hence in $L$) the letters that precede the context HE in the input text $T$. These will probably be a space, T, E, D, N, or a few others. *A fortiori* the rows that start with the longer context HEA will be adjacent in the sorted matrix and they will have at the end (hence in $L$) the letters that precede HEA in $T$, such as E, T, or few others. Therefore, the following should not surprise the reader: the longer the prefix shared by these rows, the fewer the number of distinct letters at the end of the rows, because these letters in $L$ will be preceded in $T$ by that (longer and longer) shared context.

Therefore, we can conclude that the sorted order of the rows of $M$ imposes some kind of *locality* on the distribution of the letters in the string $L$, in the sense that letters close together in $L$ will be probably the same or there will only be a *few distinct ones* because they precede contexts that may share many characters since these rows are close in the alphabetically sorted order. This rough observation, which can be made mathematically precise and formally proved, is the key property underlying the design of data compressors that hinge on the Burrows-Wheeler transform by processing the string $L$ with encoding techniques that suitably deploy this kind of *locality* in the distribution of the letters.

BWT-based compressors often *perform* better than those based on the Lempel-Ziv approach in terms of compression ratio. On the other hand, however, they turn out to be significantly slower in the compression and decompression phases because of the algorithmic complexity induced by the computation of the sorted matrix $M$ or the inversion of string $L$. The sorting of long rows (in compression) and the jumps over $L$ (in decompression) induce *random* accesses to the various memory levels that store the input text, the string $L$, and the auxiliary data structures needed for the underlying computations. From Chapter 7 we know that this pattern of memory access impacts unfavorably the overall performance of sorting algorithms. However, the recent design of new (compressed) data structures and sophisticated encoders, as well as the availability of modern computer memories of larger size and faster access, have permitted the development of compressors based on the Lempel-Ziv paradigm that use longer windows (where copies could be located). This enables dictionary-based compressors to achieve compression ratios close to, or even superior to, the ones achievable with sort-based compressors while still guaranteeing very fast compression and decompression phases. These advancements have made the dictionary-based compressors much more appealing in modern applications that need to compress big datasets, such as LZMA and Brotli.

We hope that this chapter has sufficiently stimulated the curiosity of the reader toward this advanced algorithmic topic that, 70 years after Claude Shannon's pioneering research, still poses many challenging problems that deserve increasing attention by (young) researchers.

# Chapter 11
# Recursion

Do you remember the tournament problem among $n$ players we discussed in Chapter 4? The proposed algorithm, based on the tree of matches (Figures 4.3 and 4.4), goes from the leaves, where all the players are placed, up to the root, where the champion resides, determining and storing in each level the winners of the different rounds. However, the sequence of matches could be defined the other way around, that is, from the root to the leaves, establishing that the tournament is organized as the match between the winners of two tournaments among $n/2$ players allocated to the two halves of the knockout stage; and these two tournaments are equally defined among groups of $n/4$ players, down to the matches between pairs of players in the leaves (as is known, in order to simplify calculations the organizers admit a number of participants equal to a power of two).

This new description of the algorithm is based on the concept of *recursion* that has characterized the science of computation since its inception, assuming a rigorous mathematical form in the twentieth century. Here we will give a pragmatic definition of it, explaining its basic structure, the advantages it can draw, and the difficulties it can create, without going into deep theoretical discussions.

Recursion is based on the possibility that the solution of a problem could be obtained through the solution of the same problem formulated on one or more subsets of the data, such that the recombination of the results thus obtained makes it possible to reconstruct the solution of the original problem. Subsets are processed in the same way, until they reduce to a small enough size so that the problem can be solved directly and easily without resorting to further subdivisions. In the tournament this occurs when each subset is reduced to two players and the winner is directly determined with a comparison. *Recursive algorithms* are coded in a language that allows this paradigm of computation. They call themselves inside their body to operate on subsets of data of progressively diminishing size, until a situation of termination is met that can be solved with a different (and perhaps simple) algorithm.

This mechanism opens up a sort of Chinese box in the computation, with each box containing several boxes of successively smaller size (e.g. the two sub-tournaments defined for each recursive call in the previous example). Each box will be closed when all the calculations inside it are completed (a sub-tournament ends

© Springer Nature Switzerland AG 2018
P. Ferragina, F. Luccio, *Computational Thinking*,
https://doi.org/10.1007/978-3-319-97940-3_11

---

**programma** REC_TOURN $(T, i, j)$

// returns the winner in the $T[i : j]$ portion of the knockout stage

1. **if** $j = i + 1$                     // a limit sub-tournament with two players

2.      **if** $T[i] > T[j]$ **return** $T[i]$ **else return** $T[j]$;

3. $m \leftarrow \lfloor (i + j)/2 \rfloor$;

4. $v_1 \leftarrow$ REC_TOURN $(T, i, m)$;     // $v_1$ is the winner of the first sub-tournament

5. $v_2 \leftarrow$ REC_TOURN $(T, m+1, j)$;         // $v_2$ is the winner of the second

6. **if** $v_1 > v_2$ **return** $v_1$ **else return** $v_2$;

---

**Fig. 11.1** Determining the winner of a tournament in recursive form. Participants are listed in a vector $T$ of $n = 2^k$ elements, but the program refers to a generic sub-tournament among the participants in the portion $T[i : j]$.

when all the smaller tournaments in its subtree are over). At this point, the result of the current box is returned to the box at the higher level, and this box takes control again of the computation. The logical structure is the same as that of a series of nested parentheses, each pair of open and closed parentheses contained inside another pair. Once the calculation between an inner pair of parentheses is completed, the action is returned to the outer pair.

To put this mechanism into action is far from elementary. Fortunately, however, the computer deals with it. The task of the coder and the algorithm designer is limited to indicating how the data should be subdivided into subsets, how the results on these subsets should be combined to reconstruct the result of the originating problem, and how the problem should be solved in the situation of termination. The tournament algorithm, for example, can be reformulated in recursive form in the program REC_TOURN shown in Figure 11.1. To understand how it works we notice the following:

- The program works on a set of $n = 2^k$ participants listed in a vector $T$, through a succession of recursive calls on two portions of $T$ (lines 4–5), until the limit condition in which the subsets contain only two elements is met (line 1) and the winner is determined by a direct comparison between the two (line 2). For this purpose, the program is defined for a generic sub-tournament among the participants listed in a portion $T[i : j]$ of the vector. The entire tournament is run through the initial call REC_TOURN $(T, 0, n - 1)$ that returns the champion.

- The program is written in the form of a *function*, a term used in programming to indicate that the result is associated with the name of the program itself. Assume that the participants are the $n = 16$ elements in the tree leaves in Figure 4.3, now contained in the vector $T$, that is:

| 24 | 15 | 7 | 9 | 20 | 49 | 33 | 35 | 22 | 40 | 52 | 12 | 62 | 30 | 8 | 43 |
|----|----|---|---|----|----|----|----|----|----|----|----|----|----|---|----|

The initial call REC_TOURN $(T, 0, 15)$ generates the final result 62. Within the computation, a call in the limit situation REC_TOURN$(T, 0, 1)$ (line 1) requires a direct comparison between $T[0] = 24$ and $T[1] = 15$ producing the local result REC_TOURN$(T, 0, 1) = 24$ (line 2).

- The program performs the same comparisons between elements executed by the program TOURNAMENT in Figure 4.4 but in a different order. In the present case, for example, the first internal call REC_TOURN$(T, 0, 7)$ following the initial one makes in turn the calls REC_TOURN$(T, 0, 3)$ (line 4) and REC_TOURN$(T, 4, 7)$ (line 5), followed by the comparison between the two winners (line 6). The first of these calls on $T[0 : 3]$ performs the comparisons $(24 : 15)$ and $(7 : 9)$ (situations of termination, line 1) that generate winners 24 and 9 (line 2), followed by the comparison $(24 : 9)$ between these winners. So, when this computation is completed we have REC_TOURN$(T, 0, 3) = 24$. Next, the second call on $T[4 : 7]$ performs the comparisons $(20 : 49)$ and $(33 : 35)$, followed by the comparison $(49 : 35)$ among the winners, and we have REC_TOURN$(T, 4, 7) = 49$. After these calculations, the comparison $(24 : 49)$ is performed between the winners from the two calls on $T[0 : 3]$ and $T[4 : 7]$, producing the result REC_TOURN$(T, 0, 7) = 49$. In conclusion, the first seven comparisons performed by the program REC_TOURN are, in order: $(24 : 15)$, $(7 : 9)$, $(24 : 9)$, $(20 : 49)$, $(33 : 35)$, $(49 : 35)$, and $(24 : 49)$. The program TOURNAMENT in Figure 4.4, instead, performs the comparisons between all the consecutive pairs of elements in a tree level before starting the comparisons in the higher level. In terms of time complexity, and thus in terms of the number of comparisons among participants, the two algorithms are equivalent since they perform the same comparisons, although in a different order.

Let's now discuss, starting with a well-known mathematical game, how recursion comes into different aspects of the science of algorithms; how its effects can be studied mathematically; and what benefits and difficulties it can generate.

## 11.1 A Very Instructive Game

In 1883, the French mathematician Édouard Lucas invented a math puzzle known as the *Tower of Hanoi* that unexpectedly achieved great popularity a century later among algorithm lovers. The game is well-known, but we describe it here again for its importance in understanding the recursive paradigm.

The game components are $n$ perforated disks of different diameters and a base with three pegs $A, B$, and $C$. Initially, the disks are placed on peg $A$, in order of decreasing diameter (Figure 11.2 (a)). The rules of the game require that the disks be moved one at a time between the pegs to transfer them all to $B$ without ever placing a disk over another of a smaller diameter. That is, during the process the disks are placed on each peg with their diameters decreasing bottom to top until all of them are on $B$. Of course, any disk can be placed on a peg that does not contain

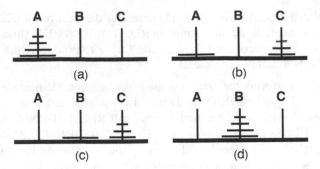

**Fig. 11.2** The Tower of Hanoi with $n = 4$ disks. (a) shows the initial disk placement and (b, c, d) show three fundamental moments in the solution algorithm.

any other disk, because the base behaves as a disk of maximum diameter, that cannot be moved.

It is only a game, but many important things can be learned from its analysis.[1] Assuming that the mental work to decide which disk to move at each step takes negligible time compared to the time needed to move the disk, we represent the complexity $M(n)$ of a solution algorithm as the number of single disk *moves*, obviously as a function of $n$.

To get an initial feeling for the nature of the problem, we first try to solve it with one or two disks. For $n = 1$ only one move $top(A) \to B$ is needed and the meaning of the notation is obvious: the highest disk on peg $A$ (the only one in this case) is moved to peg $B$ and we have $M(1) = 1$. For $n = 2$ we can solve the problem with three moves:

$top(A) \to C$:   the smallest disk is temporarily moved to peg $C$;

$top(A) \to B$:   the second disk, now the highest on peg $A$, is moved to peg $B$;

$top(C) \to B$:   the smallest disk is moved to peg $B$, over the second disk.

We now have $M(2) = 3$ and it is easy to realize that you cannot do better. For $n > 2$ the situation substantially more complicated and the problem has to be tackled systematically. Denote the disks with $1, 2, \ldots, n$ by decreasing diameters. A general solution has a recursive structure that can be summarized in three basic phases:

**phase 1:** move the disks $1, 2, \ldots, n - 1$ from peg $A$ to peg $C$, without ever moving the largest disk $n$ (result in Figure 11.2.(b));

**phase 2:** move the disk $n$ to peg $B$ (Figure 11.2.(c));

**phase 3:** move the disks in peg $C$ to peg $B$, without ever moving disk $n$ (result in Figure 11.2.(d)).

---

[1] The problem of the Tower of Hanoi is dealt with in many sources, often in a disappointing if not incorrect way. It is simple but it requires some delicate reasoning: in principle, we recommend readers to be wary of the websites where it is discussed.

```
program REC_TH (i,X,Y,Z)
1.    if i = 1                              // limit situation with a single disk
2.        top(X) → Y; return;
3.    REC_TH (i − 1,X,Z,Y);
4.    top(X) → Y;
5.    REC_TH (i − 1,Z,Y,X);
```

**Fig. 11.3** A recursive solution to the problem of the Tower of Hanoi. The disks are $n$, and the pegs are $A, B$, and $C$, but the program refers to a generic phase in which the $i$ smaller disks $n − i + 1$ to $n$ move from a generic peg $X$ to a generic peg $Y$, using the third peg $Z$ as their temporary support.

Phases 1 and 3 are recursively executed with the same algorithm on an ever decreasing number of disks until the limit situation is encountered. This occurs when a single disk is left, and requires only one move. The algorithm, called REC_TH, is coded in the program in Figure 11.3. To understand it we notice the following:

- The program is defined for a generic number $i$ of disks, $1 \leq i \leq n$, and for three pegs indicated by the generic names $X, Y$, and $Z$. It causes the transfer to peg $Y$ of the disks $1, \ldots, i$, all contained in the highest positions of peg $X$. The other $n − i$ disks are larger than the previous ones. They do not take part in the operation, and do not affect the movements of the smaller disks by acting as the base of the pegs. Transfer of the entire stack of $n$ disks from peg $A$ to peg $B$, using peg $C$ as their temporary support, is obtained with the initial call REC_TH$(n,A,B,C)$. Note that REC_TH also covers the cases $n = 1$ and $n = 2$.
- The program is written in the form of a *procedure*. The result is provided as a transformation of a data set accessible to the procedure itself and the program that calls it. In the present case the procedure changes the positions of the disks among the pegs. In the limit situation (only one disk, line 1), only the one disk is moved and the computation is resumed by the calling procedure (the command **return** in line 2).
- It is crucial to note the different order with which the pegs are specified in the two recursive calls (lines 3 and 5). In the first, the disks $1, \ldots, i − 1$ are transferred from $X$ to $Z$ using $Y$ as their support. In the second recursive call, the same disks are transferred from $Z$ to $Y$ using $X$ as their support.

The structure of the algorithm REC_TH should be clear, but a rigorous proof of its correctness requires some attention. The proof is based on the *induction principle* on $n$ (in this case on the number of disks), which we will recall in the course of the reasoning. We start from the *base case* $n = 1$: there is only one disk and the problem is solved by moving this disk from $A$ to $B$ (lines 1–2 in the call REC_TH$(1,A,B,C)$). Once the correctness of the base case is established, for the induction principle we must prove that the algorithm is correct for $n$ disks by assuming that it is correct for $n − 1$ disks. To this end we note that the problem for $n − 1$ disks implies that only these are on peg $A$ at the beginning. However, if there are $n$ disks and the larger one is not moved, we work on the other $n-1$ disks as if the larger disk were part of the base of the pegs. That is exactly what is done in the two recursive calls of lines 3 and 5. Under the inductive hypothesis, these calls correctly transfer the disks $1,\dots,n-1$ from $A$ to $C$ (line 3, recursive call REC_TH$(n-1,A,C,B)$), and then from $C$ to $B$ (line 5, recursive call REC_TH$(n-1,C,B,A)$). In between these two recursive calls, the algorithm moves the larger disk $n$ from $A$ to $B$ (line 4). At the end, the algorithm has correctly transferred all the disks $1,\dots,n$ from $A$ to $B$, and is therefore correct for $n$ and, given the inductive principle, it is correct for any number of disks.

With a similar reasoning we can evaluate the complexity of the algorithm, that is the number $M(n)$ of disk moves. This value is subject to the *recurrence relation*:

$$M(n) = \begin{cases} 1, & \text{for } n=1, \\ 2M(n-1)+1, & \text{for } n>1, \end{cases} \tag{1}$$

resulting from a direct examination of the program REC_TH applied to $n$ disks. For $n=1$ only one move is done and we have $M(1)=1$. For $n>1$ the procedure for $n-1$ disks is performed twice, followed by one move of disk $n$, and thus $M(n)=2M(n-1)+1$. For $n>1$, relation (1) can be solved by successive substitutions of the expression $M(n)$ on the decreasing numbers of disks. Since $M(n)=2M(n-1)+1$, we also have $M(n-1)=2M(n-2)+1$, and so on. We therefore obtain the following sequence of substitutions for $M(n)$:

$$\begin{aligned} M(n) &= 2M(n-1)+1 = 2\left(2M(n-2)+1\right)+1 \\ &= 4M(n-2)+3 = 4\left(2M(n-3)+1\right)+3 \\ &= 8M(n-3)+7 = \dots\dots \\ &= 2^{n-1}M(1)+2^{n-1}-1 = 2^n-1. \end{aligned} \tag{2}$$

Therefore the algorithm REC_TH has an exponential time complexity but, as we will now see, this is inevitable and we cannot do better. To this end we must determine a lower bound $L(n)$ to the number of moves needed to solve the Tower of Hanoi problem. We immediately notice that $L(n) \geq n$ because the disks need to be moved one at a time, although we can scarcely expect this limit to be significant.

Proving a stronger bound, however, requires some subtlety. First note that the moves of disks $1,\dots,n-1$ are not affected by the position of the disk $n$, which, as we have already seen, has the same effect as the peg base for the smaller disks. Second, consider a sequence of moves $\sigma$ that transform a disk configuration $C_1$ into another configuration $C_2$, with disk $n$ occupying the same position in $C_1$ and $C_2$. Then there is another sequence $\sigma'$ consisting of the same moves of $\sigma$ for disks $1,\dots,n-1$, which does not contain any moves of disk $n$, and thus generates the same effect as $\sigma$ on disks $1,\dots,n-1$. Specifically, if in $C_1$ the disks $1,\dots,n$ are all on peg $X$ (in the order that is the only one allowed), and in $C_2$ they are all on peg $Y$ (again in the same order), the number of moves necessary in any transformation (i.e. $\sigma$, or $\sigma'$, etc.) is at least $L(n-1)$, which is the lower bound for $n-1$ disks. Our third and final observation is that the problem requires that all disks are transferred to peg

$B$, including disk $n$, so this disk needs to emerge from the stack where it is placed at the beginning. This requires that the disks $1, \dots, n-1$ have been moved elsewhere and peg $B$ is free; hence, the disks $1, \dots, n-1$ must have been transferred to $C$, which requires at least $L(n-1)$ moves. Since at least one other move is required to transfer disk $n$ from $A$ to $B$, and at least $L(n-1)$ moves are necessary to move the disks $1, \dots, n-1$ from $C$ to $B$, we can write the recurrence relation:

$$L(n) \geq \begin{cases} 1, & \text{for } n = 1, \\ 2L(n-1) + 1, & \text{for } n > 1, \end{cases} \tag{3}$$

which coincides with relation (1) apart from the $\geq$ sign; and, with the same calculations, produces the result:

$$L(n) \geq 2^n - 1. \tag{4}$$

By combining the number of moves $M(n)$ executed by the algorithm REC_TH, given in relation (2), with the lower bound of relation (4), we conclude that the value of $M(n)$ is the least possible. That is, the bound given in relation (4) is *tight* and the algorithm REC_TH is optimal. It is worth emphasizing this result. In Chapter 8 we explained that there are problems known as NP-complete that we can solve solely with exponential algorithms, although it is not known whether we could do better. The "One Million Dollar Problem" is related to this issue, since we still do not know whether there is a polynomial time algorithm for their solution. The problem of the Tower of Hanoi is "harder" than these NP-complete problems because it is *intrinsically exponential* and nobody would bet a *cent* on it.

## 11.2 Comparison Between Recursion and Iteration

The problem of the Tower of Hanoi has shown us that in principle recursive algorithms are suitable for a proof of correctness, based on the principle of induction, and for an assessment of their complexity, based on recurrence relations. That is, they lend themselves to rigorous mathematical analysis. Of course, in many cases this analysis is not so simple, but the principle is always valid that a *top-down* paradigm, which uses a general property of the problem at hand to indicate the organization of the computation, is more easily analyzed than a *bottom-up* paradigm, which indicates the individual steps to be performed without thoroughly clarifying the general organization on which they are based. This is one of the main differences between recursive (top-down) algorithms and *iterative* (bottom-up) algorithms. Among the latter, incidentally, we find all those we have presented in the previous chapters.

A serious problem can, however, arise using recursion if the exact sequence of operations executed by an algorithm must be known to the user, since this sequence does not immediately appear in the recursive formulation of the algorithm. In fact, deciding this sequence is left to the computer in its interpretation of recursion, which requires keeping track of all the independent values that each parameter assumes in the recursive calls opened up within another and left in a waiting state until the computation inside them is completed.

For example, to understand the sequence of disk moves performed by the algorithm REC_TH for $n = 3$, the development of the computation shown in Figure 11.4 may be followed. Each recursive call is represented in a "box" where the parameters have local values, independent of those of the other calls. The sequence of operations is then:

$top(A) \rightarrow B$,

$top(A) \rightarrow C$,

$top(B) \rightarrow C$   (the first two disks have been moved to $C$),

$top(A) \rightarrow B$   (the largest disk has been moved to $B$),

$top(C) \rightarrow A$,

$top(C) \rightarrow B$,

$top(A) \rightarrow B$   (the first two disks have been moved to $B$).

As you can see, interpreting a recursive algorithm is not trivial, even in the present case for $n = 3$. It can be argued that this is not a real difficulty because the computation is entrusted to the computer. However, it becomes a problem, for example, in the *debugging* process (correction of program errors) if something goes wrong and it is necessary to know what happened in any single operation by examining its results. On the other hand, the sequence of operations performed by an iterative algorithm is almost immediately expressed in its coding, but it can be much more difficult to prove its correctness or to evaluate its complexity. Let us see how by discussing an iterative algorithm for the Tower of Hanoi.

Recall that in modular algebra $x \bmod y$ is equal to the remainder of the division between $x$ and $y$, so $0 \bmod 3 = 0$, $1 \bmod 3 = 1$, $2 \bmod 3 = 2$, $3 \bmod 3 = 0$, $4 \bmod 3 = 1$, etc. To solve the problem of the Tower of Hanoi, the source of our inspiration, there is a very simple iterative algorithm ITER_TH reported in Figure 11.5, which must be called according to the rule:

if $n$ is *odd*, the call is ITER_TH $(n, A, B, C)$;

if $n$ is *even*, the call is ITER_TH $(n, A, C, B)$.

Looking at the program and at its two possible calls immediately shows that the pegs are examined sequentially according to the sequence $A, B, C, A, B, C, \ldots$ if $n$ is odd, or $A, C, B, A, C, B, \ldots$ if $n$ is even, and repeats the steps:

- move the smaller disk 1 to the next peg (line 3);
- perform the only legal move between the disks in the other two pegs (line 4).

By executing these operations manually, the reader can easily solve the problem of the Tower of Hanoi, for example by transferring a tower of five disks from $A$ to $B$. However, it is very difficult to evaluate why this algorithm works and the number of operations it performs. For this purpose the recursive program is much more useful.

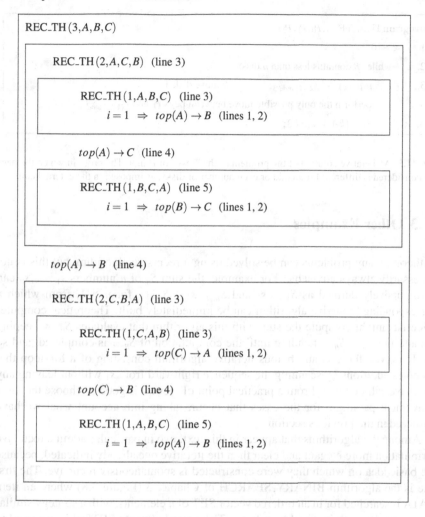

**Fig. 11.4** Simulation of algorithm REC_TH to move $n = 3$ disks from peg $A$ to peg $B$.

Now a little surprise: *REC_TH and ITER_TH execute exactly the same disk moves, in the same order.* To prove this statement, the moves executed by REC_TH for an arbitrary number of disks should be identified, which is not easy; while the moves for ITER_TH are immediately known as they are directly specified in the program. In any case, the statement indirectly ensures that ITER_TH is also correct and executes $2^n - 1$ moves.

---

**program** ITER_TH $(n, P_0, P_1, P_2)$

1.     $k \leftarrow 0$;

2.     **while** $B$ contains less than $n$ disks

3.          $top(P_k) \rightarrow P_{(k+1) \bmod 3}$;          // move disk 1

4.          perform the only possible move between pegs $P_k$ and $P_{(k+2) \bmod 3}$;

5.          $k \leftarrow (k+1) \bmod 3$;

---

**Fig. 11.5** An iterative solution of the problem of the Tower of Hanoi. The order in which the pegs are considered is different for an odd or even number of disks, as imposed in the external call.


## 11.3 Other Examples

In theory, many problems can be solved using a recursive algorithm, but this is not necessarily always advisable. For example, the sum $S_n$ of $n$ numbers $s_1, \ldots, s_n$ can be recursively defined as $S_1 = s_1$ and $S_n = s_1 + S_{n-1}$, for $n > 1$, from which a corresponding recursive algorithm can be immediately built. Theoretical computer scientists might compute the sum with this algorithm that evaluates $S_n$ by keeping the addition $s_1 + S_{n-1}$ pending until the computation of $S_{n-1}$ is completed, and so on. However, there is an obvious iterative algorithm consisting of a **for**-loop that executes additions by scanning the sequence rightward from $s_1$ without leaving any recursive call pending. From a practical point of view, it is good to choose the most convenient paradigm for the cases that occur, taking into account what we have observed in the previous section.

Among the algorithms that appear in this text, two in particular admit a recursive formulation more elegant and clear than the iterative one already indicated, because the basic idea on which they were constructed is spontaneously recursive. The first one is the algorithm BINARY_SEARCH of Chapter 3 (Figure 3.8) where an item DATA is searched for in an ordered vector SET of $n$ elements, with a strategy similar to a manual search in an address book. The central element SET[$m$] is accessed to check whether DATA is in that position. If not, the search proceeds *recursively* on the portion of the vector that precedes or follows position $m$, depending on whether DATA is less than or greater than SET[$m$].

The new recursive formulation REC_BS of the algorithm is shown in Figure 11.6. We think that it does not require any particular explanation or proof of correctness. The external call is REC_BS($SET, 0, n - 1, DATA$). Depending on the result of the comparison in the last **if**, the algorithm makes one of two possible recursive calls, respectively, on the portion of the vector that contains the elements that precede or follow the element SET[$m$] in the ordering.

The maximum number $C(n)$ of comparisons executed by the algorithm between DATA and the elements of SET is subject to the recurrence relation:

```
program REC_BS(SET, i, j, DATA)
// recursive search of DATA in the portion [i : j] of the ordered vector SET
    if i > j
        print DATA "is not present"; stop;
    m ← ⌊(i+j)/2⌋;
    if DATA = SET[m]
        print DATA "is present"; stop;
    else
        if (DATA < SET[m])
            REC_BS(SET, i, m−1, DATA);
        else REC_BS(SET, m+1, j, DATA);
```

**Fig. 11.6** The recursive version of binary search.

$$C(n) \simeq \begin{cases} 1, & \text{for } n = 1, \\ 1 + C(n/2), & \text{for } n > 1, \end{cases} \tag{5}$$

where the approximate equality symbol $\simeq$ refers to the fact that the vector portions on which the recursive calls are made do not usually contain exactly half of the elements. In particular, the two portions do not include SET[m] and therefore they may not consist of $n/2$ elements. For example, for $n = 8$ such portions contain three and four elements, respectively. Letting $2^{k-1} < n \leq 2^k$, relation (5) is solved as:

$$\begin{aligned} C(n) &\simeq 1 + C(n/2) \\ &\simeq 1 + (1 + C(n/4)) = 2 + C(n/4) \\ &\simeq 2 + (1 + C(n/8)) = 3 + C(n/8) \\ &\simeq \ldots = k + C(n/2^k) \\ &\simeq \ldots = \log_2 n + C(1) = 1 + \log_2 n. \end{aligned} \tag{6}$$

Relation (5) is referred to as the worst case situation in which DATA is not present in the vector SET and the computation goes on until DATA is searched for in an empty subset (condition $i > j$). Relation (6) indicates that the algorithm has a time complexity that grows logarithmically in the vector size $n$. The same result was obtained for the iterative version: in fact, the comparisons between the elements are the same and occur in the same order.

The second algorithm that admits a simple recursive formulation is the one of sorting a vector $C$ of $n = 2^h$ elements, already considered in Chapter 7 under the name of MERGE_SORT. The algorithm uses the procedure MERGE $(A, B, F)$ in Figure 7.4 to merge two ordered vectors $A$ and $B$ into a single ordered vector $F$. The algorithm compares the elements of $C$ in pairs to get ordered pairs, then merges the

---

**program** REC_MS $(C, i, j)$

// recursive sorting of the portion of vector $C[i : j]$ using a support vector $F$

   **if** $i < j$

      $m \leftarrow \lfloor (i+j)/2 \rfloor$;

      REC_MS $(C, i, m)$;

      REC_MS $(C, m+1, j)$;

      MERGE $(C[i : m], C[m+1, j], F[i : j])$;

      $C[i : j] \leftarrow F[i : j]$;        // the elements of $F$ are copied in $C$

---

**Fig. 11.7** The recursive version of merge sort.

pairs to get ordered quartets, and so on, until it merges two ordered halves of $C$ so that the entire vector is sorted.

The recursive formulation REC_MS of the algorithm is shown in Figure 11.7. The algorithm is put into operation by calling it as REC_MS $(C, 0, n\text{-}1)$ and contains in its body two recursive calls on two halves of the vector $C$, which are sorted and then merged with each other. Unlike in the binary search algorithm in Figure 11.6, where only one or the other recursive call is actually performed, in REC_MS both calls must be performed at each level of the calculation.

Again in this case it is easy to understand how the algorithm works. The condition for termination is met if $i = j$ (the portion of the vector to be ordered is reduced to a single element) and the next part of the program is skipped. Recalling that $n = 2^h$ the two recursive calls of REC_MS work exactly on the two halves of $C[i : j]$ and the correctness of the algorithm is proved by induction on $h$. In the base case $h = 1$ (the items to be ordered are $2^1 = 2$) the two recursive calls are invoked on individual elements, so their sorting is immediately interrupted, and the following call of MERGE sorts the two elements with one comparison. Assuming by the inductive hypothesis that the algorithm correctly sorts vectors of $2^{h-1}$ elements, the two recursive calls sort the two portions $C[0 : 2^{h-1} - 1]$ and $C[2^{h-1} : 2^h - 1]$ of $C$, and the following call of MERGE produces the ordering of the whole vector $C$. The algorithm is therefore correct for $n = 2^h$, and thus it is correct for any number of elements to be sorted.

The number of comparisons $R(n)$ executed between the elements of $C$ by the algorithm REC_MS is governed by the recurrence relation:

$$R(n) = \begin{cases} 1, & \text{for } n = 2, \\ 2R(\frac{n}{2}) + F(n), & \text{for } n > 2, \end{cases} \qquad (7)$$

that starts from the single comparison $R(2) = 1$ for $n = 2$, and then indicates that $R(n)$ is the sum of the number of comparisons of two recursive calls on $n/2$ elements plus the number $F(n)$ of comparisons made by the procedure MERGE called on $n > 2$ elements. Recalling that the latter comparisons are at most $n - 1$, which is the worst case for the algorithm, relation (7) is solved by subsequent substitutions:

$$R(n) = 2R(\tfrac{n}{2}) + n - 1$$
$$= 2\left(2R(\tfrac{n}{4}) + \tfrac{n}{2} - 1\right) + n - 1 = 4R(\tfrac{n}{4}) + 2n - 3$$
$$= 4\left(2R(\tfrac{n}{8}) + \tfrac{n}{4} - 1\right) + 2n - 3 = 8R(\tfrac{n}{8}) + 3n - 7$$
$$= \ldots\ldots,$$

which at the $i$-th step takes the form:

$$R(n) = 2^i \times R(\tfrac{2^h}{2^i}) + i \times n - (2^i - 1) = 2^i \times R(2^{h-i}) + i \times n - 2^i + 1.$$

Since $n = 2^h$ and thus $h = \log_2 n$, we set $i = h - 1$ in the previous relation to obtain:

$$R(n) = 2^{h-1} \times R(2) + (h-1) \times n - 2^{h-1} + 1$$
$$= \tfrac{n}{2} + (\log_2 n - 1) \times n - \tfrac{n}{2} + 1$$
$$= (n \log_2 n) - n + 1. \tag{8}$$

In relation (8) the first term clearly prevails asymptotically, so the time complexity of the algorithm is in the form $n \log_2 n$ because the number of all operations performed is proportional to the number of comparisons. This is the same time complexity we found in Chapter 7 for the algorithm MERGE_SORT in iterative form, and in fact the two algorithms perform the same comparisons, although in different order (recall what has been already observed for the iterative and recursive versions of the tournament algorithm). However, it is worth emphasizing the elegance and simplicity of the recursive formulation REC_MS with respect to the iterative formulation MERGE_SORT.

An issue that admits a recursive algorithm that is very compact but more difficult to understand is generating all the permutations of $n$ elements. This problem was already mentioned in Chapter 8 in relation to the algorithm FOOLISH_SORT and to the Hamiltonian cycle problem. We now show how to solve it.

The algorithm PERMUTATION, whose pseudocode is shown in Figure 11.8, is based on the idea of dividing the permutations of $n$ elements into $n$ groups, each of which contains all the permutations beginning with the same element followed by the permutations of the other $n - 1$ elements, which will be built recursively. More precisely, let us assume that the elements to be permuted are stored in a vector $P[0 : n-1]$. Then, the first group contains the permutations beginning with $P[0]$ followed by permutations of the elements $P[1], P[2], \ldots, P[n-1]$; the second group contains the permutations beginning with $P[1]$ followed by the permutations of the elements $P[0], P[2], \ldots, P[n-1]$; the third group contains the permutations beginning with $P[2]$ followed by the permutations of $P[0], P[1], P[3], \ldots, P[n-1]$; and so on.

The program is defined to construct all the permutations of the elements in a portion $P[k : n-1]$ of $P$ starting from a generic value of the index $k$, and is triggered by the external call PERMUTATIONS$(P, 0)$ for $k = 0$. The first exchange between the elements $P[k]$ and $P[i]$ (line 3) brings the element that characterizes a permutation group into the first position of the vector's portion mentioned previously. The second exchange between the same elements (line 5) restores that portion as it was before

---

**program** PERMUTATIONS $(P,k)$

// permutations of the elements in the portion $P[k:n-1]$ of a vector $P$

1.    **if** $(k = n-1)$ EXAMINE$(P)$;        // a new permutation has been built

2.    **else for** $i = k$ **to** $n-1$

3.        $P[k] \leftrightarrow P[i]$;        // exchange $P[k]$ with $P[i]$

4.        PERMUTATIONS $(P,k+1)$;        // permutations of $P[k+1:n-1]$

5.        $P[k] \leftrightarrow P[i]$;        // reconstruct the original situation

---

**Fig. 11.8** Construction of the permutations of the elements contained in $P[k:n-1]$. The procedure EXAMINE$(P)$ is defined depending on the end use of the permutations of the entire vector $P$ once they are generated.

the recursive call that constructs the permutations of the elements from $P[k+1]$ to $P[n-1]$ (line 4). The initial exchange $P[k] \leftrightarrow P[k]$ and the subsequent exchange between the same elements pertaining to the permutation group beginning with $P[k]$ do not produce any variation. As soon as a new permutation is built, the procedure EXAMINE$(P)$ is called on the entire vector $P$ (line 1), defined case by case depending on the requirements for such permutations.

The algorithm's proof of correctness is done by induction on the number $n$ of elements to be permuted, starting from the base case $n = 1$ (the vector $P[0:0]$ containing only one element). Here, the external call PERMUTATIONS$(P,0)$ terminates immediately in line 1 with the trivial permutation of a single element. We then assume, by inductive hypothesis, that the algorithm correctly permutes the elements in a vector of $n-1$ elements. The external call PERMUTATIONS$(P,0)$ for $n$ elements triggers the **for**-loop at line 2 with the resulting $n$ exchanges in line 3 that alternately put in $P[0]$ an element chosen from among all of them, followed by the call PERMUTATIONS$(P,1)$ in line 4 that generates, by the inductive hypothesis, all the permutations of the remaining elements contained in $P[1:n-1]$. The algorithm is therefore correct for $n$, and thus it is correct for the length of any vector.

To estimate the time complexity of PERMUTATIONS we compute the number $S(n)$ of exchanges of elements in the vector $P$ through the recurrence relation:

$$S(n) = \begin{cases} 0, & \text{for } n = 1, \\ n \times (S(n-1)+2), & \text{for } n > 1, \end{cases} \tag{9}$$

which indicates that, for $n = 1$, $S(1) = 0$ exchanges are performed; and for $n > 1$ a **for**-loop is repeated $n$ times and, in each repetition, the algorithm is recursively called on $n-1$ elements in line 4, and two exchanges are performed in lines 3 and 5. The value of $S(n)$ is computed by subsequent substitutions as indicated in the following relation (10). We have already pointed out that a permutation algorithm must have an exponential time complexity because it must generate an $n!$ number of permutations. In the present case, the result "greater than $2n!$" is due to the approximations made to simplify the calculations.

$$S(n) = n \times (S(n-1)+2)$$
$$> n \times S(n-1)$$
$$= n \times [(n-1) \times (S(n-2)+2)]$$
$$> n \times (n-1) \times S(n-2)$$
$$= n \times (n-1) \times [(n-2) \times (S(n-3)+2)]$$
$$> n \times (n-1) \times (n-2) \times S(n-3)$$
$$= \cdots > \cdots$$
$$= n \times (n-1) \times (n-2) \times \cdots \times 3 \times 2 \times (S(1)+2)$$
$$= 2 \times n!. \tag{10}$$

The proof of correctness and the calculations are standard, however, some nontrivial problems may arise when trying to figure out the order in which the algorithm generates all the permutations of $P$'s elements. Those who want to go deeper into this issue can manually apply the algorithm to the set $\{a,b,c\}$, similarly to what we did for the Tower of Hanoi in Figure 11.4. Three elements are enough to complicate things; permutations have to appear in the order: $(a,b,c)$, $(a,c,b)$, $(b,a,c)$, $(b,c,a)$, $(c,a,b)$, and $(c,b,a)$. Then the initial permutation $(a,b,c)$ is restored with the final exchange at line 5.

## 11.4 A Famous Randomized Algorithm

Consider a vector $C$ of $n$ elements. We will operate on the portion $C[p:q]$, where $0 \le p < q \le n-1$, with the algorithm PARTITION, whose pseudocode is shown in Figure 11.9. This algorithm picks randomly an element of $C[p:q]$, called a *pivot*, and then relocates the vector's elements in such a way that the elements smaller than or equal to the pivot appear in the first part of the vector, followed by the pivot itself, and then the larger elements.

To understand the structure of the program PARTITION refer to the examples in Figure 11.10 and 11.11, keeping in mind the following:

- The pivot is chosen by calling the function RANDOM $(p, q)$ (line 1), available in different formulations in all programming languages, which returns a random integer between $p$ and $q$. The selected pivot is $C[r]$ and it is immediately exchanged with the element in the last position $q$ (line 2) where it will remain until the last operation, when it is moved to position $s$ to separate the elements equal to or smaller than $C[s]$ from the larger ones (line 10).
- The variable $i$ indicates the position of the rightmost element among those already recognized as $\le C[q]$: at the beginning this set is empty and thus we set $i = p-1$ (line 3).
- Elements $C[j]$ are examined one by one in a **for**-loop (lines 4–8) by comparing each of them with the pivot $C[q]$ (line 5). If the test fails (i.e. $C[j] > C[q]$), the

---

**program** PARTITION $(C, p, q, s)$

// reorganization of vector portion $C[p : q]$ around a *pivot* chosen randomly
// upon exit the pivot is in $C[s]$

| | | |
|---|---|---|
| 1. | $r \leftarrow$ RANDOM $(p, q)$ ; | // $r$ is the initial position of the pivot |
| 2. | $C[r] \leftrightarrow C[q]$ ; | // exchange $C[r]$ with $C[q]$: now the pivot is in $C[q]$ |
| 3. | $i \leftarrow p - 1$ ; | |
| 4. | **for** $j \leftarrow p$ **to** $q - 1$ | |
| 5. |    **if** $C[j] \leq C[q]$ | |
| 6. |       $i \leftarrow i + 1$ ; | |
| 7. |       **if** $i < j$ | |
| 8. |          $C[i] \leftrightarrow C[j]$ ; | // exchange $C[i]$ with $C[j]$ |
| 9. | $s \leftarrow i + 1$ ; | |
| 10. | $C[q] \leftrightarrow C[s]$ ; | // exchange $C[q]$ with $C[s]$: now the pivot is in $C[s]$ |

---

**Fig. 11.9** The program PARTITION for relocating the elements of $C[p : q]$ around a randomly selected element called the pivot. The elements smaller than or equal to the pivot are placed to the left of it and the larger elements to the right of it. $s$ is the resulting position of the pivot.

loop operations are skipped and the computation proceeds with the next value of $j$. If instead $C[j] \leq C[q]$ two alternatives are considered:

1. where $i + 1 = j$ the variable $i$, incremented by 1 in line 6, keeps the role of pointer to the rightmost element among those smaller than or equal to the pivot (see Figure 11.10(a)). This case is shown in the fourth configuration of the example in Figure 11.11, where the pivot has the value 4, $i = j = p$, and both indexes point to the element 3;
2. where $i + 1 < j$ the new value $i + 1$ indicates the position of the leftmost element among those already recognized as greater than the pivot (see Figure 11.10(b)). The elements $C[i]$ and $C[j]$ are exchanged and $i$ resumes its original role of pointer to the leftmost element smaller than or equal to the pivot. This case is shown in the fifth configuration in Figure 11.11, where $i$ points to element 7 and $j$ points to element 2, and the two elements swap (next configuration) so that $C[i] = 2$, i.e. smaller than the pivot.

- The last element exchange is done in the **for**-loop with $j = q - 1$, depending on the value of $C[j]$ (in the second last configuration in Figure 11.11 we have $C[j] = 6$ which is greater than the pivot $C[q] = 4$ and thus no exchange is done). The pivot is then swapped with the element in position $i + 1$, which is the leftmost element larger than the pivot (last configuration in the example). Thus, all the elements to the left of the pivot are smaller than or equal to it, and all the elements to the right are larger.

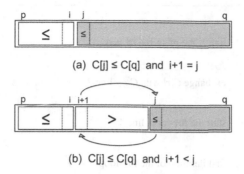

(a) C[j] ≤ C[q] and i+1 = j

(b) C[j] ≤ C[q] and i+1 < j

**Fig. 11.10** Two alternatives may occur in the algorithm PARTITION, for $C[j] \leq C[q]$: (a) $i+1 = j$, then $C[i+1] \leq C[q]$ and thus $i$ is incremented; and (b) $i+1 < j$, then $C[i+1] > C[q]$ and thus the two elements are swapped. The gray areas contain the elements that must still be processed.

The correctness of the program PARTITION is immediately verifiable on the basis of the previous points. To estimate its time complexity on a vector of $n$ elements, we note that in addition to the operations of lines 1, 2, 3, 9 and 10 that are executed only once, the **for**-loop at lines 4–8 is repeated $n-1$ times, in each of which a constant number of operations is executed. These are not always the same because they depend on the results of the comparisons in each loop-iteration but their overall number, and therefore the overall time complexity of the algorithm, is still proportional to $n$: it could not be inferior because to divide the elements around the pivot you have to examine the entire vector $C[0 : n-1]$. Therefore, even the lower bound is proportional to $n$ and the chosen algorithm is optimal.

The program PARTITION works around a randomly selected pivot. Why did we do this? Why, for instance, did we not directly choose the element $C[q]$ (7 in our example) as the pivot, thus avoiding the call of RANDOM in the first line of the program? The explanation lies in the fact that PARTITION is the heart of a famous recursive sorting algorithm known as QUICK_SORT, which we mentioned in Chapter 7 and are now going to present as an example of a *randomized sorting algorithm*, that is, an algorithm constructed to sort elements by taking advantage of the appearance of a random event inside it.

To order a vector $C[0 : n-1]$, the basic idea of QUICK_SORT is to divide the elements around a pivot using PARTITION, and then repeat recursively the process on the two portions of the vector to the left and the right of the pivot until all the portions are reduced to one element. It is easy to understand that the whole vector will be ordered using this method, but since the different portions will have unpredictable lengths, and in any case these lengths may be different from each other, it is difficult to write a program valid for an arbitrary vector without using recursion. The corresponding simple formulation of the program is shown in Figure 11.12; in this regard we note the following:

$$
\begin{array}{ll}
\begin{array}{l}p\ r\qquad q\\ 3\ \ 4\ 8\ 2\ 6\ 7\end{array} & \text{line 1, the pivot is } C[r]=4 \\[2em]
\begin{array}{l}p\ r\qquad q\\ 3\ \ 7\ 8\ 2\ 6\ 4\end{array} & \text{exchange } C[r] \text{ with } C[q], \text{ line 2} \\[2em]
\begin{array}{l}i\ j\\ 3\ \ 7\ 8\ 2\ 6\ 4\end{array} & \text{start the \textbf{for}-loop, line 4} \\[2em]
\begin{array}{l}i,j\\ 3\ \ 7\ 8\ 2\ 6\ 4\end{array} & \text{first iteration of the \textbf{for}-loop, line 7} \\[2em]
\begin{array}{l}\quad i\ \ j\\ 3\ \ 7\ 8\ 2\ 6\ 4\end{array} & \text{fourth iteration of the \textbf{for}-loop, line 6} \\[2em]
\begin{array}{l}\quad i\ \ j\\ 3\ \ 2\ 8\ 7\ 6\ 4\end{array} & \text{fourth iteration of the \textbf{for}-loop, line 8} \\[2em]
\begin{array}{l}\quad i\qquad j\\ 3\ \ 2\ 8\ 7\ 6\ 4\end{array} & \text{fifth iteration of the \textbf{for}-loop, line 4} \\[2em]
\begin{array}{l}\quad i\ s\ \ j\ q\\ 3\ \ 2\ 8\ 7\ 6\ 4\end{array} & \text{line 9} \\[2em]
\begin{array}{l}\quad i\ s\ \ j\ q\\ 3\ \ 2\ 4\ 7\ 6\ 8\end{array} & \text{line 10}
\end{array}
$$

**Fig. 11.11** Effect of the program PARTITION on $C[p:q]$, after executing the operations specified on the right. The randomly selected pivot (4) is initially located in position $r$ and immediately moved to the last position $q$. At the end of the operations, the pivot is moved to position $s$, to divide the elements $\leq 4$ from the ones $> 4$.

- The program executes two recursive calls in lines 3 and 4. The final position $s$ of the pivot, returned from the call of PARTITION, lies between $p$ and $q$, so the two recursive calls repeat the operation for the two portions $C[p:s-1]$ and $C[s+1:q]$ if one and/or the other contain at least two elements, otherwise the corresponding recursive call stops at line 1.
- Like every recursive program, QUICK_SORT is defined for an arbitrary vector of data, here specified by the endpoints $p$ and $q$ of a portion of the vector $C$.
- The entire vector is sorted by the external call QUICK_SORT$(C, 0, n-1)$.

The reader will easily be convinced that the program is correct by an inductive reasoning on $n$ without requiring an explanation, although in the present case the *strong induction principle* should be used because we have to assume that the inductive hypothesis is valid for *all* values smaller than $n$ and not just for $n-1$. In fact, as we already pointed out, the two portions of the vector on which QUICK_SORT

```
program QUICK_SORT (C, p, q)
// recursive sorting of the vector portion C[p : q]
1.   if p < q
2.       PARTITION (C, p, q, s);              // s is the pivot's position
3.       QUICK_SORT (C, p, s − 1);
4.       QUICK_SORT (C, s + 1, q);
```

**Fig. 11.12** The QUICK_SORT recursive program.

is recursively called contain less than $n$ elements, but their sizes are unpredictable because they depend on the random choice of the pivot.

This difference in the sizes of the two parts on which QUICK_SORT is recursively called also makes it difficult to evaluate its time complexity. Therefore, it is good to make some new considerations to explain why the pivot is chosen randomly.

Let us assume, whatever the mechanism of choice, that the pivot coincides with the maximum element of $C[p : q]$. In such a case, the partition would divide $C[p : q]$ into a portion $C[p : q − 1]$ containing all of the elements except for the pivot, followed by the pivot $C[q]$. The right portion would be empty and we would have $s = q$. If this event were repeated in all the recursive calls of QUICK_SORT, the calls at line 4 would always be ineffective and the total number of comparisons made by PARTITION in the calls at line 3 would be $(n − 1) + (n − 2) + \ldots + 1$. As we have seen in Chapter 7, this sum has the value $n(n − 1)/2$. Therefore, QUICK_SORT would have a time complexity quadratic in $n$.

We have considered a worst case input distribution, which actually also occurs when we choose the minimum element as a pivot at each level. However, what can we expect to happen *on average,* if this average is calculated on all the possible random choices of the pivot that are all likely to appear with the same probability? The computation, too complicated to repeat here, shows that by executing QUICK_SORT a large number of times on vectors of $n$ elements, with random choices of the pivot, the average value of the number of operations performed (that is, the average time complexity of the algorithm) is proportional to $n \log_2 n$. Of course, there will be cases in which the number of operations is greater than the average, as in the worst case seen above or in others approaching it, but in other cases the number of operations will be much less.

By comparing QUICK_SORT with the other two comparison-based sorting algorithms considered in this book, we see that in the worst case its time complexity is quadratic as with INSERTION_SORT, but on average it behaves like MERGE_SORT. Unlike this latter algorithm, however, QUICK_SORT does not require a support vector and therefore occupies only the space of the input vector $C$, which is half the space required by MERGE_SORT. This and other more subtle algorithmic considerations make QUICK_SORT the most used sorting algorithm, unless it is indispensable to set a certain limit on the duration of the program, such as for controlling an industrial process or launching a missile. QUICK_SORT is also the most well-known and probably most important example of a randomized algorithm. Many others exist, but we cannot deal with them in this book.

## 11.5 To Conclude, Let Us Be a Little Cautious

Many readers have probably already met the following table of integers:

| $j \to$ | 0 | 1 | 2 | 3 | 4 | 5 | 6 | 7 |
|---|---|---|---|---|---|---|---|---|
| $i$ 0 | 1 | | | | | | | |
| ↓ 1 | 1 | 1 | | | | | | |
| 2 | 1 | 2 | 1 | | | | | |
| 3 | 1 | 3 | 3 | 1 | | | | |
| 4 | 1 | 4 | 6 | 4 | 1 | | | |
| 5 | 1 | 5 | 10 | 10 | 5 | 1 | | |
| 6 | 1 | 6 | 15 | 20 | 15 | 6 | 1 | |
| 7 | 1 | 7 | 21 | 35 | 35 | 21 | 7 | 1 |

This is Tartaglia's famous triangle,[2] potentially infinite but limited here to the rows and columns 0 to 7. It is full of interesting properties but we will discuss only a few.

If limited to $n$ rows and $n$ columns, the triangle can be stored in a bidimensional array $T[0:n-1, 0:n-1]$, with rows and columns indicated by $i$ and $j$, respectively. In the figure we have chosen $n = 8$. The values of $i$ and $j$ are not part of the matrix and are shown in a column to the left and in a row at the top. Actually the matrix is filled only for the values $T[i, j]$ with $i \geq j$; for example, $T[4,2] = 6$ and $T[7,7] = 1$, while $T[1,2]$ is not defined and is left blank in the figure. It would be natural to put a zero or any other conventional character in the cells for which $i < j$, but from the point of view of the coding this does not matter because the algorithms acting on $T$ will never access such cells, which can thus contain any value, e.g. the ones already present in its relative memory cells.[3]

As most readers probably already know, each element of the triangle has two precise mathematical meanings:

- The elements in row $i$ are *binomial coefficients*, that is the coefficients to apply to the addends in a binomial $i$-th power. For example $(a+b)^3 = a^3 + 3a^2b + 3ab^2 + b^3$, where the coefficients 1, 3, 3, 1 are listed in row 3 of the triangle.
- $T[i, j]$ is the number of *combinations* of the elements of a set of cardinality $i$, taken in groups of $j$ elements. For example, the groups of $j = 3$ elements in a

---

[2] Often called Pascal's triangle, even though the French mathematician arrived at it a century later than Tartaglia. However, the triangle has been known to the Chinese since the twelfth century.

[3] Naturally, for large values of $n$, only the significant portion of the array is stored, even if this requires a coding complication.

set $\{a,b,c,d\}$ with a cardinality of $i = 4$ are: $abc, abd, acd$, and $bcd$. And indeed $T[4,3] = 4$.

Then, row $i$ of the triangle lists in an orderly way the number of combinations of the elements of a set of cardinality $i$, in groups containing $0, 1, 2, \ldots, i$ elements. Note that the number of groups of zero elements is $T[i,0] = 1$ (i.e. the empty set), and the number of groups of $i$ elements is $T[i,i] = 1$ (i.e. the set containing all of them). Therefore, the sum $S$ of all the numbers that appear in a row equals the number of all the subsets of the given set, including the empty subset and the complete subset. However, what is the value of $S$? From set theory we know that a set of $i$ elements contains $2^i$ subsets, so $S = 2^i$ as can be seen in the triangle; for example, for the last row, in which $i = 7$, we have $S = 1 + 7 + 21 + 35 + 35 + 21 + 7 + 1 = 128 = 2^7$.

In general, the number of combinations of $n$ elements in groups of $m$ elements with $m \leq n$, that is the entry $T[n,m]$ of Tartaglia's triangle, is indicated in math with $\binom{n}{m}$ and obeys the following recurrence relations:

$$\binom{n}{m} = 1 \qquad\qquad \text{for } m = 0 \text{ and } m = n, \tag{11a}$$

$$\binom{n}{m} = \binom{n-1}{m} + \binom{n-1}{m-1} \quad \text{for } 0 < m < n, \tag{11b}$$

reflecting two well-known properties of the triangle, that is, all the cells in the first column and the main diagonal of the table $T$ contain 1 (relation (11a)), and every other element in $T$ equals the sum of the element immediately "above" it (that is, $T[n-1,m]$) with the element to the left of the latter (that is, $T[n-1,m-1]$); for example, $T[6,4] = 15 = T[5,4] + T[5,3] = 5 + 10$ (relation (11b)).

The calculation of $\binom{n}{m}$ through relations (11a) and (11b) can be executed with a trivial and apparently "stupid" method by computing one by one all the elements of Tartaglia's triangle up to row $n$ where $T[n,m]$ resides. The obvious pseudocode of this algorithm, called TARTAGLIA, is shown in Figure 11.13.

```
program TARTAGLIA (n)
    for i = 0 to n
        T[i,0] ← 1;   T[i,i] ← 1;    // 1's in col 0 and main diagonal, relation (11a)
    for i = 2 to n
        for j = 1 to i − 1
            T[i,j] ← T[i−1,j] + T[i−1,j−1];                      // relation (11b)
```

**Fig. 11.13** Construction of Tartaglia's triangle up to row $n$.

It can only be noted that it is enough to construct the triangle up to row $n - 1$ because $T[n,m]$ is computed as the sum of two elements of this row. Moreover, not all of the other elements built by TARTAGLIA are needed, as for example all $T[i,j]$ with $j > m$ (that is, those in the columns to the right of $T[n,m]$): the algorithm would need some complication to reduce the number of computed elements, but we leave it as it is because the spared operations only marginally affect its time complexity, with which we will deal now. The number of operations performed is clearly expressed by the number of elements stored in the triangle. Limiting them from row 0 to row $n-1$ we have $1+2+3+\ldots+n = (n+1)n/2$, an expression already encountered: the complexity is quadratic in $n$.

Let us ask then whether we can use relations (11a) and (11b) more intelligently. Basically, these relations define $\binom{n}{m}$ as a function of $n-1$ and $m-1$ and then immediately provide the scheme of a recursive algorithm. Any computer scientist would be tempted to consider this solution, but would quickly realize that doing so would be a serious mistake. In fact, relations (11a) and (11b) can already be seen as a simple recursive algorithm expressed in a strictly mathematical language so they can be used to extrapolate an evaluation of its time complexity. However, such relations are complicated by the presence of two parameters $n$ and $m$, so we limit the calculation to the example $\binom{7}{3}$ interpreting the relation (11b) on the portion of the triangle on which this calculation takes place, reported below in boldface.

|   | 0 | 1 | 2 | 3 | 4 | 5 | 6 | 7 |
|---|---|---|---|---|---|---|---|---|
| 0 |   |   |   |   |   |   |   |   |
| 1 | **1** | **1** |   |   |   |   |   |   |
| 2 | **1** | **2** | **1** |   |   |   |   |   |
| 3 | **1** | **3** | **3** | **1** |   |   |   |   |
| 4 | **1** | **4** | **6** | **4** |   |   |   |   |
| 5 |   | **5** | **10** | **10** |   |   |   |   |
| 6 |   |   | **15** | **20** |   |   |   |   |
| 7 |   |   |   | **35** |   |   |   |   |

The value $T[7,3] = 35$ must be computed as $T[6,3] + T[6,2] = 20 + 15$ found in row 6. These two values are in turn computed with three entries of row 5, namely $T[6,3] = T[5,3] + T[5,2] = 10 + 10$ and $T[6,2] = T[5,2] + T[5,1] = 10 + 5$. Therefore, in the recursive paradigm, $T[5,2]$ will be computed twice independently using the values of row 4, while of course it would be sufficient to compute it once, storing the result for subsequent use. In fact, by computing the entries needed in the recursive computation going up in the table, the number of addends entering into the sums doubles at each row due to the repeated presence of the same elements (in our example there are two addends in row 6, four in row 5, and eight in row 4) so their number grows as a power of two until the value 1 in column 0 or on the diagonal is encountered, where this growth begins to decrease at the two extremes of the row. More precisely, starting from $T[n,m]$, column 0 is encountered going up $m$ rows (in the example, computing $T[7,3]$, column 0 is encountered at row 4, going up three rows from row 7). The diagonal is encountered by going up $n-m$ rows (try calculating $T[7,5]$, it meets the diagonal going up two rows). Therefore, the number of addends computed in the recursive paradigm is certainly greater than the minimum between $2^m$ and $2^{n-m}$, then the algorithm has an exponential time complexity if the value of $m$ is not close to 0 or $n$.

To conclude these observations on computing binomial coefficients we must observe that their value can also be obtained by using the formula:

$$\binom{n}{m} = \frac{n(n-1)...(n-m+1)}{m!}$$

which requires a total of $n$ multiplications. However, the exponential growth of the terms under construction makes the computation practically impossible unless it is organized as a suitable set of divisions between the numerator and denominator factors. We prefer not to go into this analysis, to leave room for another example that casts light on the comparison between iterative and recursive algorithms.

The example is provided by a famous sequence of integers introduced in 1202 by Leonardo Fibonacci in his *Liber Abaci* (The Book of Calculation). The problem was related to the development of a breed of rabbits, animals known to be very prolific. Starting from the assumption that a couple of rabbits gives life to another couple every month, but that a couple can only pair from the second month of life, how does a colony that begins with just one newborn couple grow (with the additional hypothesis, we add, that the rabbits never die, so as to extend the calculation to infinity without subtracting the dead)?

Denoting by $F_i$ the number of rabbits present at month $i$, the *Fibonacci sequence* develops as:

$$F_1 \quad F_2 \quad F_3 \quad F_4 \quad F_5 \quad F_6 \quad F_7 \quad F_8 \quad F_9 \quad F_{10} \quad F_{11} \quad F_{12} \quad ...$$

$$1 \quad 1 \quad 2 \quad 3 \quad 5 \quad 8 \quad 13 \quad 21 \quad 34 \quad 55 \quad 89 \quad 144 \; ...$$

Clearly $F_1 = F_2 = 1$ because in the first and second months only the original rabbit couple is present, which can pair in the second month to generate a new couple in the following month, so we will have $F_3 = 2$. Henceforth, the number of couples grows according to the rule that the couples present at month $i$ are the same as those present at month $i-1$, plus as many couples as existed at month $i-2$, since they are able to procreate in the month $i$. The sequence can then be defined by the recurrence relation:

$$F_1 = 1; \quad F_2 = 1; \quad F_i = F_{i-1} + F_{i-2}. \tag{12}$$

Our computational problem is to calculate the value of $F_n$ given an arbitrary value of $n$. For this purpose, all the elements $F_i$ of the sequence can be computed up to the $n$-th element by subsequent additions, using the iterative algorithm FIB$(n)$ in Figure 11.14. The algorithm uses three variables $a, b$, and $c$. The first two, which initially contain the values $F_1 = 1$ and $F_2 = 1$ (line 1), are intended to contain values $a = F_{i-2}$ and $b = F_{i-1}$ during the computation of $c = F_i$ at step $i$ of the **for**-loop (line 3), and then be updated with the two new values $F_{i-1}$ and $F_i$ (line 4). The time complexity of this algorithm is obviously proportional to $n$ if $F_n$ has to be computed.

As an alternative, the recurrence relation (12) could be used to design a recursive algorithm REC_FIB$(i)$ for calculating the generic element $F_i$ of the sequence.

```
program FIB (n)
1.      a ← 1; b ← 1;                              // set a = F₁ and b = F₂
2.      for i = 3 to n
3.          c ← a + b;
4.          a ← b; b ← c;                          // set a = Fᵢ₋₁ and b = Fᵢ
5.      print "Fₙ =" b;
```

**Fig. 11.14** Iterative computation and printing of the $n$-th Fibonacci number.

This could be done by two recursive calls REC_FIB$(i − 1)$ and REC_FIB$(i − 2)$, followed by the addition of the two results thus obtained, until the termination conditions $i = 1$ or $i = 2$ are met, and the initial values $F_1 = 1$ and $F_2 = 1$ are directly returned. As in any recursive algorithm, the external call REC_FIB $(n)$ would trigger the computation of $F_n$. However, even without describing the algorithm in detail, we can anticipate its time complexity.

As with binomial coefficients, we can note that the number of recursive calls for REC_FIB doubles for every value of $i$ because each recursive call requires two new calls, until the termination conditions are reached. These conditions are first met in the calls REC_FIB $(i − 2)$, which are the ones whose index decreases more quickly. Since that index reaches the value $i = 2$ after $n/2$ recursive levels, doubling the total number of calls goes on for $n/2$ times reaching the number of $2^{n/2}$ calls. The time complexity of the algorithm is therefore exponential. Once again, an iterative algorithm is clearly preferable.

From the comparison of the two types of algorithms (i.e. iterative vs. recursive) considered for computing the binomial coefficients and the Fibonacci numbers we can draw an important lesson. The iterative version is apparently trivial, if not silly, but it is far more efficient than the recursive version which is much more sophisticated. More importantly, the iterative one is acceptable because it takes polynomial time while the recursive one is absolutely unacceptable because it requires exponential time. Note, however, that this does not depend on the recursive paradigm in itself but on the fact that relations (11a), (11b), and (12) have a drawback; the sub-problems into which the original problem has been recursively decomposed are broadly superimposed, which causes the redundancy of the calculations we have observed. In all the recursive algorithms examined before these ones, apart from that of the Tower of Hanoi which takes *intrinsically exponential time*, calls were performed on disjoint portions of data and redundancy did not occur.

To conclude, any paradigm of computation, and recursion in particular, should be treated extremely carefully by analyzing the time complexity of the proposed algorithms before engaging in the writing and execution of related programs. And keeping in mind that the aesthetic qualities of an algorithm are not necessarily related to its efficiency.

# Index

Printed in the United States
By Bookmasters